W9-CAZ-037

SOUTH PARK TOWNSHIP LIBRARY
2575 BROWNSVILLE ROAD
SOUTH PARK, PA 15129
412-833-5585

GUMBO LIFE

Also by Ken Wells

NOVELS

Meely LaBauve

Junior's Leg

Logan's Storm

Crawfish Mountain

Rascal: A Dog and His Boy

NONFICTION

Travels with Barley:
A Journey Through Beer Culture in America

The Good Pirates of the Forgotten Bayous: Fighting to Save
a Way of Life in the Wake of Hurricane Katrina

GUMBO
LIFE

Tales from the Roux Bayou

KEN WELLS

W. W. Norton & Company
Independent Publishers Since 1923
New York • London

SOUTH PARK TOWNSHIP LIBRARY
2575 BROWNSVILLE ROAD
SOUTH PARK, PA 15129
412-833-5586

02   2019

Copyright © 2019 by Ken Wells

All rights reserved
Printed in the United States of America
First Edition

For information about permission to reproduce selections from this book, write to
Permissions, W. W. Norton & Company, Inc., 500 Fifth Avenue, New York, NY 10110

For information about special discounts for bulk purchases, please contact
W. W. Norton Special Sales at specialsales@wwnorton.com or 800-233-4830

Manufacturing by LSC Communications, Harrisonburg
Book design by Michelle McMillian
Map by David Atkinson, handmademaps.com
Production manager: Beth Steidle

Library of Congress Cataloging-in-Publication Data

Names: Wells, Ken, author.
Title: Gumbo life : tales from the Roux Bayou / Ken Wells.
Description: First edition. | New York : W. W. Norton & Company, independent publishers
since 1923, 2019. | Includes bibliographical references and index.
Identifiers: LCCN 2018048425 | ISBN 9780393254839 (hardcover)
Subjects: LCSH: Gumbo (Soup)—History. | Cooking, Acadian. | Wells, Ken—Travel. |
Louisiana—Social life and customs.
Classification: LCC TX757 .W43 2019 | DDC 641.81/3—dc23
LC record available at https://lccn.loc.gov/2018048425

W. W. Norton & Company, Inc., 500 Fifth Avenue, New York, N.Y. 10110
www.wwnorton.com

W. W. Norton & Company Ltd., 15 Carlisle Street, London W1D 3BS

1 2 3 4 5 6 7 8 9 0

To my parents,

Bonnie and Rex,

who gave me the gift of the Gumbo Life.
You are gone but never forgotten.

And to my late lamented Louisiana friends, the Louie Brothers

Delbert Louis Leggett (1950–2016)
Jerry Louis Hermann (1953–2017)

with whom I shared not just a middle name, but almost five decades
of irreplaceable friendship, often over bowls of gumbo.
I sorely miss your camaraderie, good humor,
and arch observations of all things Louisiana.
Rest you, my brothers.

CONTENTS

SOME HELPFUL DEFINITIONS

People of the Region

Cajun An Anglicized shortening of the word "Acadian." It refers to the descendants of pioneers principally from the Poitou-Charentes and Vendée regions of west-central France who settled Acadie, the French-controlled Maritime Provinces of eastern Canada beginning in the early 1600s. After about 150 mostly peaceful years there, *les Acadiens*, as they called themselves, were swept up in the nine-year territorial battle between the British and French known as the French and Indian War. Though taking no sides in the conflict, the Roman Catholic Acadians drew the suspicions of the British because of their reluctance to take a loyalty oath to the English and their Protestant king. It didn't help that the Acadians sat on some of the richest farmland in all of Canada, which the British coveted for the British settlers they hoped to coax there. In 1755, the British began confiscating and burning Acadian farmsteads and sending Acadians into exile to other colonies aboard cargo ships, where they languished under deplorable conditions. Families were often separated and almost half of the twelve thousand Acadian deportees died. This act of ethnic cleansing is known as the "Le Grand Dérangement." Clusters of survivors began arriving between 1763 and 1776 in the Louisiana territories, recently ceded to Spain by France, but which supported a robust and sympathetic French-speaking culture. The Cajuns would settle the remote bayous, swamps, and prairies of South Louisiana and live in relative isolation. Their culture, music, and antique French remained largely intact until the acculturation pressures following World War I and escalating after World War II. The French they speak, known today as Cajun French, is essentially eighteenth-century country French derived from colonial French, with borrowings from Spanish, Native American, and English forms. Cajun French has been preserved by its long isolation in both Canada and colonial Louisiana.

Creole A term of complicated etymology. Of Portuguese and Spanish origins, the word in colonial Louisiana was originally used by French-speaking, Louisiana-born descendants of continental French and Spanish settlers to distinguish themselves from newly arrived French and Spanish speakers coming from the Francophone and Afro-Hispanic Caribbean. Creole planters also applied the term to their Louisiana-born slaves. These days, *Creole* more commonly applies to mixed-race peoples whose lineage may include any amalgam of European colonists, Native Americans, African Americans, and Afro-Caribbean peoples, descending both from slaves and free people of color. Binding them today is a language known as Creole French, which is derived from the more widely spoken colonial French that came with the first French settlers from Europe, as well as from the dialects that emerged as Afro-Creoles and Afro-Caribbeans began to mix. Creole French, like its cousin, Cajun French, is kept alive by diminishing communities of speakers still determined to preserve it. One pop culture footnote: Zydeco, the Creolized, amped-up interpretation of the Cajun music repertoire, is sung in Creole French (and these days in English) while traditional Cajun music is typically sung in Cajun French.

Geography and Culture

bayou   A shallow, slow-moving, usually serpentine natural waterway, typically larger than a creek and smaller than a river, and often coursing through marshlands or swamplands. In Louisiana, some, like Bayou Teche, encompass more than 120 miles. Bayous attracted Louisiana's early settlers because they were full of harvestable fish and game, and served as transportation routes in the absence of roads. Even better, the bayou banks, formed by silt from millennia of floods, provided habitable high ground in a place where high ground was rare. Thus, the term *bayou* today has been expanded to include entire communities. Bayou Black, where I grew up, is a perfect example: It is a small town formed not around a center, but which stretches for twenty miles along opposing banks of the bayou from which it takes its name.

boucherie   A Cajun/Creole ritual involving the communal slaughtering and smoking of hogs and cattle. Colonial-era boucheries, carried out principally by Acadian and German settlers, were a necessity to preserve meat in the days before refrigeration. These days, boucheries are more often than not a feature of festivals throughout South Louisiana.

Gumbo Belt   Principally, the twenty-two contiguous south Louisiana parishes that form the heart of Francophone Louisiana and still hold the vast majority of the state's French-speaking Cajuns and Creoles and gumbo cookers.

pirogue (PEE-rawg, alternatively PEE-roe)   A Cajunized adaptation of the Native American dugout canoe. It's a wooden or fiberglass boat, typically twelve to sixteen feet long, propelled by paddling and made for navigating in shallow water. The vessel remains popular with modern-day hunters and fishermen.

poule d'eau (POOL-doo)   The Louisiana French term for the bird the rest of the world calls the American coot. Resembling a diminutive black duck, the poule d'eau (Cajun French for "water chicken") winters by the tens of thousands throughout the coastal South, with Louisiana having among the largest migratory populations.

Foods and Ingredients

andouille (awn-DOO-wee)   A lean, heavily smoked sausage made with pork and spices that originated in France but gained its special character from the butchering and smoking techniques of Cajuns of the Gumbo Belt, notably the inhabitants of the River Parishes between Baton Rouge and New Orleans, and the prairie Cajun lands of Southwest Louisiana. Andouille, a staple in contemporary gumbos, also owes a great debt to the Gumbo Belt's German pioneers, who helped teach the Cajuns and Creoles smoking and curing techniques.

boudin (BOO-dehn)   A spicy meat and rice–stuffed sausage typically using pork but often made these days with more exotic ingredients such as crawfish and alligator.

courtbouillon (coo-BEE-yawn)   A roux-based fish stew traditionally made with spicy tomato sauce and herbs and usually served over rice. Most recipes call for a whole fish, typically redfish, though catfish, turtle, and shrimp are sometimes substituted.

crawfish bisque   A laboriously prepared souplike dish in which crawfish heads stuffed with ground, seasoned crawfish tails are simmered in a stock made with a roux. It is typically served in a bowl over white rice. It is a favorite Lenten season dish throughout the still heavily Catholic Gumbo Belt.

etouffee (eh-TOO-fay)   A classic Louisiana brown stew of shrimp or crawfish made with a roux and served over rice.

filé (FEE-lay)   Rendered from dried, pounded sassafras leaves, the dusty green powdered substance, tasting of a muted hint of thyme, was a staple of Louisiana's Native American cooking and herbal medicine that eventually found its way into the gumbo pot. Many use it as a flavor booster, others to thicken gumbos that are either rouxless or whose roux needs bolstering. In bygone years, gumbos were commonly labeled either gumbo fevi (thickened with fresh or dried okra) or gumbo filé.

fricassee (FRICK-uh-see)   In the Cajun-Creole interpretation, a roux-based stew usually made with chicken. It is similar to etouffee but usually not as thick in consistency.

gumbo   A brown-colored soup, its origins running perhaps three centuries deep to the early days of the Louisiana settlement, and typically made with a roux and served in a bowl over white rice. Archetypal gumbos contain okra and some combination of vegetables—the "Trinity" of bell pepper, celery, onions is common—and some combination of meat and seafood. The two most common gumbos cooked today are chicken-and-smoked sausage and shrimp-okra. The first printed reference was spelled *gombeau*—the African Bantu dialect term for okra and the most likely origin of gumbo's name.

jambalaya (jumba-LYE-uh)   The Cajun-Creole adaptation of Spanish paella, it's a one-pot dish in which rice is simmered with finely diced vegetables—typically celery, onion, bell pepper, and garlic—and some combination of sausage and seafood. It can be served on a plate or in a bowl.

mirliton (MURL-ee-tohn)   Known also as the chayote or alligator pear, this crunchy member of the gourd family finds its way into a lot of Cajun and Creole casseroles as a substitute for zucchini, whose taste it somewhat resembles.

poboy   Invented in New Orleans by the Martin brothers, Cajuns born in Raceland, Louisiana, this Cajun-Creole version of the hoagie or submarine sandwich is typically made with fried oysters, shrimp, catfish, or roast beef and served "dressed" on French bread with lettuce, tomatoes, and mayonnaise.

roux   A base for soups and gravies made by browning flour in hot oil, butter, or lard. While there is a long history of rouxless gumbos, which substitute filé or copious amounts of caramelized onions or okra as a thickener and color enhancer, the roux style has come to dominate gumbos served today.

sauce piquant (sauce PEE-kawn)   The spiciest of the Cajun-Creole offerings, it's a stew served over white rice and made with diced vegetables—typically the Trinity plus garlic—and simmered in a tomato-based sauce fired up by diced jalapenos. Some recipes call for the addition of crushed red pepper, ground black pepper, and/or cayenne. Shrimp, turtle, alligator, chicken, rabbit, venison—all may find their way into sauce piquant.

tasso   Lightly cured and smoked pork shoulder that is sliced and used in a variety of dishes, including gumbo.

Cajun Cooking versus Creole Cooking

Cajun The food that evolved from the Acadian settlement in Louisiana starting in the mid-1760s. Cajun is at its heart home cooking that features robust, savory, simple dishes. They can be cooked with indigenous ingredients and are traditionally made in a big cast-iron pot in amounts adequate to feed a large family. Many Cajun dishes are made with a roux and, more often than not, served over or cooked with rice.

Creole Creole cooking is as complicated as the definition of Creole itself, with classical Creole owing its roots to France and continental Europe. Creole tends to be more refined and complicated fare than Cajun cooking, often incorporating sauces based on wine, liquor, and cream. Iconic New Orleans restaurants like Arnaud's, Commander's Palace, and Galatoire's have long been the embodiment of high-end Creole cuisine. Creoles of African American/mixed-race descent have taken classical Creole and given it an earthier, often spicier interpretation, melding the style into boundary-stretching gumbos, for example, and spicy fried chicken. It's a cuisine that liberally borrows from African, Native American, Spanish, German, Italian, and even Cajun influences to produce food with a style of its own. Dishes that come out of Li'l Dizzy's Cafe and Dooky Chase's Restaurant are embodiments of this evolution.

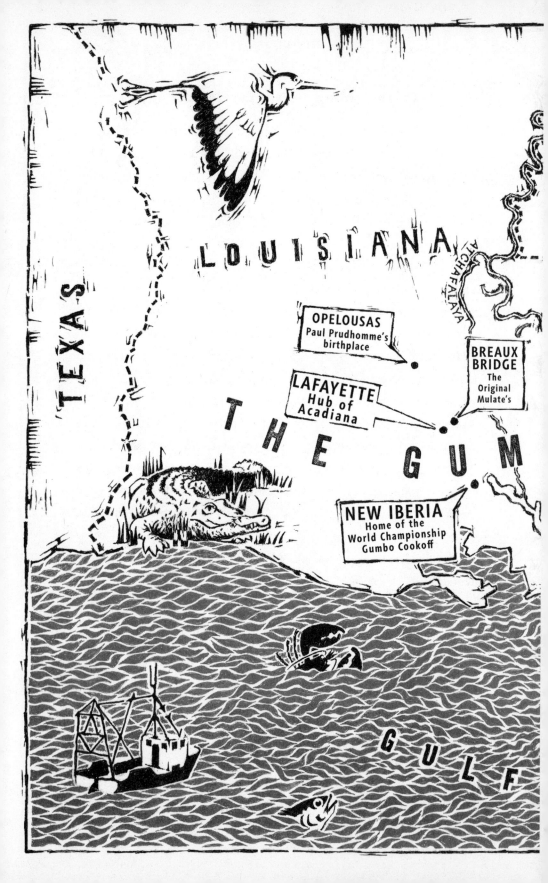

PREFACE

Boy Drooling, Man Wondering

In South Louisiana's Gumbo Belt, babies eat gumbo as soon as they go off the breast or the bottle. The mommas make sure of this.

My mother, Henrietta "Bonnie" Toups Wells, certainly did.

Now, I wish I could say I have a toddler's memory of tasting my first gumbo, but I don't. My first recollection was when I was six or seven years old.

We were still town people, three years before my dad moved us to the country. I was seated at the kitchen table of our tidy, slate-sided beige house near the banks of the Intracoastal Waterway, the broad, muddy-brown canal that runs through Houma. My little town, fifty-five miles southwest of New Orleans, would grow into a lively oil-and-gas hub by the time I finished high school in 1966. But back then it was a drowsy Cajun hamlet of about ten thousand people with an entrance sign proudly proclaiming itself "Oyster Capital of the World."

A red plastic cloth, decorated in ornate white roses, draped our table. In the center were the condiments that sat on the tables of many South Louisiana households: Tabasco Sauce; a bottle of homemade, pickled pepper–infused vinegar; a jar of filé or ground sassafras leaves.

These first two are gumbo enliveners, the last a thickener and flavor booster. Cajuns, like many cultures, have a tradition of adjusting their seasonings at the table. Reaching for the hot sauce is an ingrained reflex.

My mother was serving shrimp-okra gumbo over white rice, as she believed all proper gumbos are served (it usually needed no enlivening). It was her favorite gumbo to cook and my favorite one to eat. She had learned to cook it from her mother who had learned to cook it from hers who had most likely learned to cook it from hers.

Gumbo cooking days were joyous occasions. The simmering dish filled the house with such exquisite anticipatory aromas that I could scarcely wait to get to the supper table. I often arrived early, picking up the spoon my mother had so carefully placed on the white cloth napkin alongside my gumbo bowl, and waited. Of course, when you grow up in a family of six hungry boys as I did, getting to the table early is a good idea.

I recall it being late spring for it was warm, windows open to a mild breeze, an electric fan drowsing in the background. The okra, I'm surmising, had come from a friend's garden or a nearby roadside stand since the supermarket was not yet a ubiquitous fixture of South Louisiana life. The shrimp—not too big, not too small—had been procured that morning from French-speaking Cajun fishermen who worked the docks of a small seafood-processing plant just down the street from us.

Bonnie usually did the bartering in her native tongue, Cajun French, and I often walked with her the short block, past pungent mounds of cast-off oyster shells, on these shrimp-buying errands. After the haggling was done, muscular men in sweat-stained T-shirts, smudged jeans tucked into white rubber boots, would scoop the glistening crustaceans from big wire hampers and onto a hanging metal scale.

Satisfied that the weight was correct, Bonnie would have them dump the shrimp, and a little chipped ice, into a bowl she'd brought along. Off we'd head to the kitchen, where she would start to prepare her pots. My mother liked to put her gumbo on in the morning for she knew that a gumbo begun early in the day and simmered slowly would be at its tastiest by the time it was served for supper.

"First, cher, you have to make a roux," she would proclaim, in her mild Cajun accent.

I had no real concept of roux back then. But I liked the sound of the word and often rolled it off my tongue—*roo, roo, roo*. Even now the mere thought of a roux brings back those memories: the lilting, exotic voices of the Cajun French speakers; the watercolor of idled shrimp and oyster boats creaking in their ropes; the wild, salty sea smells mingled with the pungent odor of the creosoted docks; the aroma of diced onions, celery, and bell pepper; the squall they made when they met the roux.

We moved from that little house near the banks of the Intracoastal when my father, William "Rex" Wells, an outlander from Arkansas, took a job with a local sugarcane mill and settled us on the banks of the Cajun enclave of Bayou Black on the western outskirts of town. Bayou Black seemed happily stranded in a previous century. We lived on a dusty road paved in clam shells, got our water from a large cypress cistern, and swam and fished from a dock on the bayou. Indoor plumbing had arrived but the fully functioning cypress outhouse at the entrance to our chicken yard reminded us that it was a recent improvement. The sugar company still kept mules in a corral a mile away and each spring, Dad paid the mule handler five dollars to bring his favorite animal to plow our narrow bayouside vegetable plot, the strip of land between the road and the bayou that the Cajuns call the *batture*.

We lived in large part off what John Folse, the iconic homegrown Louisiana chef and serious Gumbo Belt food historian, calls Gumbo's Pantry, the great sweep of woods, fields, bayous, bays, marshes, and swamps of the immensely fertile deltaic plain that defines South Louisiana's geography and fed and nurtured our gumbo-cooking forebears. Gardening, hunting, and fishing supplied most of the ingredients for our gumbo pots, as they did for our bayou neighbors. Central to that life were family, friends, respect, and love of the low country that nurtured us, and a gritty sense of self-reliance, born in part because if we didn't do for ourselves, we did without.

This was Bayou Black when we arrived in 1957: a place that had not changed materially in its rustic rhythms, customs, and sense of place for a hundred years. There, my brothers and I lived what I call the Gumbo Life much as my mother's and grandmothers' generation had experienced it, a time before the homogenizing influences of things like supermarkets, processed foods, television, and the internet. A chicken gumbo more often than not started with a chicken chased down in the farmyard and a crawfish stew began with baiting our homespun crawfish nets with chicken necks and tossing them into the shallows of a nearby swamp.

Back then, gumbo was pretty much a Cajun and Creole secret, a peasant dish, a concoction that we cooked with passion and tradition. Historians believe the primordial form of Louisiana gumbo is at least 250 years old, perhaps much older. Just as in my mother's family, recipes and methods had come down through generations, passed on almost exclusively by word of mouth in families living in isolation where schools were rare and illiteracy high. Outside of a smattering of historically significant cookbooks, written recipes were uncommon until after World War II. This helps to explain why gumbo's origins are so clouded in mystery and why, as well, we probably have as many gumbo recipes in the Gumbo Belt as we have gumbo-cooking families.

We made gumbo because, when properly done, it is consistently delicious, can be crafted from simple, inexpensive ingredients and cooked in a giant pot. Served over rice as is customary, it fed lots of mouths in the big families common to predominantly Catholic South Louisiana. We made it because it also fed our souls. Something this good being lovingly and patiently passed down through the generations spoke to the vibrancy and optimism of our ancestors and the culture they'd created, even amidst the poverty in which we often lived.

I grew up, moved away, lived abroad, and traveled the world. Gumbo has grown up, too, and has been doing quite a bit of traveling itself. Our once cloistered soup is in the midst of a long and expansive Diaspora, embraced, cooked, and enjoyed by peoples and cultures virtually worldwide. These days, London, New York, Paris, Toronto, Madrid, Sydney, Copenhagen, and Tokyo are but a few of the world's great cities with Cajun and Creole restaurants that feature gumbo on the menu. I'd hazard to guess that most American cities with over two hundred thousand in population have a restaurant dishing out some version of gumbo. My father-in-law in Chicago orders in a perfectly authentic chicken-and-sausage gumbo from a Cajun place called Heaven on Seven not far from downtown's Magnificent Mile. It's one of seven gumbo-serving restaurants in the city.

On a recent visit to my daughter, Sara, who lives in the Richmond District of San Francisco, I walked past an Asian-Cajun restaurant called Swamp with gumbo and crawfish on the menu. I couldn't resist going in to sample the gumbo. It was authentic gumbo, obviously made with a roux, but it was more like jambalaya in consistency and rather bland. But I was more disappointed that the Asian owner wasn't around so I could've gotten firsthand the full story of how a place that served both gumbo and garlic noodles had bloomed in San Francisco. (I later learned that the San Francisco family has a branch living in New Orleans and visits and eats there often.)

While visiting the University of Montana School of Journalism in 2016 to give a lecture, I learned there was a good Cajun restaurant in Missoula with a gumbo that locals raved about. More recently, a friend sent a link to a story in the *Times of Israel* with the headline: "In a Black Jew's Yiddish Gumbo, the Secret Ingredient Is Diversity." The story was about a chef and food writer dishing out his international-

ized version of gumbo in New York City. How much more of a global
and cosmopolitan mention can gumbo get?

As any gumbo-loving Louisiana expatriate of a certain age will tell
you, this is a rather recent phenomenon. It wasn't so long ago that you
could drive the length and breadth of the land beyond South Louisiana and queries about gumbo almost always drew blank stares. Back
then, if you moved from the Gumbo Belt and wanted gumbo, as I did
in 1975, you had to cook it yourself.

Now, with gumbo practically everywhere, you can make a reasonable argument that gumbo has joined the pantheon of world-famous
soups. Our gift to ourselves has become a gift to the planet. But when
did the Gumbo Diaspora begin and what explains its phenomenal
reach? And what of gumbo's roots?

Historians, who for decades had doggedly combed the musty stacks
of libraries and archives, assumed that no one would ever find a written
reference to gumbo earlier than those dating to 1803 and 1804. The latter, recorded by C. C. Robin, a Frenchman and journalist traveling deep
into Louisiana's rural Cajun communities, was particularly important
because it seemed to place gumbo's creation solidly in the Cajun camp.
Robin was invited to attend a Cajun *bal de maison*, or house party, along
the Mississippi River between Baton Rouge and New Orleans. He
noted that after a long night of dancing and drinking cheap, watered-
down rum called tafia, "always everyone has a helping of gumbo."

That seemed to settle the matter until Gwendolyn Midlo Hall, a
noted historian sleuthing into New Orleans slave genealogical records,
stumbled upon a written reference to gumbo dating to 1764. (The discovery, made in the early 1990s, went largely unnoted until it burst
into the gumbo blogsphere almost two decades later.) Why was what
it said about gumbo such a shock to Gumbo World?

This matters because for the vast majority of Gumbo Belt natives,
gumbo has never been merely a dish. It's a cultural metaphor and
anchor that both explains and bonds our food-centric part of the world.

It is the star example that shows how the natives of the Gumbo Belt invented the only truly indigenous regional cuisine in all of America; not just a dish but a style and a way of cooking.

Perhaps because of this, gumbo has also become something of an obsession among academics, culinary historians, chefs, and pundits, for they correctly see that the story of gumbo is inextricably linked with our own. Gumbo, like blues and jazz, had come out of the crucible of a history that has been at turns uplifting and heroic, dark and dispiriting.

It is a story of intrepid French, Spanish, and German pioneers, but also a story of hardship, slavery, racism, and poverty, stretching into the encampments of Louisiana's Native Americans and deep into West Africa and the islands of the Afro-Caribbean. It is a story inextricable from the cultural upheaval of the Cajuns and their cruel expulsion from their ancestral maritime lands in Canada by their British overlords. And yet the coda of the Cajun story is their triumphant assimilation in a low country that they have forever stamped as their own and their unquestionable influence in the evolution and spread of gumbo.

This complex and kaleidoscopic history has produced this thing—gumbo—that today transcends race, class, religion, and politics. Gumbo's creation, evolution, and triumphant ascension is a beautiful story with a happy, ever-evolving plot line. Nobody wants to or should be left out of it.

Although I am a lifelong journalist, I came to this story more in the manner of a pilgrim on a journey, inspired by my roots in the Gumbo Life and bearing no bias except the one for which I know I will be readily forgiven: My mother made the best gumbo on earth and the way my mother made her gumbo is the way all gumbo should be made. Everyone who makes that claim is allowed to, for in a way it is the elixir of the gumbo story, a spunky testament to the pride in family and place and history that has propelled the gumbo story forward. Here is my telling of it.

GUMBO LIFE

ROUX AWAKENING

On an early sunny Saturday morning in August 1975, I stood in the front yard of my parents' suburban South Louisiana home hugging my mother, who was sobbing. Dad stood by stoically, ready to shake my hand. Parked in the driveway was my two-tone, bronze-and-white 1968 Chevy pickup with camper top and gun rack. It was packed to the brim with most of my earthly possessions.

My mother's tears were complex. Second of six sons, I was the first to finish college, a matter of considerable pride to my parents, whose impoverished childhoods crimped their educational ambitions. Now I was going off to school again to seek a master's degree. That part my mother loved. But I'd gotten my bachelor's degree from Nicholls State University, the small state school in Thibodaux, my mother's birthplace, a mere sixteen miles up the road. This time I was moving eight hundred miles away to Columbia, Missouri, to attend the University of Missouri School of Journalism. Bonnie hated the moving away part.

I'd been working on my feisty hometown paper, the *Houma Courier*, since my freshman year and had the good sense to understand how providential my landing there had been. The kindly editors had

hired me on a hunch rather than any particular qualifications, knowing that I had recently flunked out of college and was having second
thoughts about ever going back. But within a few months, I discovered I had an unexpected aptitude for the work and had not just found
a job, but my life's calling. My bosses steered me back to college. I
graduated and went full-time at the paper and had worked my way
into the managing editor's job. Truth be told, I was leaving not without misgivings.

Houma lies in the heart of Cajun bayou country. I'd grown up on a
six-acre farm outside of town, fishing, hunting and trapping with my
father and my five energetic, goodhearted brothers. With my mother
helping out and commanding her aroma-filled kitchen, we grew big
family gardens and raised chickens, pigs, and other farm animals. If
Bonnie's forte was gumbo, she also cooked all manner of Creole and
Cajun specialties like sauce piquant and courtbouillon that kept her
sons and husband rushing to the table. My large, extended, French-
speaking Toups family lived forty-five minutes away in Thibodaux.
We saw them often. I practically moved in with some of my Thibodaux
cousins during the summertime.

The Toupses could cook, too. During my undergrad years, I seemed
to coincidentally show up at the door of my Maw-Maw Toups' house
around lunchtime, where the odds were good there would be gumbo,
chicken stew, or red beans and rice or white beans and rice on the
stove. Like many Cajuns, they kept an open kitchen. No invitation or
phone call necessary. Just come on by and come hungry.

My Wells grandparents, who had both grown up in rural Arkansas, lived with us on and off and I was very close to them. Granny
Wells was an excellent fry cook who brought a traditionally Southern
cooking dimension to our table—think melt-in-your-mouth homemade biscuits and succulent chicken and dumplings. Pop Wells was
an extraordinary outdoorsman who, despite a tendency to tell a story
to death after a beer or two (or three), had with Dad helped to instill

in all of the Wells boys a deep love of the woods, hunting, fishing, and nature. I had tons of friends, the steady company of winsome Cajun women, and a fulfilling job. I was pretty happy with my life, so why would I want to leave it behind?

Well, I was also restless. As much as I liked my job and coworkers and felt a true debt to the editors who had given me such a providential break, I was soon to turn twenty-seven years old and felt I'd already had the full cycle of experience at the Houma paper. While I reveled in my title as managing editor, I didn't particularly like the managing part. I knew in my heart of hearts that my true love was feature writing and I already had some concept of my dream job. A local banker passed on his copy of the *Wall Street Journal* each day and I read the front page religiously, particularly the light and always beautifully written feature story in the center column.

I often fantasized about writing for the *Wall Street Journal* one day but talking this ambition over with Al Delahaye, my Nicholls mentor, we both concluded that it was unlikely that it or any other big-name publication was coming to Houma to find me. A Louisiana native, Al had gotten his PhD at Mizzou and suggested I enroll in the graduate program where he still had friends and could put in a good word for me. The *Journal* and many fine metro dailies sent recruiters to campus each spring. If I got in and did well, I'd have a chance to get noticed.

I applied with mild trepidation (what if I *didn't* get in?) and screamed with joy when my acceptance came in the mail. I sold my motorcycle to help raise the first semester's tuition and living expenses. That and $1,200.00 in savings was all the money I had in the world. I'd just figure out the rest when I got there.

As I stood hugging my mother that sultry August morning, I was doing my best to reassure her—and maybe myself—that I was doing the right thing.

Bonnie, drying her tears, had her mom's demand list at the ready: Write often, call once a week, don't skip breakfast.

Then she stopped for a moment and looked at me with great seriousness.

"Now I got a question for you, Kenny," she said. "So where do you think you're gonna find gumbo way up there in Missouri, eh?"

The question came with an intonation that made it sound as if it might make me change my mind about leaving.

Truth be told, though gumbo was my chief comfort food, a dish I never grew tired of no matter how many times I ate it, I hadn't really given that question any thought. I'd never been to Missouri and I had no real idea what Missouri people ate. Down here, in the South Louisiana Gumbo Belt, *everybody* ate gumbo and many mom-and-pop Cajun and Creole restaurants now served it. For all I knew, Missouri people fixed gumbo, too.

It had also not dawned on me that, if gumbo could *not* be found in Missouri, I was out of luck because as much as I loved my gumbo I had not yet mastered the gumbo pot. This was not, I can say truthfully, a matter of chauvinism. I had no aversion to cooking and had become reasonably adept at barbecue. And in South Louisiana, it's absolutely common for the man of the house to not just cook but to cook proudly and well, although in many cases he limits himself to one or two signature dishes.

Gumbo, jambalaya, and boiled seafood are prime examples of South Louisiana Man Cookery. Dad, for example, was the crawfish, crab, and shrimp boiler in our family. My brother, Pershing Wells, married into a big family of Cajuns from Bayou Petit Caillou below Houma and his then father-in-law, Myo Pellegrin, was such a renowned jambalaya chef that he was invited to cook his recipe at the White House. (The only negative part of this story is that the president at the time was Richard Nixon.) My Uncle Pershing Toups (for whom my brother Pershing was named) turned out terrific Cajunized chicken and ribs on his barbecue pit in his Thibodaux backyard.

Since my mother cooked so well and since nothing pleased her more than cooking for her husband and sons, and since gumbo was her tour de force, I'd seen no need to learn the gumbo pot. So, I more or less laughed off my mother's question about gumbo prospects in the State of Missouri. I would soon find out, however, that Bonnie knew more about the intensity of my gumbo cravings than I knew myself.

I got to campus, found a dark but livable basement apartment that I shared with two easygoing roommates (one of them, Rans Pierson, coincidentally from Louisiana) and settled into classes. Columbia, population about fifty thousand at the time, was a pleasant enough town with one attribute I truly admired—the tons of cheap downtown beer bars. I liked my classes, my profs, and my fellow students. I was doing well academically. But I had severely misjudged Missouri as a place closer to the South than to the Midwest.

Weatherwise, I was in for a shocker. Thanksgiving arrived in a snowstorm and by Christmas the campus was in the grips of a winter that seemed downright Canadian and would last deep into April. In bayou country, the buttercups are in full bloom by thc first of March. I began calling it the State of Misery instead of the State of Missouri. The cold, ice, snow, and short, gloomy days led to cabin fever, which intensified my homesickness and my need for comfort food. On that front, I was out of luck.

I had nothing against burgers, fries, BLTs and a sandwich called the Reuben, which I'd discovered in a popular campus diner. And since I'd managed to snag a job as a graduate teaching assistant—which paid what seemed like a fortune at $330.00 a month—I would now and then splurge. One of my indulgences was dining at a local chicken shack where they served up a three-piece special of tasty fried chicken drenched, almost as an afterthought, in tangy barbecue sauce. The sides included mashed potatoes and collard greens—but they were bland compared with the same dishes cooked back home.

As for gumbo, no way. One person I asked thought gumbo was some version of voodoo. The better restaurants in town served Midwestern food—pot roast, pork chops, baked chicken, steamed green beans and cauliflower, middle-of-the-road sausages that tasted nothing like the well-seasoned andouille or boudin I'd grown up on.

Where was the spice, the bold flavors, the passion?

At some point, it dawned on me that I might not survive till spring without my gumbo fix.

So one desperate evening, I did a thing I'd never done in all the years I'd lived in Louisiana. I called my mother and asked her how to make gumbo.

There was a silence on the phone that night. And then our conversation went something like this, Bonnie unable to keep the "I told you so" tone from her voice:

"Well, cher, it's kind of hard to do over the phone."

"How come?"

"Well, it's easier to show than tell."

"OK. But just tell me what you put in it."

"Oh, that's the easy part."

As my mother began her list and I began to scribble, I realized it wasn't going to be that easy. For one thing, she now confessed that she'd never written down her recipe. For another, she might change things up now and then.

Also, what gumbo did I have in mind? She knew that I loved her shrimp-okra gumbo slightly more than I loved her chicken-and-sausage gumbo. But, ah, fresh shrimp and okra, she surmised (with a "Tsk, tsk, tsk" in her voice), might be hard to find up there in the Midwestern cornfields. Meanwhile, I should easily be able to get chicken and some kind of smoked sausage, even if it's not authentic andouille.

"If you even say *andouille* up there, they're gonna look at you like you're crazy."

I said nothing but realized Ma had a point.

"Then there's the Trinity," she said.

"The Trinity?"

"Yes, you remember," my mother replied, "the three vegetables that go into every gumbo—celery, onion and bell pepper. If you don't have the Trinity, it's not gumbo in my opinion. Now, some people add a little fresh diced garlic to their Trinity. I do, sometimes. It depends on how I'm feeling. Surely, Kenny, you can find celery, onion, bell pepper, and garlic up in Missouri, right?"

I ignored this gratuitous dig at my obviously foolish decision to attend graduate school in a place so ill located that a person couldn't find fresh shrimp, okra, and andouille for a proper gumbo. I switched the subject to spices.

"Salt and pepper to taste," my mother replied. "Maybe some cayenne or Tabasco—I know you like your gumbo a little hot. Some bay leaf. I put it in toward the end. Can you find bay leaf up there?"

Bonnie didn't wait for an answer. "Some people put in a little oregano, but just a pinch. I don't, usually. Some people throw in a pinch of thyme, too. Sometimes I'll put in a little of that. Maybe some paprika. Just a pinch. This all goes in after you've married your vegetables and the roux and poured in your stock and simmered that for a while. I make my stock from the chicken trimmings, but you can get canned stock from the supermarket. Oh, and filé, but remember, don't put the filé in while you're cooking the gumbo. It goes in afterward. If you cook your filé your gumbo will turn bitter."

Filé, I knew, was rendered from ground sassafras leaves and its application in gumbo was subject to a rather robust debate even in the deepest part of the Gumbo Belt. Some people do stir in filé as the gumbo is cooking, a fact that always drew one of my mother's patented "You've got to be kidding" looks.

While filé was now ubiquitous in South Louisiana supermarkets and some older Cajuns and Creoles made their own from sassafras trees growing in their yards, I doubted filé existed in Missouri.

My mother read my mind. "You'll never find filé up there. Nobody will even have heard of it. You'll have to stock up next time you come home. Oh, a couple more things. Don't add your sausage too early. Otherwise, your gumbo will be too oily and your sausage tough. You can also throw in a sliced hard-boiled egg, if you want to. It goes in with the file, after the gumbo's cooked. It absorbs the gumbo's flavor."

If this seems like a lot to take in, it was. I had not fathomed gumbo cooking to be this complicated. Still, I dutifully wrote down the ingredients. But then I realized I had to back up. I'd not given much thought to the roux thing.

"So, Mom, explain the roux again."

Another silence.

"It's hard to explain over the phone," she said.

"I know. You keep saying that. But I'm desperate."

So, my mother laid out, as best as she could, the proper procedures for making a roux. "It's just flour browned in hot oil," she explained.

"OK, that doesn't seem too hard."

"Yeah, well, the thing is, Kenny, you can't stop stirring 'cause you'll burn your roux if you do. And if you burn the roux, you might as well throw it out and start over. Your gumbo will never be anything but bitter. Now, if you undercook your roux, that's bad, too. Really bad. Your gumbo will be weak and pasty. You have to get exactly the right color."

"And what color would that be?"

"Depends. How dark do you want to make it? The color affects the flavor. Mine, well, I usually bring it to a dark café au lait color. Or maybe pecan. My roux for my chicken-and-sausage gumbo is usually darker than my roux for my seafood gumbo. That's just how I like it."

So, there wasn't really a *right* color, only a color in a range depending upon my mother's whims that day and some amorphous idea of the roux's relation to taste and ingredients.

This roux business was presenting itself as a wrench in my gumbo-making ambitions.

"What if I don't make a roux?" I asked my mother.

Another "Tsk, tsk, tsk."

"Then, if you want my opinion, whatever you're making, it won't be gumbo. You can call it a soup but not a gumbo. The roux is the soul of the gumbo."

I repeated this silently to myself: "The roux is the soul of the gumbo."

I had no idea my mother could wax so poetic.

It was also kind of scary. Gumbo wasn't just a soup. It had a soul, for heaven's sake, a soul that would be in my hands!

Like every child observant of the basic dispositions of their parents, I had come to realize that my father and mother had certain polar-opposite tendencies. Bonnie, maybe because of the rather strict regimen of Cajun Catholicism she grew up in, preferred to think of the world as good but was inclined to a certain strain of pessimism. If things can go bad they usually will. Rex, despite his impoverished Arkansas upbringing—or maybe because he survived it—tended to think that everything would work out, even in cases where it was pretty clear they wouldn't.

In that way, I suppose I am my father's son. Armed with Bonnie's instructions, I not only went out and bought ingredients for my first chicken-and-sausage gumbo, substituting a generic smoked sausage for andouille, I invited my roommate and some grad school chums to come over for dinner on the Saturday I planned to cook it.

In retrospect, learning to cook a gumbo based on notes taken over the phone is a little like learning to have sex by reading a manual or asking your friends how to do it. It's never going to come out well. Showing or doing is always going to be better than telling.

Afraid that I would burn my roux—and scorch its soul!—I woefully undercooked it. My gumbo came out looking pale and pasty—more or less the color of Campbell's Cream of Mushroom Soup. Lumps of flour floated in the broth. It tasted doughy, bland—pathetic, really. My gumbo had no flavor. My gumbo had no soul.

I ladled some out into a small bowl and offered it to my cat. She sniffed and turned away. No thanks.

All this transpired before my guests arrived. I dumped the zombie gumbo in the garbage and ordered in pizza for everyone.

At Christmas break, I drove home in the Chevy, marched into my mother's house and said, "Show me."

Bonnie smiled and said, "It's about time, cher." She bent down before her kitchen cabinet and got out her well-worn, stainless-steel gumbo pot.

We made that first gumbo together and then a second one, my mother patiently guiding me through all her little rituals and methods. The roux, I learned, was truly the tricky part. You couldn't be in too much of a hurry; a good roux can't be rushed. Your burner can't be set too high or too low (especially if you're a rookie uncertain of your timing). You can't stop stirring or watching for that magic moment when the roux rotates to just the proper, rich café au lait color.

At that very moment, you toss in the Trinity and stir like crazy over the sizzle and the stunning aromas that well up from the bottom of the pot.

Like magic—or some religious moment—your roux stops darkening as your vegetables transfigure themselves into a caramelized state. As you pour in the first few cups of warm stock, just enough to cover the Trinity, the soul of the gumbo reveals itself in aromatic glory.

I cooked my first solo gumbo, made with chicken and supermarket-bought smoked sausage, back at Missouri. (I'd brought a stash of filé from home.) It wasn't exactly my mother's gumbo, as close as I tried to hew to the recipe. Still fearful of a burnt roux (and ruined soul!), I didn't get this one quite as dark as I should've.

No matter. It was a fine gumbo, light chestnut in color. It tasted like *real* gumbo. I liked it. My rice, I'm happy to say, turned out perfectly. I savored every bite and when I served it to my friends, all them admittedly unpicky graduate students chained by budget and schedule to fast food, the oohing and aahing went on and on. I had become a star chef overnight, even if my repertoire was a single dish.

I also had the good sense to realize it wasn't exactly *me*. I was only the vessel stirring the roux. It's what I came to realize was the Gumbo Effect. It was the *dish* itself. Gumbo, if you just stuck to the plan with love and attention, transformed itself into food magic.

It took me slightly longer to realize I had found something deeper. By learning to cook gumbo at Bonnie's side, I had sealed a connection to my family and our ancient roots in a place so intricately woven by history, culture, and geography that gumbo could only have come from there.

{ 2 }

ACADEMIC GUMBO

It's a Swamp Out There

But what of that history?

While much of the world views gumbo as a Cajun and/or Creole invention, gumbo's history is far more complex than that; in fact, it took a veritable gumbo of cultures to create the dish as we know it today. Just who and how many is still being debated.

Many food scholars, notably among them John Folse, whose book, *The Encyclopedia of Cajun & Creole Cuisine* is in its fourteenth printing, subscribe to the theory of the seven nations. In this view, New Orleans and South Louisiana, in a period roughly between 1700 and 1850, received wave after wave of culinary-minded cultures—first the French, then the Africans, then the Spanish, followed by the Acadians, who fit under the French rubric. Then came the Germans, then the Americans with the Louisiana Purchase in 1803, with the Italians bringing up the rear.

In the first half or so of what might be termed "the Great Compression," these settlers found in place a Native American population with its own gifts to the pot. The result was a fusion of tastes, ingredients, recipes, and techniques that not only would produce gumbo, but the best regional cooking in America. "Where else in America did these different culinary influences come together within, historically speaking, such a relatively short period to produce a cuisine like this?" says Folse, whose name adorns a culinary institute at my alma mater, Nicholls State University. "The answer is—nowhere."

I think the seven-nations theory is utterly convincing as it applies to the evolution of South Louisiana's signature style of cooking in general. But what of gumbo specifically? Were some of these nations/ cultures more influential than others in gumbo's development during this period of the Great Compression? Central to this question is the French/European impact on gumbo and that of the African/Creole "black hand in the pot."

Until the last decade or so, many food writers, scholars, and chefs tended to downplay or even outright ignore the Creole role. Sure, the Africans, who began arriving as slaves in 1719, came with okra, rice, knowledge of how to cultivate both, and their word-of-mouth recipes for okra stews and soups. And, yes, their name for okra in the Bantu dialect was *ki ngombo* or simply gombo or gombeau—a logical explanation of how gumbo got its name. One fanciful telling has it that Louisiana-bound slaves smuggled okra seeds in their hair braids, so desperate were they to retain the ability to cook their traditional okra stews and soups. More likely, cultivatable quantities of these staples were larded aboard ships by the slave traders themselves in quantities large enough to feed their captives on the long voyage to America and to sustain them in their involuntary new homes. Both okra, and eventually rice, would thrive in Louisiana's sultry subtropical climate.

But according to the Eurocentric view of gumbo's evolution, it was the European influence, most notably that of the French and later the Acadians (who were of French stock), Spanish, and Germans, who would be responsible for the creation and refinement of gumbo. The Italians, who arrived toward the end of this great compression, are credited with bringing more gusto to the dish.

And everyone knows that France, Spain, and Italy constitute three of the great cooking cultures, not just of Europe, but of the world. The Germans, if they didn't cook with the sophistication of the southern Europeans, were famous for their advanced knowledge of charcuterie and sausage-making in particular.

But the cooking of Native Americans and the Africans? Not so much. History told us that, all the way back to the colonial times of Bienville and Iberville, the French elite came with their chefs as did Louisiana's Spanish overlords who followed. But could anyone comb the history books and name a great and influential African or Native American chef during that period? No.

An opening salvo against this Eurocentric interpretation came in 2010 from the pen of Lolis Eric Elie, an African American journalist who would go on to be a script editor for the hit HBO TV series *Treme*. (It's set in the historically significant African American neighborhood in New Orleans of that name.) He wrote an essay for the literary quarterly *Oxford American*, titled, "The Origin Myth of New Orleans Cuisine." Elie, who grew up in New Orleans eating his momma's Creole gumbo (declaring it, as he should, "the best gumbo on earth"), did a serious survey of New Orleans food literature going back to the writings of journalist Lafcadio Hearn in the 1870s and beyond.

What he found was basically a whitewashing of the "black hand in the pot" role. Too many contemporary food writers, in Elie's view, were perpetuating the myth that Creole cuisine's basic roots lay with the more "elegant" cuisine of Europe. "Most portrayals of the black contributions to Creole cooking," he wrote, "assume that black people had a mysterious talent for cooking and that, unlike the Europeans, they didn't include any of the techniques from their homeland in their cooking in the Americas."

As the preface to the first edition of *The Picayune Creole Cook Book*, (1901), asserts, the city's great cooking emerged when "the Creole negro cooks of nearly two hundred years ago carefully directed and instructed by their white Creole mistresses"—themselves schooled in the "gastronomic lore of France"—dutifully followed and absorbed these cooking lessons and "improved upon the product's [*sic*] of Louisiana's mother country." In this view, black cooks were merely the vessels into which their white overlords poured their culinary knowledge.

Elie also quotes from the 1992 edition of *The Plantation Cookbook* by the Junior League of New Orleans, which gives the "black hand in the pot" absolutely no credit: "French colonists brought a wealth of recipes that were to form the basis of Creole cooking. Robust Spanish colonials followed and imposed their own spicy touches to established dishes. . . . German immigrants who farmed near the mouth of the river became the largest producers of local rice. Like corn in the uplands, rice was the staple of lowland tables. Italian colonists increased the use of garlic and hot peppers."

Elie, however, pointed out that the Junior Leaguers actually didn't provide any of those French recipes and overlooked the fact that those hot peppers they attribute to the Italians and Spanish are actually New World foods that the Europeans got from the people they colonized.

Also overlooked was the fact that the Senegambians—the West African ethnic group that comprised the largest component of Louisiana's slaves—had been cooking spicy stews and soups with okra, rice, and even thickeners for centuries. Jessica B. Harris, the African American writer and culinary historian who has taken food-sampling trips throughout former slaving ports of Senegambia, sees a direct parallel to gumbo's evolution and contemporary okra dishes like superkanja (sometimes spelled soupoukandia) still cooked in countries like Senegal and Gambia. Like gumbo, superkanja is a one-pot dish served over rice. It features copious amounts of okra and onions and bell pepper and often a mixture of both meat and seafood as is the case of some contemporary Creole gumbo recipes. But it doesn't employ a roux and is typically more stewlike than souplike; the addition of hot peppers often give it a fiery kick.

As for blacks and cooking, Harris also notes that there are records of slaves being pressed into serving as cooks aboard the slaving ships. During the Louisiana plantation period from the time of the French settlement from about 1699 until the end of the Civil War in 1865, African women often labored in the kitchens of "the Big House" and the slaves obviously cooked for each other.

Giving the argument for the "black hand in the pot" a boost was the startling discovery by Louisiana-born historian Gwendolyn Midlo Hall, professor emeritus of history at Rutgers University, who has won wide acclaim for her groundbreaking research into slave genealogy. Dr. Midlo Hall's work is aimed at restoring names, family, and social context to African captives who in the main lie buried and forgotten on the plantations where they toiled.

Reviewing extensive depositions in a 1764 court case involving runaway slaves before a New Orleans colonial court, Midlo Hall not only found a written reference to "gombeau" but also a reference to "giving a gombeau," i.e., what historians say was a term commonly applied to social gatherings in which gumbo was served. She was able to piece together a stunning social portrait of a group of African slaves, some of them runaways, who dined regularly on "gumbo filet." The gumbo was cooked by two female African slaves, Comba and Louison, both from the Mandinka ethnic group, in the kitchen of the house of their master, a Monsieur Cantrell, while he was away. The frequent gumbo parties, according to Midlo Hall's account, were lively, with the runaways, mostly men from the Bambara ethnic group, whooping it up. "According to Mama Comba, these Bambara men amused themselves very much," Midlo Hall writes.

And what was being cooked is unambiguously, in Hall's view, the dish we call today filé gumbo. "And it was being cooked by Africans, not Europeans," she notes.

This is important because Midlo Hall's 1764 findings show a form of gumbo already being cooked by the time the first Cajuns started to arrive in Louisiana. Recall that the previously known oldest written references to gumbo dated to 1803 and 1804. The 1804 record was particularly significant because it referenced gumbo in a Cajun context.

No recipe exists for this filé gumbo and so the question remains: Did it resemble the okra stews that the slaves had cooked in Africa or had it by that time mutated into a dish (perhaps with a roux borrowed from the French?) that we would easily recognize today?

There are other tantalizing hints about the influence of the black hand in the pot in gumbo's evolution. Though the first African American cookbooks weren't published until after the Civil War, the recipes in some cases seem to reach back to the slavery period. One of these shows that a dish called gumbo was being cooked elsewhere in the slaveholding South—though not nearly as widely as in Louisiana—and that blacks were likely cooking it.

The evidence is in the 1881 cookbook, *What Mrs. Fisher Knows About Old Southern Cooking* by Abby Fisher. She was born in South Carolina in the 1830s, daughter of a French-born slave owner and a Carolina-born slave. At some point before the Civil War, Mrs. Fisher moved to Mobile, Alabama, where she lived with her husband, a minister. In the late 1870s, the Fishers moved to San Francisco, where she made a living as a cook and started a successful pickling business. Her cookbook notes that she was the mother of eleven children.

Mrs. Fisher could neither read nor write but she dictated her book to well-placed San Francisco friends who admired her gifts and wanted to make sure they would be preserved for posterity. Food scholars who have studied Fisher's book—at that point only the second recipe book written by an African American—are reasonably convinced that the recipes come from her years cooking during the antebellum period when she lived in South Carolina and Alabama. She included two gumbo recipes: Ochra Gumbo and Oyster Gumbo Soup.

"Ochra" gumbo sounds more like a stew: diced okra cooked in beef broth and served over "dry boiled rice." Oyster Gumbo Soup begins with browned chicken to which are added oysters, but no fresh okra, and then finished off with a tablespoon of an ingredient she called "gumbo."

Could this be dried, powdered okra or could she have meant filé powder, the gift of the Native Americans? The latter is the most likely. And these recipes certainly could bolster the case that early New Orleans Creole gumbo was a rouxless variety adapted from the African tradition of okra stews and soups.

Some gumbo historians, while acknowledging the evidence of gumbo's African provenance, proffer an alternative prototype for gumbo's original template: The French seafood soup from Provence known as bouillabaisse. It's a spicy fish stew cooked in a broth of herbs and vegetables, including celery and onions, and made with at least two and often three kinds of fish, both finfish and shellfish. The bouillabaisse theory of gumbo's origins drives many in the black-hand-in-the-pot camp crazy because it puts gumbo's invention solidly into the French-cooking camp.

Bouillabaisse would certainly have been known to Louisiana's French founders who began to carve the city they called *La Nouvelle-Orléans* out of the wilderness in 1718 and came with cooks. According to lore, that same year French Louisiana's first governor, Jean-Baptiste Le Moyne de Bienville, employed a relative known as Madame Langlois to essentially open a cooking school for young French women "poor but of good character" who had been recruited from convents and orphanages in Paris and its environs to become the wives of New Orleans' male colonists. In some circles, Madame Langlois, who was said to have learned some techniques from Native American cooking, is called "the mother of Creole cuisine"—though there is no record that she cooked bouillabaisse (and some now believe her Bienville lineage may be a construct or that she, in fact, may have been an arche-type and not a real person).

And it's not implausible that the Acadians brought bouillabaisse recipes from France to Maritime Canada and cooked some form of the dish before they were exiled to Louisiana, although there is no record of this. The French Acadians and their Louisiana Cajun ancestors didn't reliably start writing down recipes until the mid-twentieth century.

The French and the Acadians also had the mirepoix, a preparation of onions, green bell peppers, and carrots still used in many classic French dishes. The mirepoix could have served as a prototype for the Trinity of onions, bell peppers, and celery of modern gumbos. And two of its ingredients, onions and bell peppers, make it into some bouillabaisse recipes. Bouillabaisse isn't made with a roux, but the broth is sometimes served separately and is often paired with a thick *rouille*, a mayonnaise made of olive oil, egg yolks, garlic, saffron, and cayenne pepper, slathered on grilled slices of bread.

Folse is among the numerous proponents of the bouillabaisse the-ory, arguing that the French not only came with their cooks and a knowledge of bouillabaisse and shellfish soups but with what would become the gumbo game changer, the roux. "So, it's easy to see that these things would naturally find a way to marry," he says.

In his *Oxford American* essay, Elie counters that the elaborately prepared dish of France leans heavily toward the use of finfish. "Sea-food gumbo," he writes, "by contrast, never contains finfish. Moreover, gumbo in Cajun Louisiana often consists of sausage and fowl and no seafood. That dish lacks any connection at all to the seafood soup of Marseilles." The Charleston-based food writer Robert F. Moss takes Elie's position on bouillabaisse and, in an otherwise evenhanded essay on gumbo's history for the website Serious Eats, declares any assertion of bouillabaisse's gumbo provenance "nonsense" and a "red herring." According to Moss, "This notion is repeated everywhere from slapdash food blogs to peer-reviewed academic books. It's also completely wrong."

I don't have a dog in this fight (I have never cooked bouillabaisse and only eaten it once). Moss and Elie have done serious, thoughtful gumbo research and a number of chefs I interviewed were also skeptical of the bouillabaisse model, among them Patrick Singley, owner of the New Orleans high-style Creole restaurant, Gautreau's, and Marcelle Bienvenu, who did a turn at New Orleans's iconic Commander's Palace. I respect their opinions but I'm not convinced that bouillabaisse as a gumbo template can be dismissed out of hand.

Some who have sleuthed deeply into gumbo's history, among them Ryan Brasseaux, dean of Davenport College at Yale University and a southwest Louisiana native, take a kind of middle position. Brasseaux, in an email, writes, "I'm not convinced that there is much traction (to the bouillabaisse connection) though I cannot completely dismiss the claim. . . . Moreover, seafood does not move beyond coastal communities before the advent of refrigeration" in the late 1800s and early 1900s. But it's not implausible, in Brasseaux's view, that bouillabaisse was being cooked in colonial Louisiana's coastal towns which, like New Orleans, had ready access to fresh seafood.

The other argument against bouillabaisse is in a way aesthetic: Why would any cook, having labored for hours over an intricate soup that is crafted to be both delicious and pleasing to the eye (and that includes the world's most expensive spice, saffron) want to turn it into something else?

When I interviewed Folse about these matters, his point was not that he was dead certain about the link or that it in any way obviates the African/Creole contribution to gumbo to which he gives homage in his continually updated encyclopedia. His view is that home cooks can be as restlessly experimental as professional chefs and particularly in frontier settings where improvisation is often necessary. And in the great tradition of experimentation and the concept of fusion cooking, it's hardly implausible.

Or as Folse said to me, "Maybe you have a simplified bouillabaisse and maybe you have a roux and maybe one day you say, 'Oh, I wonder what this would taste like if we put these things together?' Bouillabaisse becomes the stock for the gumbo."

Maybe it never happened. But the idea doesn't strike me as nonsense. The more gumbo I sampled in my ramblings throughout the Gumbo Belt, the more I encountered intricately prepared gumbos that, even if bouillabaisse was not the conscious template, were bouillabaisse-like in their complexity. The gumbo at Liuzza's by the Track in New Orleans is one example, in my opinion. The Gumbo Ya Ya at Mr. B's Bistro in New Orleans is another. Neither is cooked with finfish, but my point is that in their taste profiles and intricate preparation and mix of ingredients, they seem closer to the bouillabaisse model than to the simple okra stews that seem clearly to be the template for early Creole gumbos. So even if the dish isn't gumbo's original inspiration, it could have served as a pathway to some of the more complex versions of gumbo we find today.

There are multiple examples of fusion dishes, both historical and modern. You may think of the spicy curry, vindaloo, as an Indian dish but it actually is a fusion of Portuguese and Indian cooking dating back to the four centuries of Portuguese rule over the Indian region of Goa. Ramen noodles that have satisfied the dorm-room cravings of millions of college kids? The result of nineteenth-century Japanese assimilation and spicing up the traditional Chinese noodle for their own tastes, at a time when the Chinese and Japanese were at each other's throats. There is even a distinctive version of Korean ramen known as ramyeon.

I attended the 2016 Festivals Acadiens et Créoles, a celebration of regional food and music held annually in Lafayette, Louisiana, and dined on crawfish tamales and crawfish tacos, the Cajun/Creole rendering of two Mexican staples. (They were delicious, by the way.)

On the other hand, Elie is right about the absence of finfish in contemporary seafood gumbo. I ate seafood gumbo in restaurants and homes in New Orleans and all across the Gumbo Belt and not one had finfish in it. I also would never put finfish in my gumbo because my mother was resolute that no finfish belonged in any gumbo of any kind.

That said, I discovered in my travels and in scores of interviews that there is widespread ignorance—mine included—about what other people put in their gumbo. I learned from older gumbo cooks in particular that the protein that went into the dish in previous decades could be far more eclectic and exotic than today's dominant repertoire of chicken, duck, sausage, and shellfish.

Folse told me that back in his grandfather's day, his family, who help to settle Louisiana's River parishes, put squirrel, smoked raccoon, and rabbit in their gumbos—whatever they could catch. I was having my hair cut by a young woman in a Houma salon who swore her Cajun maw-maw once made a gumbo out of the skinned carcass of a snake. It was that or go hungry. (Full disclosure: I emailed her for the recipe but never received it. But I don't think she was pulling my leg.)

Retired Houma judge Timothy Ellender, nephew of the late gumbo-cooking U.S. senator Allen Ellender, told me he makes a gumbo out of oyster drills. These are whelks that the Cajuns call *bigorneaux* (bee-gah-NO). It's based on a recipe he got from an old Cajun friend. I've never heard of anyone else cooking such a gumbo.

And combing through archives, I did stumble upon a gumbo recipe with finfish in the 1990 edition of *Bayou Gourmet Cookbook*, published by my old employer, the *Houma Courier*. The recipe titled Cost a Lot Gumbo calls for crab, oyster, shrimp, and speckled trout. Made with a roux, it's not bouillabaisse, but the ingredients would be at home in bouillabaisse.

Consider, too, that in some of the earliest written references to gumbo, all manner of what today would be considered nontraditional ingredients got stirred into the pot. In his memoirs, the French colonial prefect overseeing the transfer of Louisiana from France to the United States in 1803, Pierre Clément de Laussat, writes of hosting a twelve-hour dinner for the acting governor of Spanish Louisiana, Marqués de Casa Calvo. "As a local touch, twenty-four gumbos were served, six or eight of which were sea turtle," Laussat wrote.

I know of no one today who makes sea turtle or even turtle gumbo; among other things, sea turtles are a federally protected species. But if in New Orleans in 1803 they were making six to eight varieties of sea turtle gumbo, is it really much of a stretch to think they might be making finfish gumbo?

In *The Picayune Creole Cook Book* (1901), whose preface implies its compilation of recipes could date back two hundred years to the very founding of Louisiana, there are nine gumbo recipes with numerous ingredient we don't normally find in gumbo today, among them ham, squirrel, and steak. A recipe for cabbage gumbo requires cooks to stir a pint of milk into the stock. (This is a dish that bears some resemblance to *soup de la Toussaint*, a cabbage and turnip soup that the Acadians brought with them from Canada and which they cooked assiduously for Sunday dinner until the coming of gumbo.) There's a rabbit gumbo finished with oysters.

And there are historical references of bouillabaisse in New Orleans, one of which Elie himself cites in his *Oxford American* essay. It comes from the British novelist, William Makepeace Thackeray, whose 1861 essay, "Mississippi Bubble," collected in *Roundabout Papers*, tells of dining at a New Orleans restaurant on Lake Pontchartrain: "It seemed to me the city of the world where you can eat and drink the most and suffer the least. At Bordeaux itself, claret is not better to drink than at New Orleans. . . . At that comfortable tavern on Pontchartrain we had a bouillabaisse than which a better was never eaten at Marseilles."

The Picayune Creole Cook Book contains a bouillabaisse recipe that calls for using two Louisiana fish, the red snapper found in the deep gulf and redfish from its saltwater bays. (And, yes, the recipe employs saffron.) Again, these are recipes that could go back decades, if not centuries.

The other undercurrent I detected in this debate is a Creole back-lash of sorts against the hagiography of Cajunized gumbo during the long reign of superstar Cajun chefs like Paul Prudhomme and Folse, and the total ascension of the roux in the gumbo pot. There is no doubt that roux is French, that the Acadians had it in Canada, employing it in dishes such as poutine, and that the Louisiana Cajuns amped it up in their new home. These days, the roux has so come to dominate gumbo that it is hard to find even a Creole restaurant in New Orleans that serves gumbo made without one. But if you go back and read the gumbo recipes in *The Picayune Creole Cook Book*, only two of the nine gumbos were cooked with a roux.

When Cajun and other Louisiana cooks began employing the roux in gumbo isn't clear. Some, like the Charleston food writer Moss, argue that the roux, despite a smattering of historical mentions, came late as a fixture to gumbo. True, there is mention of a roux-based gumbo in an 1880 letter to the *New Orleans City Item-Tribune* news-paper. And Lafcadio Hearn's 1885 cookbook *La Cuisine Creole* has an oyster gumbo calling for browning flour in a tablespoon of oil. That's a roux, even though he doesn't call it a roux by name. These citations aside, Moss, in another essay for Serious Eats, writes that "it wasn't until the 1950s that roux become the standard in Creole gumbo recipes—and in Creole cooking in general."

Creole cooking perhaps, but not Cajun. My Toups family was most certainly making gumbo by 1900 and probably well before that and every recipe that came down by word of mouth used a roux. Randy Cheramie, a former restaurateur who teaches, among other things, gumbo-making at the Chef John Folse Culinary Institute in Thibodaux, has roux-based gumbo recipes from his great-grandmother dating back to the late 1800s. When I interviewed one-hundred-year-old Matine Verdin, who recalls eating gumbo as a child growing up in a French-speaking Native American enclave of Pointe-aux-Chenes in the marshlands south of Houma, her clan's gumbos were made with roux.

Indeed, roux is so ingrained among Cajun cooks that my mother had no concept of a gumbo without one. In her big Cajunized Catholic family and among Cajun friends who lived in the cloistered world that was the Cajun experience back then, rouxless gumbo was blasphemy.

Lest you think this is an antiquated notion, not really. In 2006, the effervescent Ms. Bienvenu, who teaches at the Chef John Folse Culinary Institute, published a food memoir of her Cajun upbringing. The title: *Who's Your Mama, Are You Catholic, and Can You Make a Roux?*

Historians, among them Ryan Brasseaux, note that the ingredients for the roux—flour and some form of animal fat or lard—were in place even during the earliest days of colonial Louisiana. True, wheat wouldn't grow in Louisiana's hot, subtropical climate, making flour an expensive import in Louisiana's first century. But it could be had. The first mention of a bakery in New Orleans dates from 1725. A 1971 cookbook, *Recipes and Reminiscences of New Orleans*, noted of flour during that period that "the only source of supply was France, whose vessels, loaded with food stuffs for the little colony, would arrive in port every two or three months."

As for the browning agent for the roux, forget butter. It was rarer than flour in early colonial Louisiana. But animal fats were not simply present but ubiquitous, one in particular: bear lard. Or as Brasseaux explained, "With butter generally absent from the diets of most colonial Louisianans, early roux relied on oil rendered from local bear lard. Bear oil was not only in wide circulation. . . . With a higher smoke point than butter, cooks could achieve a darker, more robust roux." In Brasseaux's view, bear lard was "the initial game-changing ingredient in Louisiana's interpretation of roux."

To modern thinkers, at a time when even conventional pig lard has largely been banished from diets due to health concerns over its high fat content, bear lard no doubt sounds, in contemporary parlance, gross. Yet, a bit like the Cajuns who make a fetish of coot gumbo, a small subset of American hunters and back-to-the-land types continue to render bear lard from the carcasses of animals harvested in hunts. And they declare it a treasure. Consider this rather rapturous description in a May 2014 blog by Clay Newcomb on the *Bear Hunting Magazine* website, titled "Bear Grease 101": "When you hold a slab of bear fat you are literally holding the assimilated nutrients of the food that the bear has been eating. In Arkansas, when I see a slab of cream-white bear fat I know that I am seeing the harvest of the Eastern Deciduous Forest—primarily, white and red oak acorns."

The piece also notes—to Brasseaux's point about the ubiquity of bear lard in colonial times—that in the 1800s and before, there were no restrictions on hunting bears and bear lard was a lucrative and readily available commodity. According to the *Bear Hunting Magazine* post, "One small town in Independence County, Arkansas, named Oil Trough, got its name because of the volume of rendered bear fat it produced."

In fact, the state of Arkansas's official tourism website provides details on Oil Trough's colorful connection to bear grease: "In 1811, a band of hunters camped along the White River and staged bear hunts into the dense canebrakes that covered hundreds of acres in the area. Over 100 bears were killed and soon the hunters ran out of a place to store the oil, which was a valued commodity on the world market at that time. Huge trees were cut and fashioned into troughs to hold the oil until shipment could be arranged downstream."

And where was the bear lard headed in 1811? According to a Wikipedia entry of the town's history: New Orleans. This is entirely plausible since the White River is a major tributary to the Mississippi. To me, this all greatly strengthens the possibility that the Cajun gumbo C. C. Robin saw consumed at that 1804 Cajun house party had been cooked with a dark, bear grease roux.

That said, the rise of the roux in the hands of the Cajuns doesn't in any way obviate gumbo's Creole/black-hand-in-the-pot provenance but in fact makes a case that gumbo could easily have developed on separate tracks before evolving into the more cohesive dish we know today. That is, the early forms of New Orleans gumbos did owe their provenance to the Creole okra stews and soups that came out of Africa, both often served over rice. The Cajuns, meanwhile, would transform gumbo with their robust application of the roux. And some creative colonial cooks may have been inspired by fond memories of the bouillabaisse they tasted in the old country and melded it into a roux, creating a more complex gumbo

As for the African connection, others who have traveled in that region can't help but remark upon the similarities to modern-day Gumbo Belt cuisine. Frank Pezold, a Louisiana native who is dean of the Texas A&M University College of Science & Engineering, recalled for me his culinary experiences on numerous research trips to Guinea, Mali, and Liberia. "What struck me from the beginning was the great similarity in flavors between our south Louisiana foods and what we had there," said Pezold. "The spices, in particular, but also the common occurrence of items like okra, greens, and eggplant. There were differences, but the influence was undeniable, especially when put against the relatively bland flavors of many French foods sampled in Paris and Belgium."

A point not overlooked by the black-hand-in-the-pot camp is that it wasn't just that the roux became ascendant, but that since the Cajuns were the main drivers of the roux, there followed an assumption that gumbo was a Cajun invention. And as gumbo's fame began to spread around the nation and the world, particularly in the late 1970s and early 1980s, the myth of the Cajuns as gumbo's sole creators followed it.

I can bear witness to this, being old enough to remember those naïve days when pretty much everything French about Louisiana got labeled Cajun by outsiders and even many in the Gumbo Belt. Creole was a style of cooking generally associated with New Orleans or a term to distinguish some vibrant forms of Louisiana music such as Zydeco and Dixieland jazz. This was a time before people became more aware of and sensitive to cultural and ethnic distinctions and the web made genealogy far easier to trace. As I noted earlier, my Toups family thought of themselves as actual Cajuns—not Cajunized Swiss-Germans—until a cousin began to research the family tree in the 1980s.

Doing my own research around the same time, I stumbled upon the 1969 work of Neil J. Toups, a Lafayette, Louisiana, academic, titled *The Toups Clan and How It All Began*. It documents my mother's family going back more than four hundred years to the German-speaking part of Switzerland. In the old definition then, when Creole meant the Louisiana-born offspring of European settlers, the Toupses are actually Creoles, not Cajuns. Of course, there are Cajun grandmothers everywhere in my mother's family tree since intermarriage between German settlers and the Cajuns was common. So, what are we? Creolajuns? Cajoles?

The myth of Cajuns as gumbo's sole creators hasn't entirely died out. Consider this passage from the 2014 book, *Southeast Louisiana Food: A Seasoned Tradition*: "While the exact origins of gumbo are not fully known, once it hit the scene, it was quite popular with the Cajuns as well as the city dwellers up on New Orleans. It is fitting that the Cajuns probably invented gumbo, a dish widely known for its ability to incorporate everything."

It's also worth noting that while chefs such as Prudhomme, who passed away in 2015, and Folse may have won fame, they didn't ask for that fame or ask to become the standard-bearer for all things Cajun or claim to make the world's best gumbos. Prudhomme was often ecumenical in his praise of African American Creole cooks and cooking, as has been Folse, and both have extolled the Creole distinctions and contributions to Louisiana's food tapestry. "The Creole pot has been boiling in Louisiana for a long, long time," Folse says, "and the contributions to gumbo and the cuisine in general are substantial."

But it wasn't lost on the Creole camp that in New Orleans in particular, African American Creoles had over the decades produced their own superstar chefs, among them Eddie Baquet of the Baquet family restaurant dynasty; Buster Holmes, whose red-beans-and-rice eatery had attained local cult status; and most notable, Leah Chase who, in her mid-nineties, is still a force in her family's iconic restaurant, Dooky Chase's Restaurant. That they are rightfully ranked these days in the pantheon of great Louisiana cooks like Folse and Prudhomme is in part thanks to corrective essays like Lolis Elie's. Elie, for his part, isn't convinced that the struggle for Creole recognition has been fully won. "Younger scholars, more liberal scholars are more inclined to credit West Africans with their foundational role in developing Creole/Cajun cuisine," he wrote to me in an email. "But for folks who have not studied these things, or whose racial politics tend toward the more traditional, the idea that the Senegalese, Nigerians, Haitians, and Angolans could have been as important as the French is such a preposterous notion that they can't quite digest it."

To be clear, Ms. Chase is a bona fide celebrity in this City That Never Stops Eating. In 2016, she was given a James Beard Foundation Lifetime Achievement Award. Among other things, her gumbo z'herbes—an everything-but-the-kitchen sink, pre-Lenten gumbo made with a roux, several kinds of meat, and greens that include collards, mustard, turnips and spinach, thereby breaking with almost all gumbo orthodoxy—has gained a kind of cult status. It's that good. And when Barack Obama visited New Orleans in 2016, it was Leah Chase's gumbo that he dined on.

Meanwhile, what of the other nations' contributions to gumbo's evolution?

Like Lolis Elie, I am skeptical that there is a traceable Italian contribution to gumbo during the time of the Great Compression, i.e., the primal period of gumbo's evolution. This is not a knock on Italian culinary creativity or Italian cooking of which I'm extremely fond. I simply think they got to Louisiana too late for that. True, a small group of Sicilian immigrants were living in and around New Orleans before the Civil War but by 1850 the Italian population of New Orleans numbered only a few hundred souls in a city of about one hundred twenty thousand.

According to U.S. Census data, most Italians arrived from the old country in New Orleans on waves of immigration in the late nineteenth and early twentieth centuries. At that point, they certainly could have contributed to gumbo's refinements, perhaps introducing garlic as an add-on to the Trinity. It's not implausible—though no one knows for sure—that they were also responsible for introducing celery as part of gumbo's Trinity. Celery is thought to be of Mediterranean origin and history records that the Italians were the first to learn to cultivate it in the seventeenth century.

One student of gumbo's history, Cynthia Lejeune Nobles, in her essay "Oysters Rockefeller" for the 2009 book, *New Orleans Cuisine: Fourteen Signature Dishes and Their Histories*, also seems skeptical of an Italian contribution to early gumbo. She notes that by 1812, the year Louisiana obtained statehood and before, there was much Italian presence in New Orleans, "all the essential ingredients had arrived" and it was the city's "adventurous Creoles" who were embracing tomatoes and adding them to gumbo. And while the Italians would bring "impressive ingredients to the city's food stalls" and win acceptance of pastas and olives, these immigrants "do not seem to have significantly affected the preparation of Creole gumbo."

Both Nobles and I are also doubtful that the arrival of the Americans with the Louisiana Purchase in 1803 had much influence on the early evolution of gumbo per se. They transformed New Orleans from a failing colony into a global trading port and in that way helped to elevate the quality of life and standard of living, and by extrapolation perhaps elevated the general level of cooking. But the frontier Americans would have contributed mainly a British-Scotch-Irish sensibility to the pot. In truth, there was not much intermarriage between the predominantly white, Protestant Americans and the Cajuns and Creoles until after World War II.

And if you scan back through Southern cookbooks from the middle 1800s, you'll find a cuisine that, in general, is devoid of the spices, creativity and variety of dishes being cooked in New Orleans and the Gumbo Belt at the time. One example: in *The Housekeeper's Encyclopedia of Useful Information*, published in 1861, there is a recipe for Calf's Brains. The ingredients are one calf's brain; vinegar or lemon juice; a pint of water and an unspecified amount of butter. The recipe calls for "removing all the large fibers and skin" and soaking the brains for four or five hours in water. Then, "Lay them in boiling water with a little salt and vinegar in it, afterwards soak them in a strong white vinegar, a solution of citric acid, or lemon-juice. Dry them well, dip them in nice butter, and fry slowly in butter until done and nicely browned. Serve with drawn butter, or a sour sauce."

Anecdotal evidence should always be taken with a grain of salt, but I offer a contrast between what my Wells grandparents were cooking and eating in backwoods Arkansas in 1930 compared with what my mother's family was eating in sleepy Thibodaux around the same time. Granny Wells often said a typical meal was wild game, fatback, and hardtack biscuits over which you poured white gravy, if available. The Toups, though equally poor, had grown up eating gumbos, jambalayas, etouffees, and sauce piquants. It seems obvious to me that the Cajuns and Creoles of Louisiana, far from giving up their food for Southern recipes, largely converted the Americans to the local way of cooking and eating.

What of the Spanish?

The Spanish arrived in the Louisiana territories before the French, but they didn't think much of what they found. The Spanish explorer Hernando De Soto and his party, on May 21, 1541, were the first Europeans to set eyes on the Mississippi River. Still, Spanish settlement was halfhearted and fitful. After it became clear there was no gold to be mined, they ceded the region to the French. In 1763, as a result of the treaty that ended the French and Indian War, the Spanish took back control of all of France's former territory on the western side of the Mississippi. The British were ensconced on the other side of the river.

The Spanish would rule Louisiana until 1802, but numerous historians note that New Orleans, in particular, never stopped being other than a French city. And by the time the Spanish arrived, the African/Creole and Native American influence on traditional French cooking had already begun to transform the cuisine into something far earthier and spicier than the cuisine of France.

Successive Spanish governors brought their cooks who, trained in the traditional cooking of Spain, introduced notable Spanish dishes to the Creoles, the one-pot rice dish paella among them, and clearly, according to most food historians, the prototype for jambalaya. Spain would also help to jazz up the food because, trading with Africa and the Caribbean, the Spanish had access to all manner of spices, particularly hot peppers, and imported them by the ton.

Traditional Spanish food is savory, with spicy North African notes that the Moors, who starting in AD 711 ruled Spain for eight hundred years, had brought into the cuisine. Hot peppers, however, aren't common in classic Spanish cooking; but in the fusion of tastes in colonial Louisiana, they would soon find their way into Spanish-influenced dishes such as paella. In fact, Spanish-imported hot peppers would help to transform Louisiana colonial cooking because they had usefulness beyond taste: Cooking with hot peppers retarded bacteria growth and thus food spoilage at a time before refrigeration.

In "A True and Delectable History of Creole Cooking," in the December 1986 issue of *American Heritage* magazine, Bethany Bultman noted the ubiquitous presence of Spanish peppers among the early Cajuns, "From the Spanish period onward, no matter how poor, each household could easily grow one or two varieties of hot peppers. The flavors of foods, from old raccoon meat to 'mud bugs' (crawfish), were greatly enhanced by the addition of a little salt and a dose of red pepper."

The Spanish also brought other influences. They loved their sausage, the chorizo, as much as the German Coasters and Cajuns loved theirs. They used bell peppers, garlic, and celery in other dishes, with echoes of the gumbo Trinity. Some suggest it was the Spanish who introduced red beans to the Louisiana colonial palate; the beans are thought to have come to the New World from Spain's southern Andalusia region. Some also credit the Spanish with bringing the concept of cooking fish in tomato sauce to the colony, thereby inspiring what are now the Cajun/Creole classics of sauce piquant and courtbouillon.

The Spanish made other major contributions to the cultural and culinary landscape, among them stepping up to rebuild the French Quarter—the beating heart of the New Orleans food scene—after the great fire of 1788. They also made indirect contributions to the evolution of gumbo. For one, the Spanish warmly welcomed several hundred bedraggled Acadian refugees who arrived by chartered ship in New Orleans in and around 1767 after being stranded in Maryland and Pennsylvania for years.

Spanish hospitality, in part, was practical because the Spanish recognized the need for more farming-minded colonists, and men to staff its military garrisons, if the Louisiana experiment was going to succeed, according to Louisiana historian Carl A. Brasseaux, in his essay, "Acadian Immigration into South Louisiana, 1764–1785." Brasseaux also notes that the Spanish brought thousands of Spanish pioneers from Málaga and the Canary Islands who would settle the lower end of the Mississippi River below New Orleans in modern-day St. Bernard and Plaquemines parishes.

A primary purpose was to supply soldiers to man the Spanish garrisons along the river as a foil against any British incursions. The Isleños, as the Canary Islanders were known, joined Andrew Jackson and his

SOUTH PARK TOWNSHIP LIBRARY

ragtag bunch of regulars and pirates to defeat the British at the Battle of New Orleans in 1815. But for that victory, New Orleans would have fallen to the British, and its cuisine might have devolved into chicken fried steak, white gravy, and New England boiled dinners.

By the mid-nineteenth century, the Isleños, some of them inter-marrying with Cajuns, had asserted themselves in a different way, having become master boat builders and fishermen. For generations, they were the chief suppliers of fresh seafood—oysters, crabs, and shrimp in particular—to the New Orleans markets and restaurant trade. Basically, they formed the supply chain for seafood gumbo, a role they continue to play today.

As for the Germans, the first German settlers began arriving in Louisiana in 1721 in and around the modern-day Mississippi River town of Hahnville. They were essentially indentured servants who had been lured from Germany by the John Law Company of the Indies. Law's outfit had been granted a twenty-five-year concession by the French to help bring settlers to their struggling Louisiana holdings. I have a personal interest in this. My sixth great-grandfather, Caspar Dubs—later changed in the French census to Caspar Toups—was one of them, as was John Folse's original Louisiana forebear. In fact, it appears, based upon genealogical records, that Chef's ancestor and mine shipped out from the same port in France a year apart.

The Germans were in for a lot of surprises, most of them unpleasant. To gain the Louisiana concession, Law, the Scotsman who was one of the eighteenth century's great financial speculators and promoters (and, some might argue, con men), had in return pledged to bring at least six thousand Europeans and three thousand Africans to the Louisiana French colonies. He knew where to look for the Europeans.

Germany at that time was a mess. Besides sporadic outbreaks of war, violence, and famine, Germans suffered both political and religious repression. Moreover, recruiters like Law used glowing and misleading pamphlets to entice would-be émigrés into believing Louisiana was a veritable paradise instead of a harsh, untamed wilderness. In reality, the low country around New Orleans was subject to hurricanes and seasonal flooding against which there was almost no infrastructure; it endured periodic outbreaks of killer illnesses like malaria and yellow fever; it was populated by Native Americans who would grow resentful and at times violent toward the settlements forced upon them.

The Germans were targeted by Law because they were considered to be hardy and industrious, with a deep knowledge of farming that was critical for settling and cultivating the territory's fertile farmlands of the Mississippi River delta. While Continental French settlers made for good cooks and bakers, they tended to make lousy farmers, and France desperately needed hardworking, skilled landsmen if its money-losing colony was to survive.

A pamphlet put out by Law's company in Germany shows the depth of fabrication Law went to in his recruiting efforts. The flavor is captured in J. Hanno Deiler's 1909 book, *The Settlement of the German Coast in Louisiana and The Creoles of German Descent*. Besides great soil and the ability to raise four crops a year, "There is also game, which every person is permitted to kill: leopards, bears, buffaloes, deer, whole swarms of Indian hens, snipe, turtle-doves, partridges, wood-pigeons, quail, beavers, martens, wild cats, parrots, buzzards, and ducks. Deer is the most useful game, and the French carry on a great 'negotium' in doeskins, which they purchase from the savages. Ten to twelve leaden bullets are given in exchange for such a skin."

And then there are the mines. "The land is filled with gold, silver, copper, and lead mines. If one wishes to hunt for mines, he need only go into the country of the Natchitoches. There we will surely 'draw pieces of silver mines out of the earth.' After these mines, we will hunt for herbs and plants for the apothecaries. The savages will make them

known to us. Soon we shall find healing remedies for the most dangerous wounds, yes, also, so they say, infallible ones for the fruits of love."

So, imagine upon landing after a sea voyage of many months, the
Germans find themselves greeted by a company of previous German
pioneers who had tried to settle the Arkansas River about 350 miles to
the north. Their wilderness experience was so horrible that they were
demanding passage back to the Old World. (They were refused.)

A census conducted in May 1722, showed 492 persons in the
Louisiana German colony—413 colonists, 297 of them of German
origin, plus 79 slaves (72 blacks and seven Indians). Two years later,
owing to hunger, storms (including a horrific hurricane in the summer of 1722) and other deprivations, the Germans had lost 128 of
their number.

According to documents in my Toups family genealogical research,
my relative, Caspar Dubs, sometimes spelled Doubs, appears in a
French census of 1724, living with his wife, two sons, ages ten and
twelve, and having cleared "one and one half arpents" (about an acre)
of land on his farm. He is the owner of three pigs. (It's at this point
that the name Doubs gets recorded as Toups by the French census-
takers and the name sticks.)

Law turned out to be right about the German work ethic and
farming abilities. After this fitful start, the so-called German Coast
flourished, and by the middle 1700s the Germans were not only self-
sustaining but became major suppliers of pork, beef, sausages, rice,
vegetables, and milk to the New Orleans market, on more than one
occasion saving the town from the brink of famine. C. C. Robin, the
Frenchman who attended that 1804 Cajun dance party where gumbo
was served, makes special note of the German presence on the same
trip: "These Germans living among the French have retained their tac-
iturn character, their language and their manners. . . . They work their
own farms, without Negroes, and although originally northern they
have become well acclimated. . . . These Germans, who are the food

suppliers of the city [New Orleans] . . . live well, without having made any fortunes," Robin writes.

Also, as mentioned earlier, the Germans took in the Acadians, and marriage with Cajun women was commonplace, in part because unlike my ancestor, Caspar Dubs, most of the German pioneers were single men. The Germans clearly taught the Cajuns the art of sausage-making and the evolution of the modern andouille sausage, now a gumbo staple, is one result of this bicultural accommodation.

And after a rough start with area Indian tribes—in and around 1748, Indian raids caused my relative, Caspar, to quit his farmlands and retreat for a while to the safety of New Orleans—relations greatly improved. Again, according to Deiler, who at the time was a German professor emeritus at Tulane University, "In the nineteenth century, the relations between the Germans and the Indians became very friendly. As late as 1845, thousands of Indians, following the migrating game, used to come from Illinois, Missouri, and Arkansas to Louisiana, to spend the winter in the south. They were given quarters in the out houses of the farmers and spent their time in hunting and making baskets. Like the migrating swallows, these Indians for generations visited at the same farms and became well acquainted with the white families, and much attached to them."

The import of this may be in evolution of the smoked sausage. According to Folse and others, the Germans clearly brought an elevated knowledge of sausage-making to the Louisiana colony, holding ritual "boucheries," the annual communal slaughtering of hogs, which were then rendered into all manner of products, sausage most notably. They also operated some of the colony's first commercial slaughterhouses.

The Native Americans, lacking refrigeration, had their own keen knowledge of meat preservation, smoking techniques in particular. It seems not implausible that, in this period of rapprochement described by Deiler, the Germans and Indians traded recipes and food-preservation techniques, and the smoked sausage took a leap forward.

The Native American contribution can't be overstated. Perhaps most influential among the Native Americans greeting the Europeans were the Choctaw, whose tribal branches inhabited not just the modern state of Louisiana, but Mississippi, Florida, and Alabama as well. They farmed and hunted. They knew butchering techniques since deer and buffalo were staples of their diet, and they knew how to slow-smoke meats to preserve them. They had a technique for browning crushed acorns, which were a dietary fixture. It's not a roux but the principle isn't all that different. And they clearly gave one gift to gumbo: the ground-sassafras powder known as filé.

And, by the way, the Choctaw term for filé was *kombo*—rhymes with *gombeau*.

This fact has emerged as a not implausible alternate explanation of how gumbo got its name since filé gumbo is among the most iconic and oldest of gumbo references. It's well known that Native Americans, during the time of the Great Compression, traded with the French, Spanish, Cajuns, and Germans and shared with them ingredients and hunting, fishing, and cooking techniques—smoking and curing of meats, for example. The natives borrowed from the Europeans and Cajuns as well.

The Cajunized canoe, known as the pirogue, was another gift from the Native Americans, who hollowed out logs to make a shallow-draft, easy-to-paddle vessel perfect for navigating the marshes and swamps for hunting and fishing expeditions. "We know, for example," says Folse, "that in Bienville's time the French traded black iron pots with the Indians for pirogues—one pot bought two boats." Before that time, Native Americans slow-cooked over open fires using gourds. Moreover, notes Folse, "they were already pounding filé and selling it in the market in New Orleans."

But were the Choctaw themselves cooking something in those pots that might resemble modern-day gumbo? Today's filé gumbo is interpreted most often as a traditional gumbo, chicken-and-sausage or seafood, into which the filé is typically stirred in at the time a gumbo is being served. This is how my mother used it, how Folse uses it, and how I use it. (A minority of filé users, among them Chef Randy Cheramie, whisk it into the gumbo while it's at a boil.)

And the early Creoles clearly used filé. In 1784, a French journal, *Observations sur la physique*, published a piece on American sassafras. Its author, a Frenchman who traveled widely in Louisiana, noted powdered sassafras was used in cooking there. "These leaves are used in sauces. A pinch of this powder is enough to make a viscous broth." He went on: "This is the dish that is called gombo in America. However, this American stew must be distinguished from the one called gombo févi. This is made with the pods of a species of mallow, known to botanists as the sabdariffa."

Sabdariffa is a plant that produces an okralike pod and is, in fact, in the okra family. *Févi* is the Louisiana Creole term for okra. So, in essence, Creole cooks had labeled the two kinds of gumbo they cooked as either gumbo filé or gumbo fevi.

This would certainly seem to strengthen the argument that the Choctaw ingredient, kombo, beat out okra as the chief thickener in the first gumbos. It was in Louisiana hundreds of years before okra arrived, and thus gumbo took its name from a corruption of *kombo*. The problem with this theory is that while we have those 1764 and 1803 and 1804 references to dishes called gumbo, gombo, or gombeau—and tons of written references by the early 1900s—no one has been able to yet find a reference to a dish called kombo, either historical or modern.

That said, Folse, during one of his many travels among ordinary gumbo cookers, interviewed a ninety-year-old man of Houmas Indian descent in southern Terrebonne Parish, whose recipe for filé gumbo is three cups of filé, salty water scooped directly from the gulf, and fresh-caught gulf shrimp, all brought to a boil. To this he sometimes added smoked garfish.

Might this have been the primordial gumbo being cooked back in those cast-iron pots the Choctaw obtained for pirogues during Bienville's day? Folse breaks with orthodoxy here. "I think gumbo was already here," he says. "I think the Native Americans were already doing their green gumbo of sassafras, sea water, and shrimp. They thickened it only with pounded sassafras."

It's an intriguing theory. But it's hard to see how the taste profile of that filé-based green gumbo by the Native Americans (even or especially with smoked gar in it) would have passed the taste test of either the French and the spice-loving Africans who were in the first wave of the Louisiana colony, or the Cajuns and Spaniards who got here later. In my view, a little filé goes a long way. But, perhaps like the Midlo Hall discovery documenting gumbo in 1764, such a reference may yet emerge.

It's interesting to me that not much has been made of the gumbo possibilities involving the frequent intermarriage in the nineteenth century of Native Americans and the *coureurs de bois*, in English, "runners of the woods." They were freelance French-Canadian fur trappers and traders who explored the lower reaches of the Louisiana territories. If colonial Louisiana had a shortage of flour and butter it also had an extreme shortage of European women. In the early days, the colony was judged too dangerous for women and children to inhabit safely. Thus, among the *coureurs de bois*, Native American women became the mates of both choice and circumstance.

How widespread this practice was is captured in the book *The Louisiana Journey*, which states, "Many *coureurs de bois* dressed like Indians, followed their customs, and married their women. . . . The French had hoped to convert the Indians to Christianity, but it seemed to Bienville that the Indians were converting the French."

Surely, the French Canadians had the roux and would have known how to render animal fats, particularly bear grease, for cooking. Their Native American wives knew how to smoke meats and process filé. It's not implausible that the tradition of smoked-game gumbo had its roots there.

When I arranged to see Jessica Harris about all this, over a leisurely New Orleans breakfast, hers is basically an ecumenical take. She's a thoughtful woman with a measured way of speaking and an intense love of her work. Ask her about her favorite gumbo and she doesn't miss a beat. "Anything that comes out of Leah Chase's pots," she says.

Harris is willing to spread a lot of the credit around. But she basically sees a straight line between the okra soups and stews of West Africa and gumbo, and believes the evidence shows that African hand in the pot "is the gumbo unifier and I think plays the dominant role" in gumbo's evolution.

Folse, though, poses an interesting question. He notes that there was slavery in the New England colonies one hundred years before slavery came to Louisiana. Moreover, the Senegambians, who were predominant among Louisiana's slaves and are the African ethnic group credited with having the biggest impact on the evolution of Louisiana colonial cuisine, were also present in large numbers throughout Colonial America. Indeed, statistics from the New York–based Schomburg Center for the Research of Black Culture show, for example, that Senegambians constituted a third of the slaves going to the Chesapeake Bay region.

"We know they were cooking American food in these places," says Folse. "So, where's their gumbo?"

The fact that gumbo, despite the presence of okra-cooking Senegambians, did not take firm root in the Chesapeake Bay region or elsewhere in New England seems evidence to me of another affirmation of the beauty of the theory of the seven nations and/or the first five nations. The difference is that the Gumbo Belt was settled early on by clearly food-centric cultures whose gifts were not merely that they liked food and could cook it, but also cultures exceptionally receptive to one another's gifts to the pot.

French, Spanish, African, Native American, German, Cajun—if you tasted it and thought it was good, you didn't care who cooked it. You wanted to know how to do it. It's how bland sauerkraut became smothered cabbage and andouille. It's how paella became jambalaya. It's how a simple African okra stew morphed into the more complex and intricately flavored dish we know as Creole gumbo. It's how gumbos cooked for generations without roux became gumbos with roux when somebody saw and tasted that dark Cajun roux and exclaimed, "Oh, my. I'd like to cook that."

It's the story of jazz but writ in food, and gumbo is the high note.

{ 3 }

GUMBO GETS GOING

Hank, Ted Kennedy, and the Great Wall of China

The Gumbo Diaspora began as a trickle and then turned into a rol-licking flood.

One of the first modern pop culture mentions of gumbo came from a seemingly unlikely source—the legendary country-music crooner and song writer, Hank Williams Sr. Williams was an Alabamian by birth, but he lived for a while in the northwest Louisiana town of Bossier City, across the river from Shreveport. Shreveport hosted a popular country music live-broadcast venue called the Louisiana Hayride—think Grand Ole Opry—where Hank often performed. (A young Elvis Presley was also a Hayride regular.)

Bossier City, 327 miles northwest of New Orleans, sits amidst the pinelands of the Protestant Bible Belt. Residents back then consid-ered the heavily Catholic, socially liberal Gumbo Belt as pretty much another country, not just another part of the state. Hank, raised by a mother who played the organ at the local Baptist church, never took to religion and was intrigued by the freer-living ramparts of South Louisiana. At some point before 1952, Williams, and/or a songwriting partner named Moon Mullican, wandered down to the Gumbo Belt.

There, they heard an up-tempo Cajun French ballad called "Grand Texas" (pronounced grohn-tex-AH, "Big Texas" in English). Williams and Mullican loved the melody, but Grand Texas was a song about loss and heartbreak. Sung in French, it was never going to get airplay on the radio in that form.

Hank and/or Mullican (biographers are split on whether the song was a collaboration) borrowed the melody, then rewrote the lyrics in English, transforming it into "Jambalaya on the Bayou." It was recorded in June 1952 with country music guitar icon Chet Atkins as part of the studio band. It hit the radio in July and stayed at the top of the country music charts for fourteen weeks and has endured to this day as a kind of Cajun pop-culture anthem. It's a joyous song about a Cajun suitor hopping in his pirogue to attend a party for his cher amio, Yvonne, at a Thibodaux dancehall called Fontenot's. Debuted in 1952, the song's chorus immortalizes the food: jambalay', crawfish pie, and, most notably, filé gumbo.

Music would continue to play a major role in the Gumbo Diaspora when, starting in the 1960s, Cajun and Creolized Zydeco began to break out of the swampland. One pivotal event, notes Cajun historian and folklorist Barry Jean Ancelet, came in 1964 when a band led by Cajun fiddle phenomenon Dewey Balfa drew a raucous, standing ovation from the mostly Yankee crowd at Rhode Island's Newport Folk Festival. It was Cajun music's first exposure to a national audience. Could these really be Americans playing toe-tapping fiddle and accordion tunes and melodic waltzes, all sung in exotic eighteenth-century country French? Who knew such people existed?

Later, according to Ancelet, musicians such as Clifton Chenier, Doug Kershaw, Michael Doucet, Buckwheat Zydeco, Zachary Richard, Steve Riley, and Wayne Toups, among them, expanded Cajun and Zydeco's reach and began to play at folk festivals and roots-music concerts all over the U.S. and the world. This began to fuel not just an interest in the music, but the culture that created it and the food that nourished it.

The seeds of gumbo's inescapable deliciousness were also being planted by an unlikely clutch of expatriate gumbo ambassadors in Washington, D.C. One of them was U.S. senator Allen J. Ellender, a Democrat from the Cajun hamlet of Montegut in the bayou lands south of my hometown of Houma. First elected in 1936, he served for thirty-five years in the Senate and was elected the Senate's president pro-tempore in 1971, putting him third in line for the presidency. He died the following year of a heart attack during a re-election campaign at the age of eighty-one.

Senator Ellender, who was fluent in Cajun French, didn't mind spending long months in Washington but couldn't bear to be there without his gumbo. So he frequently cooked large batches of shrimp-and-crab gumbo in his Senate hideaway office, serving it to senators and congressmen of both parties. President Lyndon B. Johnson and Lady Bird Johnson ate Ellender's gumbo, as did First Daughter Tricia Nixon. The lunches were packed; gumbo was attracting a large following of political bigmouths. I don't mean this as a pejorative. It's just that extremely influential people were giving gumbo rave reviews and word of its deliciousness was rapidly spreading.

I was still working for the Houma paper then and covered Senator Ellender's funeral, which drew several thousand people. President Richard Nixon came to our little town to pay his respects, as did Vice President Spiro Agnew. So did Massachusetts Senator Ted Kennedy. I snatched a five-minute interview with Kennedy outside St. Francis de Sales, the graceful Catholic church where Ellender's body lay in state. All he wanted to talk about were his memories of dining on Senator Ellender's gumbo.

Marcelle Bienvenu, who hails from St. Martinville, Louisiana, had an early career around the edge of politics before becoming a chef and culinary instructor. She recalls being on Capitol Hill as a congressional intern around the same time. Homesick for gumbo, she set up her own little gumbo-cooking operation with a small clutch of other Louisiana expatriates. Soon, they found lines outside their door of hungry Hill staffers who, having gotten one taste of gumbo, wanted more.

One day, Bienvenu was waiting for a bus home in the rain near the Capitol when a stretch limo pulled up. It was Minnesota senator Hubert Humphrey offering the Louisianans a ride.

How did he know them? The senator had heard about their gumbo feasts and was angling for an invite. "It was an eye-opener about gumbo's appeal," Bienvenu says.

Gumbo also got a ringing endorsement on national television in 1977 when the comedian Bill Cosby, at the height of his popularity, went on the Johnny Carson show and raved about an astonishing dining experience he'd had in New Orleans. The venue was a Creole restaurant called Eddie's run by an old-line New Orleans Creole family, the Baquets.

Cosby spun out an elaborate story of how, to get to Eddie's, you had to drive over railroad tracks and highway overpasses, along often deserted streets with car-swallowing potholes, only to arrive at a decrepit-looking building with nary a sign indicating it actually might be a restaurant. But inside, the gumbo and fried chicken were so good that Cosby declared it not just the best place to eat in New Orleans, but maybe best place to eat in all of America.

New Orleans itself was doing its part to spread the gumbo gospel. By the mid-1960s, its annual Mardi Gras had begun to attract tens of thousands of hungry out-of-state tourists. In 1970, private organizers launched the New Orleans Jazz & Heritage Festival. The first year it drew a small and fitful crowd to its sole Gospel tent and four open stages in Treme's Congo Square. But by 2001, celebrating a centennial in honor of city-born trumpeter Louis Armstrong, it attracted 650,000 people, perhaps half of them tourists. One of New Orleans' great gumbo shacks, Liuzza's by the Track, sits at the main Jazz Fest entrance. And these days, Jazz Fest has mutated into an annual April celebration in which the city's endemic food—including lots of varieties of gumbo—gets equal billing with the music.

Back in the Cajun part of the Gumbo Belt, gumbo was about to get another lift. In 1980, Kerry Boutté (pronounced boo-TAY), a Cajun entrepreneur blessed with his momma's gumbo recipe and a love of traditional Cajun music, recognized the need for a culturally authentic place that combined both. Oh, there were plenty of Cajun dancehalls and plenty of restaurants that served a Cajun dish or two, mostly gumbo. But, odd as it may seem, Boutté's integrated vision didn't exist. Thus, he opened Mulate's, a combination restaurant and Cajun-music honky-tonk, in the southwest Louisiana Cajun hotbed of Breaux Bridge. (You can still get world-class gumbo in Breaux Bridge—start in Glenda's Creole Kitchen on the pastoral outskirts of town—although Breaux Bridge prefers these days to bill itself as "the Crawfish Capital of the World.")

Boutté's timing was impeccable for another reason. The Gumbo Belt, where most of the state's 250,000 French speakers still reside, was in the midst of an energetic effort to revive its endemic language, then called either Cajun French (spoken by white French speakers) or Creole French (spoken predominantly by black French speakers). The state had even formed an agency, The Council for the Development of French in Louisiana, CODIFIL for short, to be the chief torchbearer for these efforts. These days, the consensus is that Louisiana French is basically an amalgam of Colonial French with roots principally in seventeenth-century northern and western France and the Canadian Maritime provinces from whence the Cajuns came, with some borrowing from the Francophone Caribbean. I suppose you could call it Gumbo French. Whatever the case, a large majority of South Louisiana's Cajuns and Creoles who, like my mother, were born before 1940, spoke some form of Louisiana French as their first language.

But then came the acculturation pressures following the two great world wars and particularly the post–World War II oil-and-gas boom. New roads, bridges, and things like telephones and television were already starting to peel away the Gumbo Belt's isolation when out-landers, many from Texas, Mississippi, and Oklahoma, flooded South Louisiana to work the oil patch. The Cajuns and Creoles found them-selves often mocked for their rustic ways, thickly accented English, "bad" French, and in many cases, lack of much formal education. In an effort to "Americanize" the Cajuns and Creoles, kids were sometimes punished for speaking French on the school grounds.

Little wonder, then, that French speakers like my mother and huge numbers of others of her generation declined to pass their language on to their children, even as they came later to regret the decision. That French had been kept alive for centuries by oral tradition, and that link had been severely stressed to the point of breaking.

As for the "bad" French criticism, this was nonsense. The refugees who would become the Cajuns had brought their perfectly fine coun-try French with them from France as they settled into the Canadian maritime wilds in the early 1600s. By the time, 150 years later, they found themselves exiled to Louisiana, they still spoke that French. But like any language isolated from the mother tongue, the language had mutated, holding on to forms and idioms that had fallen away in the Old World while inventing new ones.

Think about Appalachian English where, not so long ago, people still spoke of farmyard predators as varmints. Nobody uses that word much anymore but it's an archaic form, not an example of "bad" English. Or how about the expression, "Lookee yonder"? In Shakespeare's day it was, "Look thee, yonder." It's an archaic elision, not an abomination.

Monsignor Jules O. Daigle, the Cajun Jesuit priest who in 1984 published the first dictionary of Cajun French, made this very point when I interviewed him for a profile the year his dictionary came out. "To call Cajun bad French," he told me then, "is to call French and Italian bad Latin."

Meanwhile, the African slaves who worked the Louisiana plantations during the French colonial period from 1699 to 1762, and many
enslaved Africans who followed, learned a simplified but perfectly useful form of standard French from their old country French plantation
owners. People started calling this Creole French even if the original
Creole French was the continental French brought to Louisiana by
early explorers and the landed gentry who followed.

After the Civil War freed South Louisiana's slaves, the vast majority settled in the countryside where they had toiled, putting them in
proximity to the Cajuns. The Cajuns and Creoles had little problem
understanding each other and to some extent their French began to
meld and overlap. True, this was not then and still is not the French
spoken in Paris, but neither is the French spoken in Belgium, Switzerland, Montreal, or Quebec. Still, it is French, not some pidgin dialect.

By the time Mulate's opened, the effort to reclaim Louisiana
French had cranked up into overdrive. After a long and lively debate
about what French to speak, the decision was made to teach standard
French as a foundation and let the Cajun- and Creole-speaking parents and grandparents fill in the idioms and idiosyncrasies. French
immersion classes returned to Louisiana's public schools. All across
the Gumbo Belt, clutches of Louisiana French speakers and French-
speaking wannabes began gathering in cafes, church halls, and bars to
converse in the endemic tongue. This was and is frequently done over
bowls of gumbo.

Mulate's caught the steam and spirit of this effort and became a
must-go place for anyone looking to show the flag of Cajun and Creole
culture. Music and food had made Cajun and Creole cool, and we now
had a fighting chance to save Louisiana French. Suddenly, everybody
wanted to be Cajun-Creole—even goodly numbers of the transplanted
oil-field rednecks (who the Cajuns called *cous rouges*) from places like
Texas, Mississippi, and Oklahoma, who had previously ridiculed us.
Settling in large numbers in towns like Houma, Morgan City, and

Lafayette, many had begun to rethink their snobbery as it dawned on them that the food, music, and joie de vivre of the Gumbo Belt made for a happy place to live.

Mulate's had already become a booming local success by the time New Orleans hosted the World's Fair in 1984. Boutté, with pitch-perfect instincts, convinced the World's Fair officials to include his joint on the list of places fairgoers could visit if they wanted to venture outside of New Orleans and into the heartland of Louisiana French culture. Over time, Mulate's found itself mobbed by thousands of out-of-state and international visitors who went back to wherever they came from talking about, among other things, that gumbo they ate there. Gumbo and Cajun cooking had another toehold. (Boutté has since sold the Breaux Bridge property and recreated Mulate's in New Orleans where it continues to feature Cajun music, serve gumbo, and thrive.) These days Boutté is a man who likes his privacy. When I finally catch up with him by phone to talk about Mulate's storied place in the Gumbo Diaspora, he tells me he was as surprised as anyone at how Mulate's rocketed to success. In a way, the idea was foreign-born. Boutté was in Germany on holiday in 1969 and went into a packed traditional German beer garden where the beer was flowing, the sausages and sauerkraut were flying out of the kitchen by the plattersful and the oom-pah band on stage was rocking the crowd. "Substitute chank-a-chank music and gumbo and I'm thinking that's us in Louisiana. That was my original inspiration."

As for his serendipitous timing? "It was accidental," he says, laughing. "Or maybe divine intervention." After a brief stint as a restaurateur in New Orleans, Boutté found the physical space he'd been searching for in Breaux Bridge in a rambling honky-tonk called Mulate's, owned by a man of that name. He thought about naming his creation Boutté's Cajun Kitchen but stuck with Mulate's—which had been in business for more than 35 years—because he feared "if I changed the name, nobody would be able to find me." Soon enough, the entire world found him, particularly after the 1984 World's Fair. "Seriously, everybody came. The world was at Mulate's doorstep." He ticks off celebrities—Bob Dylan, John Fogerty, Paul Simon, Robert Duvall—who not only visited but passed on their accolades about the food, music, and ambience to their famous friends. Saturday Night Live's Lorne Michaels showed up one day and "seriously wanted to shoot an episode of SNL in Mulate's," Boutté recalls. It didn't happen because of logistical issues "but that's how crazy it was. Mulate's became world famous in a very short period of time."

Four years later, in 1988, gumbo got another lift when the Republican National Convention came to the New Orleans Superdome. With George H. W. Bush having locked up the nomination and little drama coming out of the four-day event, the national press—numbering four thousand strong—went looking for feature stories and food and gumbo got huge play in publications like the *New York Times* and the *Washington Post,* and on network TV. Another five thousand delegates plus politicians and their entourages fanned out over the nearby Central Business District and French Quarter, all looking to partake in the city's sybaritic pleasures, notably its food. Or as Bush's deputy press secretary, Mark Goodin, told local reporters, "I intend to eat myself into obesity." Indeed, by this time, if you visited New Orleans, you absolutely had to go to Café du Monde for those sugary beignets and you simply *had* to pop into some place to eat gumbo. Gumbo's press notices were almost uniformly effusive, making the dish a requisite experience for many of the millions of tourists who would travel to New Orleans and the Gumbo Belt region in coming years.

Then came Saint Paul and the Gumbo Missionaries.

By the mid-1980s, the Gumbo Diaspora had gained speed, owing in no small part to the cooking skills and creative energies of a charismatic Opelousas, Louisiana–native chef named Paul Prudhomme. The portly, restlessly inventive, gregarious, self-taught Chef Paul had mutated from a hometown burger flipper into one of the most innovative chefs in America.

There was nothing in Prudhomme's early childhood that suggested superstar chef. He was the youngest of thirteen children raised on an Opelousas farm by parents who struggled financially. He didn't like his name—given to him by the family priest who had high regard for St. Paul the Apostle—and took to calling himself Gene Autry Prudhomme after the 1950s cowboy television star.

At seventeen, Prudhomme, whose kitchen experience was entirely cooking gumbo and other Cajun specialties at the hip of his mother, opened a burger joint called Big Daddy O's Patio. It failed in about nine months. But Prudhomme, after a tour as a New Orleans magazine salesman and busboy and then a long sojourn away from the Gumbo Belt, returned to his Louisiana roots in 1970. He was determined to cook and reinvigorate the Cajun fare that he'd dined on at his mother's table.

Among other things, he created a grilled dish, blackened redfish, that took Louisiana and the nation by storm. Its popularity bordered on the insane, an irony since redfish, though Cajuns and Creoles ate it in dishes like courtbouillon, was nowhere near as prized for the pot as other bay species such as speckled trout and flounder. Or as Ti Adelaide Martin, who helps to oversee Commander's Palace in New Orleans, says, "To many down here, it was considered trash fish."

But so great was the demand for redfish fillets that in 1986, state wildlife officials were forced to outlaw gill-netting to save the species from extinction. (The Feds closed the nearshore Gulf of Mexico to commercial fishing of redfish the same year.) These days, redfish, technically the red drum, are farmed for the restaurant trade and wild Louisiana stocks have spectacularly recovered.

At heart, though, Prudhomme was a gumbo man. Before pop-up restaurants became a fad, he opened one in Los Angeles and then Chicago, cooking gumbo and other Cajun specialties. They were packed. In 1985, he took on New York City, opening a pop-up at Columbus Avenue and 77th Street on Manhattan's Upper West Side. Trouble soon reared its head when city health inspectors, saying they'd spotted flies in the kitchen, threatened to shut the restaurant down. However, none other than Mayor Ed Koch intervened. Conducting his own investigation (and sampling Prudhomme's gumbo), he declared the Health Mounties' ruling "bullshit" and told Prudhomme he could continue to operate. This ended what the New York press had dubbed the "gumbo war."

The restaurant was a rollicking success, with lines, often including Hizzoner, stretching blocks long. Celebrities—Elton John; Dr. Ruth, the TV therapist; and pop-art icon Leroy Nieman, among others—visited the kitchen before tucking into bowls of gumbo. The Big Apple had gone gumbo gaga.

By then, gumbo had begun to head abroad. The first wave was spearheaded by émigré native home cooks unable to bear life without their chief comfort food. I knew lots of Cajuns who, starting in the early 1970s, were among the thousands of Gumbo Belt expatriates working the international oil patch from the North Sea to Nigeria as the era of global offshore oil exploration took off. It wasn't just that the Cajuns already had three decades of oil field experience from the post–World War II oil boom at home. It was also that a great deal of the oil-rig and workboat technology that served places like the North Sea had been invented by Cajun entrepreneurs from the Gumbo Belt. These Cajuns, wherever they went, took their gumbo with them (and shared it generously as Cajuns are wont to do).

I lived in London from 1990 to 1993 and found gumbo the perfect elixir for its gloomy, wet fall and winter days. I cooked it for colleagues and friends to rave reviews. I cooked a big pot of it once while on assignment in South Africa in the mid-1990s and my South African friends didn't leave the table until the pot was empty. "How do you do this?" one asked, as if I had created magic. Another said with a straight face, "This is almost better than sex."

Again, I'm not trying to be immodest. I cook a good gumbo, but I know a ton of people who cook excellent gumbos. It was the Gumbo Effect again. If prepared properly, it's just always a winner.

The big push, however, came from homegrown professional missionaries who, like Kerry Boutté, were in the vanguard of those who understood that Louisiana's indigenous cuisine was about to become a phenomenon. If cooked authentically, with gumbo as its marker dish, there were no boundaries or cultures that our food couldn't cross. Chief among those was John Folse.

With Prudhomme zigzagging the nation to satisfy America's gumbo and blackened redfish craze, Folse, a Vacherie, Louisiana, native whose Lafitte's Landing Cajun and high-style gumbo restaurant was perennially packed, headed overseas as requests came in from around the globe. He opened gumbo-serving pop-up restaurants in Japan in 1985, Beijing in 1986, Hong Kong and Paris in 1987. They were sold out every night.

His first inclination that gumbo had intense cross-cultural appeal was when Japan's sumo wrestling champion, known as Yokozuna, clamored into his Kyoto dining room with an entourage of ten extremely big and hungry wrestlers. The sumo champ began not just gorging on the gumbo but loudly proclaiming how good it was. "Oh, my God," Folse says. "People were kneeling before him. He was like the emperor and he was loving his gumbo."

Another sign that the world had changed came a year later when Folse, sitting with his driver and an interpreter at the Great Wall of China, overheard the driver, who spoke almost no English, saying something about New Orleans. He then turned to Folse and sang out part of the chorus to Hank's Cajun anthem, "Jambalaya (On the Bayou)"—"jambalay', crawfish pie, filé gumbo."

"I was stunned," Folse recalls. "This phrase had made it into the music of a driver in China who otherwise spoke no English. I said to myself, 'What am I missing here?' This was a sign that the world was ready for the food of Louisiana and gumbo in particular. . . . This was the dawning of a new world and a new life for me."

The following year, Folse cloned the experience of Lafitte's Landing, dishing out gumbo and other Cajun-Creole classics in Moscow for the Reagan-Gorbachev summit. Not only did the Gipper and Gorby love their gumbo but at the opening dinner, "I look and who's at my table eating gumbo?" recalls Folse. "It's Yuri Gagarin," the Russian cosmonaut who was the first man in space.

In 1989, Folse became the first non-Italian chef to be invited to cook for the Vatican state dinner in Rome, serving gumbo to Pope John Paul II. The pope died in 2005 and was canonized by the Catholic Church in 2014. This allows Folse to proclaim, with more than a wry smile, that he has cooked gumbo for a saint, and that perhaps gumbo has a savory reputation in Heaven as well.

In the early 1990s Folse would go on to open pop-up restaurants to enthusiastic crowds in London, Bogota, Taipei, and Seoul where gumbo was the star dish. Flash forward to 2015, when Tory McPhail, Commander's Palace's executive chef, was sent not once but twice by the U.S. State Department on a food ambassadorship to Australia to teach gumbo-cooking down under. When I caught up with McPhail to talk gumbo and spend a morning in Commander's busy and aromatic kitchen, he said he was startled at how "Australian chefs were totally obsessed in their desire to master Cajun and Creole cuisine." Gumbo was at the top of that list.

Gumbo's spread is undoubtedly a testament to the dish's universal appeal and deliciousness—when done properly. But in the hands of outsiders not properly trained, sometimes it is gumbo in name only and cooked in ways and with ingredients that make Gumbo Belt natives cringe. My pal Michael Doucet, Cajun fiddler extraordinaire and founder and mainstay of the band BeauSoleil, recalls being on a series of multistate tours in the early 1980s. He was constantly being bombarded with well-intentioned promoters insisting on sending localized versions of Cajun food to the band's dressing room.

"People really wanted to get on the Cajun bandwagon and so pots of gumbo and jambalaya would appear," Doucet says. "After politely explaining that gumbo roux is not green but coffee brown, we just had to find a way to ward off this sudden Cajun cuisine experiment on the road. It got to be too much."

Michael has a wry sense of humor, so BeauSoleil, which eventually would tour every state in the union, included a rider in its contract that explicitly stated, "Please, under no circumstances serve the band Cajun food." Some "northerners"—defined by Doucet for gumbo purposes as all people living north of Alexandria, Louisiana—still couldn't take the hint and "pots of green gumbo and mushy jambalaya" kept being sent backstage. "We played a lot of gigs on an empty stomach," he says.

The misfires continue, sometimes in a spectacular way. In the fall of 2016, Disney, the entertainment giant, posted a video recipe for "Tiana's Healthy Gumbo" on the Facebook page for *The Princess and the Frog*, a 2009 animated movie that featured a culinary-minded princess with New Orleans roots. It seemed flattering enough until the recipe unfolded. The ingredients: quinoa, kale, other nonstandard greens, and worst of all, no roux.

The online backlash from Gumbo Belters, fired up by the hashtag #gumbostrong, was so swift and strong that Disney was forced to take the video down. One example that caught the spirit of the reaction was posted on a NOLA.com website: "I'm from Lafayette, Louisiana, and I gotta say, I've never seen a recipe before that actually made me mad. And this recipe right here makes me mad enough to wanna punch a baby right in the face."

Had the Disney flaks spent any time at all in Louisiana, they would have realized gumbo chauvinism is an unavoidable feature of gumbo culture. Not only do I know a lot of Gumbo Belt people who refuse to eat gumbo cooked beyond the borders of the South Louisiana (unless they know the chef has bona fide Louisiana credentials), I know New Orleans people who will not eat gumbo in Lafayette, and Lafayette people who will not eat gumbo in New Orleans. These people are totally convinced that the gumbo of their home place is the only true gumbo.

I understand these reservations. But that's not me. I've long been intrigued with wanting to know how others might interpret our gift to the culinary world.

Have I sometimes suffered for my gumbo adventurism? Yes! In 2001, while researching a book on America's love affair with beer, I drove the length of the Mississippi River in a quest to find the mythical "perfect beer joint." At one point I stopped into an attractive brew pub in a Wisconsin river town. It not only had an impressive beer list but, gazing at the menu, I was surprised to see "Creole gumbo" on the menu.

Of course, I ordered it. When it came, I got another surprise. It was served on a plate, not in a bowl, and more resembled jambalaya, except that it had beans, tomatoes, bits of fish (!), and some other chunks of mysterious ingredients I could not immediately divine. All this covered in a thick, not particularly tasty, brown gravy. It wasn't inedible, perhaps because I was totally starved after five hours in the car. But it sure in the hell wasn't gumbo.

But so what? I'm glad I tried it. In mimicry, even when it falters, lies flattery.

I'm hardly alone in this adventurism. Tim Gautreaux, elegant writer of Gumbo Belt–based short stories and novels (and a former classmate at Nicholls State), shares my enthusiasm for sampling gumbo in places where, well, it's probably a bad idea. But you just have to do it. He emailed me to say, "I recently walked into a North Carolina restaurant in a small mountain town and saw that the daily special was chicken gumbo. I ordered a cup instead of a bowl so I could limit my suffering and was brought a serving of 'chicken, green bean, carrot, and okra gumbo!' After poking around in it a long time I managed to find one small perfectly square piece of chicken remarkably similar to one of the lumps in a can of Campbell's Chicken with Rice soup. There was also some suspiciously familiar tasting rice in the gumbo. The color of the concoction was brown, but not roux brown, rather canned gravy brown with maybe some sort of non-okra thickener. What this all seemed to be was a mildly pleasant vegetable soup that went well with a sandwich I'd ordered. But it's about as close to gumbo as a spice-deprived borscht."

Meanwhile, I'm going to make the heretical statement that in America's foodie towns, notably New York, Chicago, San Francisco, Seattle, and Los Angeles, you can find perfectly authentic Cajun and Creole gumbo—gumbo cooked with a roux and all the traditional ingredients—assuming you know which restaurants are authentic. One example: When I still lived in New York City, I dined at a Cajun place called the Delta Grill in Hell's Kitchen and ate the gumbo on several occasions. It was perfectly good—not Momma good, not John Folse or Paul Prudhomme restaurant good—but I ate it with pleasure. Of course, it should have been perfectly fine because as my waiter told me more than once, the gumbo chef had trained in a Paul Prudhomme restaurant.

That was also my experience after I sampled the takeout gumbo from Heaven on Seven at my father-in-law's apartment in Chicago. My skepticism turned to surprise at how perfectly fine it was. I more recently visited the restaurant itself in the company of a neighbor to see if, upon eating a second bowl, I'd have the same opinion.

And I did.

There's no reason that outlander chefs, if they get good training and take the time and care to hone their gumbo skills, and pay attention to our gumbo traditions, can't make a decent bowl of gumbo. And they are now doing that all over the country.

{ 4 }

GUMBO INC. AND THE GUMBO IDENTITY CRISIS

I have thus far left out New Orleans, still my favorite food town, the variety of cooking in Chicago, New York, and San Francisco notwithstanding, because it deserves special attention as the obvious urban cradle of gumbo, if not its birthplace. The city is also the thriving hub of what I call Gumbo Inc. Gumbo is not only the marker dish for a thriving restaurant scene, but the driver of a sprawling collateral business in spices, condiments, prepared meats, jarred and powdered roux, and pre-packaged foods that could easily make gumbo a $1 billion-plus a year industry.

If a $1 billion gumbo market seems far-fetched, consider that in 2017, Louisiana attracted 47.1 million domestic and international visitors, who spent $17.5 billion. The gumbo hub of New Orleans alone accounted for 10.5 million of those visitors and $7.4 billion of that revenue. And about $1.75 billion of that went to dining. And these days, who goes to New Orleans without trying the gumbo? Moreover, a supplementary report on Louisiana's 2017 tourism economy prepared for the state by Tourism Economics, a consulting firm, puts the total value of the 2017 tourism industry, when the value of job creation and tax generation are included, at $21.6 billion. And according to that report, almost 20 percent of that total was generated by food and beverage sales.

And dining dollars are only part of the gumbo market which, while New Orleans is the hub, includes many lucrative satellite operations. Consider that Tabasco Sauce alone, a hot sauce empire operated from Avery Island, Louisiana, generates an estimated $250 million a year in worldwide sales, according to a 2007 book written about the privately owned, family-run McIlhenny Company (I asked the kindly people at McIlhenny if they had ever estimated how much Tabasco goes into gumbo each year but, alas, they said an accurate estimate simply isn't possible.)

Or think about the family-owned Tony Chachere's Creole Foods in the southwestern Louisiana Cajun hub of Opelousas. Its Creole Seasoning often finds its way into my gumbos and the gumbos of untold others all over the world. That's because Tony's, as my family and legions of others of its faithful customers fondly call it, can nowadays be found on supermarket shelves where we live in Chicago and in places we frequently visit like New York, San Francisco, Austin, Texas, and Ellsworth, Maine. (Not to mention you can order it on Amazon and find it at Walmarts almost everywhere if you are so inclined.) Not bad for a company begun in 1972 by a retired Cajun chef who first sold his spices out of the trunk of his car.

Ditto for the privately held Savoie's Companies in the same town, whose powdered and jarred roux, prepared and packaged foods, and other gumbo accoutrements sell briskly and not just in Louisiana but in national grocery chains such as Walmart, Winn-Dixie, Texas-based H-E-B, Kroger, and Albertsons. Savoie's, like the other of these privately held companies, doesn't publish its revenues. (When I phoned Savoie's offices hoping to get a tour of their roux works, my request was met by a most un-Cajun response: Under no circumstances, an officious young woman informed me, would a journalist be allowed to see how Savoie makes its products.)

And you can't forget Zatarain's, the old-line New Orleans producer of Cajun and Creole seasonings, packaged foods, and condiments, and perhaps most famous for its crab, shrimp, and crawfish boiling concoctions. Founded in 1889 by Emile Zatarain, a New Orleanean of Basque descent, Zatarain's product line includes packages of Gumbo Mix with Rice, Gumbo Base (a roux substitute), jarred filé, and its own proprietary Creole Seasoning mix that often finds its way into gumbo. A testament to Zatarain's long-running success and popularity: It was acquired in 1993 by food giant McCormick & Co. Inc. for $180 million. Its operations remain in the New Orleans area, where it employs about two hundred people and has annual sales of about $250 million.

Meanwhile, walk into any of the sprawling, state-of-the art food stores operated by the family-run, Thibodaux-based Rouse Supermarkets chain, whose fifty-five stores sprawl across the Gumbo Belt and into Mississippi and Alabama, and you may be stunned—as I was—at entire shelves given over to the sale of gumbo ingredients. These include everything from jarred and powdered roux to filé, hot sauces, and all manner of spices and quickly prepared rice mixtures. And that doesn't include its prepared food sections where everything from pre-cut chicken to prechopped and packaged vegetables for the Trinity can be had—all this dedicated to hastening gumbo's preparation. (You can also pick up bags of frozen gumbo.)

Many other Louisiana supermarket chains have shelves and cooler cases solely dedicated to the gumbo trade, as do the dozens of mom-and-pop specialty stores throughout the Gumbo Belt—think T-Boy's Slaughter House in the southwest Cajun hamlet of Mamou, for example—whose andouille, tasso, and various smoked meat and poultry products are specifically aimed at the gumbo market. And owing to the web, these gumbo products are now available all over the United State thanks to sites like CajunGrocer.com, where you can buy not just pretty much every commercial spice and roux mix available but also order twenty different kinds of gumbo shipped to you frozen in dry-ice containers. Some of CajunGrocer's gumbo offerings are made in Donaldsonville, about sixty miles upriver from New Orleans, where Chef Folse presides over a seventy-thousand-square-foot USDA-sanctioned factory making gumbo on a scale I had not imagined existed.

Prudhomme's enterprises are another example of a business streaming in the contrails of gumbo. Though Chef Paul made his name as a chef, he was also a brilliant mixer of seasonings and spices. These days, his Magic Seasoning Blends company operates out of a 125,000-square-foot New Orleans warehouse and books probably half of its considerable annual revenue selling tons of premixed bulk and packaged spices, many of them ending up in gumbo, to all fifty states and thirty-seven countries around the world.

So, if you're living on a Greek Island and wish to sample Cajun blackened fish, for example, you can buy a two-ounce jar of Prudhomme's Blackened Redfish Magic for about five dollars and liberally sprinkle the concoction—containing several different kinds of pepper, paprika, dried thyme, and oregano—on the fish of your choice. I know Blackened Redfish Magic is available in Greece because when I phoned the Prudhomme people seeking an interview, they told me the person I most needed to speak with had just left on a regular spice-selling trip to that country. Gumbo-inclined Greeks can also buy Chef Paul's Gravy and Gumbo Magic which is a spiced-up flour concoction that can help produce a tasty roux.

New Orleans is also the place to trace how gumbo rose from a peasant dish born and nurtured in South Louisiana's rustic home kitchens to an honorable, even star, place in the city's top restaurants. This is an achievement in which Prudhomme again played a huge role, beginning in 1975, after Ella Brennan, the grande dame overseeing Commander's Palace, dumped her latest European chef, and his typically European propensity to replicate staid classical French cooking. She replaced him with Prudhomme.

He electrified Commander's kitchen by spicing things up and Cajunizing the food, with gumbo as a centerpiece. (It's a little-known fact that blackened redfish actually began as a Prudhomme experiment in Commander's kitchen, but he didn't perfect the dish until he opened his own place.) Until that moment, Cajun and Creole food could not be found on the same menu in a New Orleans restaurant. Gumbo would soon become a staple at many high-end Creole restaurants that had declined to serve it before. If a patron saint of gumbo is ever canonized, I suspect that Chef Paul, who died at the age of seventy-five, will be a shoo-in.

These days, a Yelp search shows that the city is awash in gumbo, with more than three hundred restaurants identifying as Cajun, Creole, or a hyphenated version of both. Most have gumbo on the menu. I dined on gumbo in sixteen New Orleans restaurants and searched actual online menus for about twenty more. What I learned is that they produce a dizzying array of gumbo styles, some with two or three different gumbos on the menu; with gumbos made with roux that run the color spectrum from pecan to café au lait to dark chocolate to nearly cast-iron black; with densities as thin as bouillabaisse to gumbo so thick you can practically stand a spoon up in the bowl; gumbos served over rice like my mother's were and gumbos whose chefs declare that rice would be an overload, even a violation, for their rich versions. You can even find a gumbo served over potato salad instead of rice, even though that technique is far more common to the towns of the Cajun prairie in southwest Louisiana.

What's interesting is that it wasn't so long ago that you could draw a pretty clear geographic distinction in gumbo styles: New Orleans Creolized see-the-bottom-of-the-bowl seafood and okra gumbos with their medium roux and the diced tomatoes that the vast majority of Cajuns don't put in their gumbos; the medium thick, pecan-colored roux of the Cajun and Creole southeast Louisiana bayou region, which trend to okra with seafood because of that area's access to the estuaries of the Gulf of Mexico; the dark roux chicken-and-andouille gumbos of the southwest Cajun prairies in towns like Opelousas, Crowley, and Lafayette, where making the lean, spicy pork andouille sausage has long been an art.

But as my incessant Gumbo Belt sampling revealed, that's changing. Styles are traveling and evolving. The isolation and culinary parochialism that once froze gumbo styles in place is crumbling. While it's true that some subset of gumbo cookers still guard their recipes jealously, our digital world is making that harder and harder to do. Stuff leaks out. Gumbo is now on the internet with recipes by the hundreds free for the downloading. Old Tante Lulu might not have wanted her gumbo on the web but now that she's gone to Gumbo Heaven, her great-niece has shared the recipe on Facebook.

Moreover, good local roads and freeways now connect the once isolated Cajun and Creole bayous to towns and cities in ways they didn't until well after World War II. My home place is an example. Houma, an hour's drive from New Orleans, sits at the nexus of a crow's foot delta, i.e., the intersection of four natural waterways, Bayous Terrebonne, Petit Caillou, Grand Caillou, and Dularge, all flowing south through sprawling marshland to the Gulf of Mexico. That explains why the fishing is so good and we have some of the best and most plentiful seafood in the world.

When I was a kid, getting to the Cajun fishing and farming settlements strung out along the banks of these bayous—places with names like Theriot, Dulac, Chauvin, Montegut, Cocodrie, and Pointe-aux-Chenes—was honest adventure. It meant traveling south by car for twenty or more miles along bayou-hugging, potholed roads served by rickety bridges and paved in clam and oyster shells. Getting down there without at least one flat tire was considered a miracle. There were almost no amenities. Live bait stands far outnumbered gas stations and mom-and-pop grocery stores. A few Cajun honky-tonks lined the roads but there were no real restaurants.

Storms, tides, and poor maintenance often rendered the roads impassable. Before we could afford a boat big enough to fish the open saltwater bays south of Houma, Dad would drive us down to these places because you had a reasonably good chance of catching redfish, speckled trout, or flounder from the bank. These trips were often occasioned when Bonnie declared she was ready to fix a big pot of redfish courtbouillon, a tomato-based fish stew.

I recall one trip, during a rare dry summer, when the chalky-white clamshell dust kicked up by passing cars was so thick that we turned around and drove home. On another, we debarked the car at a favorite fishing hole called Robinson Canal, whereupon a cloud of mosquitos blacker than any tornado that ever existed descended upon us from the marsh, causing even my unperturbable Arkansas-born father to yell, "Lordy, boys, back in the car!" Dad had to turn on the wipers of the old Jeep station wagon to get through the mosquito cloud.

To go between, say, Theriot (pronounced Terry-O) along the banks of Bayou Dularge, and Dulac on the banks of Bayou Grand Caillou (ky-yoo), was simply impossible save by a long, roundabout journey by boat or by motoring all the way up to Houma along one bad shell road and driving all the way back down along another. Until the 1950s, few people there had cars anyway.

That isolation explains why the gumbo cooked by the Cajuns in Theriot could be quite different than the gumbo cooked by Cajuns living in Montegut. There was simply little or no gumbo intercourse. As a young reporter for the Houma paper, I was a witness to this isolationist effect. Every Saturday morning, converted school buses ran from these bayou communities to Houma, filled up with riders wishing to be dropped off at a convenience that didn't yet exist where they lived—a supermarket. I'd had enough experience on assignments down in these bayou communities that I could tell you, based upon a person's accent and the French idioms they used, which bayou they lived along.

For generations up until World War II, South Louisiana families stayed put; it was common to find three or even four generations of a family living next door to each other on ancestral plots of land passed down through the generations. If Gumbo Belt residents still haven't quite caught up with the mobility of other states, they are nonetheless migrating to other states and countries in numbers unthinkable in my mother's generation. My own family is a testament to that: As of this writing, I have a Houma niece living in New York City; another in Chicago; another in Austin, Texas; another just outside Atlanta. Their gumbo goes with them.

Houston, Texas, is a gumbo hotbed. How'd it get there? Initially, from the thousands of Cajuns who moved to Houston and the surrounding area starting after World War II to work in the oil patch.

And if restaurant gumbo was rare in New Orleans restaurants until Chef Paul got to Commander's and Mulate's opened in Breaux Bridge, that's just not true anymore. Houma probably has at least a dozen restaurants serving gumbo. Partly, this is about prosperity. The debate about the environmental impact of the oil industry on Louisiana aside, it's incontrovertibly true that the industry pulled the Gumbo Belt from the scenic agrarian poverty in which many people had lived since Louisiana's colonial days. Restaurants proliferated as paychecks swelled and diners who were once homebodies began to eat out more, and especially if they'd heard that the gumbo served at, say, Big Al's, a popular Houma seafood joint, tasted like Momma's.

The truth is, Houma restaurant gumbo too tends to be all over the map in terms of style. In part, it's that mobility again. Maybe the cook learned his gumbo-cooking in Opelousas, worked in a restaurant in Lafayette, and brought his southwest Louisiana style with him when he moved to Houma. People used to "bayou gumbo," tasted it one day and said, "Not bad. I wonder how he made that roux?" Then they look it up on the internet, where they will more than likely find it or something close to it and try it themselves. They change their recipe into something of a hybrid.

Professional gumbo chefs have the internet, they watch cable cook-ing shows, and they travel and eat in one another's restaurants. If it's something they like, they borrow freely. "Most of the top chefs in New Orleans have eaten at my place," says Wayne Baquet Sr., proprietor of the hole-in-the-wall Li'l Dizzy's Cafe in the city's Treme neighbor-hood, which dishes out a kind of everything-but-the-kitchen-sink Cre-ole gumbo. It defies every rule my mother had about gumbo-making. But, sorry, Ma, it's killer-good.

Pat Mould, a newly minted friend of mine in the Cajun cultural cap-ital of Lafayette, invented what became a regionally famous smoked-duck-and-andouille gumbo when he worked as a chef in Lafayette's Charlie G's restaurant more than twenty years ago. (Mould's secret is to smoke the ducks well in advance of starting the gumbo and then to use bones and fat from the deboned ducks to make a smoked-duck stock. He likes to cook with teal, the fleet-of-wing wild duck that is a favorite of Gumbo Belt hunters.) I sampled some version of that gumbo in restaurants in New Orleans and Thibodaux and it's doubt-lessly served in many other places. "I should have patented the recipe," Mould told me one day, laughing. "If I had a dime for every pot of it that got cooked, I'd be rich."

Meanwhile, an older generation of gumbo-cookers is passing on its art to a younger generation and the young folks aren't just sitting still. While taking those recipes with them around the state, country, and the world—and still proclaiming the sanctity and unmatchable flavors of Momma's sacred recipe—they are also engaging in a fair amount of cross-pollination and experimentation. All this is amplified by our fluid, digitally wired, always-switched-on culture.

I don't think it's a stretch to say that gumbo is in the middle of something of an identity crisis—in itself not necessarily a bad thing, even though it may mean that some endemic style of gumbo perfected in some once isolated bayou community is in danger of being lost. The gumbo made from the breasts and gizzards of what the Cajuns call the poule d'eau (translation, water chicken) is one example. But new styles are being invented, old styles reimagined and refined, and the gumbo world is exploding with an unmatched energy and creativity.

Consider one experience: In spring 2016, I paid a visit to St. Bernard Parish, the Katrina-ravaged enclave that sits east and south of New Orleans. I dropped in on my friends Monique Verdin, a coastal-preservation activist, and her hundred-year-old French-speaking grandmother, Matine Verdin, whom I'd met during the reporting of my post-Katrina book, *The Good Pirates of the Forgotten Bayous*. Matine, ninety at the time, had with her two sons and a nephew been washed out of her house when failing levees unleashed a titanic surge and plunged 95 percent of all habitable St. Bernard Parish buildings under water. They barely escaped with their lives and endured a long and harrowing journey to safety.

This time I'd come to discuss a far more pleasant topic—gumbo. After all, Matine had been cooking and eating gumbo for most of her long, long life. Monique's thirty-three-year-old husband, Blaise Pezold, was there, cooking up a chicken-and-sausage recipe for a gumbo-cooking contest. Rather nonchalantly, Blaise mentioned that he was adding sweet potatoes and some nontraditional spices to his otherwise traditional recipe. A former cook who now works in coastal restoration, Pezold's view is that it doesn't hurt to experiment. If it doesn't work, you can fall back on the basics or try something else.

I can see my mother rolling her eyes at the idea of sweet potatoes anywhere near her gumbo, and the truth is, upon sampling the dish I can't say I divined a sweet potato presence. No matter. Had I been blindfolded and ignorant of the presence of that outlier ingredient I'm pretty sure I would've pronounced Blaise's an archetype of an authentic chicken-and-sausage gumbo—not my momma's but a gumbo I would eat without hesitation.

THE MEANING OF "T"-MAN IN THE LAND OF A ZILLION CHEFS

What everybody in the Gumbo Belt knows, and which sooner or later occurs to outsiders who spend any time there, is that the restaurant gumbo is so good because it has to be. Professional chefs are competing with hundreds of thousands of extremely picky and proud home chefs like Pezold in a place that has, hands down, the best regional cooking in America. Or as Ella Brennan of Commander's Palace was fond of telling her highfalutin European chefs about their cooking before Paul Prudhomme arrived: "That's good, yes, but not as good as the food I ate growing up in my house."

In the Gumbo Belt, and in New Orleans in particular, eating out is somewhere between pastime, sport, and religion. In fact, the sly joke is that New Orleans people discuss at lunch where they are planning to go for dinner. They talk. If a restaurant's gumbo is lackluster, word gets out and that's a bad thing. Or as Commander's Palace's McPhail told me, "If the gumbo is just so-so, people become suspicious of the rest of your menu."

When in 2002 the *New Yorker* writer and New York City resident Calvin Trillin went searching for what was truly remarkable about indigenous American cooking, he didn't go to New York, Los Angeles, or Chicago. He went to Breaux Bridge, Jeanerette, and Opelousas, Louisiana, and bought some boudin, our spicy meat and rice–stuffed sausage, from truck stops. Boudin is typically made with pork, though inventive chefs these days also employ crawfish, alligator, and smoked chicken, to name a few varieties. In an essay he penned about his experience, Trillin noted that Louisiana's boudin is so sublimely delicious that outsiders pretty much have to visit the state to sample it. That's because the locals eat it with such fervor that there's almost none left to export. In fact, most boudin gets eaten in the parking lot or in the car on the way home.

Trillin learned what we all know down there, that the tastiest boudin comes from the home kitchens of Cajun and Creole cooks, often the "maw-maws and paw-paws" of grandparent vintage. Since people kept telling these maw-maws and paw-paws their boudin was good enough to be sold commercially, some obliged and opened shop, usually renting counter space in the back of somebody's gas station.

That's still where a lot of the best boudin is found. When I was reporting on Katrina's aftermath for the *Wall Street Journal*, driving daily from a hotel room in Baton Rouge because there was no place to stay in storm-ravaged New Orleans, I discovered a boudin stand in the rear of an Exxon station near the Baton Rouge airport. I bought everything they had (because there was no food in New Orleans, either) and shared it with some Kansas relief workers. One of them cried, and not just because she was hungry. It was that good.

Now, you may live in Dubuque and dread that Sunday dinner invitation to Aunt Sally's because, well, that three-bean salad with onions dished up before the main course of calf's liver with lumpy white gravy has you longing for a frozen Costco pizza or a detour to Applebee's. If so, I feel bad for you. But in the Gumbo Belt, if you get invited to someone's home to dine, go.

I'm not saying everyone is a star chef or that it's impossible to get bad food. We have our share of fast-food joints, mall food, and tourist traps cooking bad versions of our real food. But I am saying that the vast majority of people in South Louisiana like to cook and know how to cook. The truth is, we are the last redoubt of Southern Europe in America and like the Continental French, Spanish, and Italians, our people don't eat to live, they live to eat. And, yes, while gumbo is the signature dish, there are many, many other staples—the aforementioned boudins, plus etouffees, jambalayas, courtbouillons, sauce piquants, fricassees among them—that are cooked with the zeal and care of gumbo.

My mother grew up with five brothers and a sister. They all married into Cajun French–speaking families and for a while three of the families lived in a cluster of tidy houses in Thibodaux. I grew up knowing that an invitation to dine at any of these houses was going to be a tasty adventure (and usually no invitation was necessary). Maw-Maw Toups, born Anna Virginia Keller, made a yummy chicken-and-sausage gumbo, being extremely picky about her sausage, which she acquired from a neighborhood sausage-maker. She also made her roux with lard, which is really old school. She usually served her gumbo over rice with fresh baked French bread and a side of her spectacular Cajun potato salad, with a dash or two of cayenne pepper stirred into the mayonnaise, making it Cajun potato salad instead of simply potato salad. (Yes, yes, I know. Gumbo served over rice with French bread and a side of potato salad puts you into carbohydrate overload. However, my view is there is health food and then there is mental health food. A gumbo lunch with potato salad and fabulous French bread qualifies as the latter.)

Maw-Maw Toups lived with my Uncle Pershing Toups, the family's talented barbecue chef, and his kindly wife, Ann Adele Naquin (pronounced knock-ehn). Aunt Ann Adele's white-beans-and-rice, flavored with a bit of salt meat and finished off with fresh parsley, was to die for. I have a first cousin, Cookie Toups Dupont, who decades later still swoons over the memories of Aunt Ann Adele's pork stew. Wander next door to Uncle Norman's and just the aroma of the chicken stew made with a dark roux coming from the stove would get you salivating. Aunt Heloise's red-beans-and-rice with sausage—oh, my. You get the picture.

And as Tory McPhail pointed out, and as the boudin example demonstrates, the common cooking is as good as the high cooking. And that's become largely true of Gumbo Belt restaurants; the meal you'll get at a gumbo shack like Liuzza's by the Track or a corner New Orleans poboy stand can be every bit as tasty, and prepared with the same care and zeal, as a five-course feast at Commander's.

One day, over a lunch not involving gumbo because it was a week in which I had sampled so many gumbos that I just could not eat one more, I was talking this over with Patrick Singley. He's the affable owner of Gautreau's, a fine dining restaurant in New Orleans' Garden District. I'd been introduced to Singley by a Houma pal, the gifted surgeon-turned-writer-historian Chris Cenac. He and Singley are duck-hunting and fishing-camp buddies ("podnahs," the Cajuns would say) and Chris turned me on to the fact that Singley was no ordinary restaurateur.

Patrick, a Florida native, trained at the Culinary Institute of America and cooks a gumbo, the ingredients and preparation of which are extremely fastidious. Singley was happy enough to discuss his gumbo and give away at least one secret: He makes his roux with peanut oil because he believes its higher smoke point than vegetable oils imparts a special silky quality. But what he really wanted to talk about was T-Man Gregoire's crab stew, which by description lay somewhere between a gumbo and a thicker, stewlike fricassee.

Now, I'm pretty sure you've never heard of T-Man Gregoire Sr. I hadn't until I was introduced to him by Cenac. He lived in extremely modest circumstances in my hometown of Houma. He was a slight, humble man with a roux-thick Cajun accent, a mustache and goatee, and a recipe, if his admirers like Singley and Cenac are to be believed, from God Himself. Antoine was his proper first name but like a lot of Cajuns he preferred his nickname (which is actually a shortening of Petit Man, i.e., 'tit Man or Little Man but rendered in the vernacular to T-Man. There are a lot of T-Mans and T-Boys in the Gumbo Belt; it's often the moniker conveyed upon the youngest or smallest son in a Cajun or Creole family).

T-Man is a variation of the Gumbo Belt archetypical self-taught chef. A few thousand hunting and fishing camps dot the marshes, swamps, and lakes of South Louisiana and when the hunting or fishing is done, the other fun begins: cooking and eating. True, some minority of camp owners may crack open that can of Van Camp's Pork and Beans and eat them cold with an aluminum spoon. But in the main, South Louisiana camp food, largely the domain of male chefs taught by their grandfathers, fathers, or uncles, is the kind of cooking that eventually finds its way out of the camp and onto restaurant menus down here. Pat Mould told me that his smoked-duck-and-andouille sausage gumbo was inspired by the time-honored smoking and cooking methods that come out of the hunting-camp tradition. The idea was to give discerning locals not just something good to eat but a dish that also flattered local cooking and cultural sensibilities.

T-Man was a cook for hire at Chris Cenac's camp, set on a roomy white houseboat that is towed from duck marsh to deer swamp, depending on the season and the inclination of its owner. Singley is often aboard and sat down one day to T-Man's crab specialty after a day of wing shooting. T-Man never took formal cooking classes and certainly never read a cookbook. He learned by watching his elders and friends and cooking what he liked. Like Paul Prudhomme.

"Ken, seriously," Singley tells me with an almost pained expression on his face, "I've never eaten anything that good ever in my life. It was almost embarrassing. I kept going back and back and back to that pot. I could not get enough."

This from a guy who owns one of the top restaurants in the city, voted by *Travel + Leisure* magazine in 2016 as the best place to eat in America.

Alas, this story took a tragic turn. Cenac had introduced me to T-Man by text and T-Man and I had spoken twice on the phone about a cooking date. T-Man was as curious about my intention to write an entire book about gumbo as I was to watch him cook and eat his magical concoction. ("Really, Ken?" he told me on the phone as he laughed about my gumbo project. "Who gave you a job like dat?")

Our first date got canceled because T-Man is picky about his crabs, selecting only the freshest and fattest, and the fisherman who catches the best ones for him wasn't crabbing that week. Then, having set another date, T-Man, when next we spoke, told me he was ill and would have to postpone again. But, not to worry, we'd reschedule. And then on April 30 Chris Cenac phoned me with the shocking news—T-Man had died in his sleep of an apparent heart attack or stroke the night before he was to go into the hospital for a stent procedure. He was only seventy years old and his short obituary in the *Houma Courier* newspaper mentioned nothing about his beloved crab dish.

If I was crestfallen, Singley and Cenac were honestly heartbroken. They'd not only lost a pal, but in their opinion, South Louisiana and America had lost one of its greatest camp cooks. If there's an uplifting note to this story, T-Man had given his secret recipe to his son, Simon, who had cooked it at T-Man's side for quality control shortly before he passed away. And T-Man himself, knowing he was going into the hospital, had cooked a batch of his magical dish and delivered it to Cenac, who, having stowed it in the freezer, shared it with Singley upon news of T-Man's passing.

"Maybe he knew something," Singley told me that day over lunch. "What a tragedy."

Still, the greater point of my T-Man digression, beyond honoring his memory, is this: Whether his dish was closer to a stew than a gumbo, he epitomized the joie de vivre, passion, and skill of Gumbo Belt cooks and the deep appreciation that people like Singley and Cenac have for those like him who carry on our art. And gumbo is the signature dish of that art and not just a dish but an attitude; in its preparation and eating, gumbo is the Zen food of an otherwise un-Zenlike culture.

This reality has unfolded to me slowly over the years, for it is one thing to be a boy on the canal banks in love with your mother's gumbo; it is another to learn to cook it properly, with the right ingredients, attitude, and love; to come to appreciate all that goes into it. To begin to understand how, as a fixture of our culture, gumbo unifies and, in a way, translates us to ourselves and a wider world.

Now, if you think I'm getting carried away, fine. But I'm all about reality checks. I've experienced the Gumbo Effect in the unlikeliest of places.

So, there I am on a fair summer's night on the banks of Little Tunk Pond in Maine, where my wife and I are fortunate enough to own a little lakeside log cabin. It's a place far, far away from the Gumbo Belt. I'm in casual conversation with a man I've just met, Giff Ewing. He turns out to be a talented, old-school photographer who shoots big-format black-and-white film in the Ansel Adams tradition and develops photos in his own dark room. He and his wife split their time between Colorado and a summering place in Sorrento, Maine, a gorgeous harbor town awash in lobster boats maybe twenty minutes from our lakeside cabin.

We were all guests of Jim and Jane Levitt, friendly Bostonians and Tunk Ponders, who have a lovely log home just up from our place. They were hosting an event for a grassroots conservation organization, the Frenchman Bay Conservancy, that is helping to protect all that is special about our little slice of pristine Maine.

At some point, I mention to Giff my gumbo book project and he stops me right there. He gets an animated look in his eyes.

"Gumbo?" he says.

He can't contain himself. He has a Colorado neighbor with Louisiana roots and she cooked a gumbo for them one evening. "I took a bite and said, 'What the hell is this? How can anything be this good? Seriously. What *is* this?'"

I smiled knowingly at Giff. Like a revival preacher, he was testifying.

Except it wasn't about God, but the Gumbo Effect. It's real.

{ 6 }

FEASTING AMONG THE POULE D'EAU COOKERS

"What you think, Ken? Good?"

The question comes from Leeward "Sou" Henry, a spritely eighty-five-year-old overseeing an oversized gumbo pot.

His gumbo is something to behold, even if it's being dished into disposable white plastic bowls with requisite white plastic spoons. It's a luscious pecan brown and not quite gravy-thick, with chunks of breasts and gizzards floating atop a bed of white long-grain rice. I take a bite and then another and delay my answer until a third.

Gumbo is traveling and mutating. Gumbo cooks are innovating like mad and I've been impressed with that vibrancy and creativity. But what of the old ways? I've come to the Cajun fishing hamlet of Chauvin, on a balmy December day to see if a gumbo tradition I'd witnessed during the days of my youth was still alive: the ritual cooking of poule d'eau (pool doo) gumbo.

The heart of Chauvin, on the banks of Bayou Petite Caillou, lies about twenty miles south-southeast of Houma. To drive Highway 56, which hugs the contours of the bayou that eventually empties into a bay fronting the Gulf of Mexico, is to drive into another world. Hand-hewn shrimp and oyster boats still idle at bayou-side docks. Road-side bait and seafood stands still do a brisk trade in minnows, mullet, shrimp, crabs, and oysters. Another fifteen miles south will get you to the end of the road at Cocodrie (Cajun French for alligator), where one-hundred-foot work vessels serving the nearby offshore oil rigs ply the same bayous and bays where fleet sports-fishing boats search for redfish, speckled trout, and flounder.

Cajun French fiercely hangs on here as do gumbo cooking traditions. When I still resided in Houma, Chauvin's St. Joseph Catholic Church each fall hosted a gumbo throw-down called Lagniappe on the Bayou (pronounced LAN-yap, it means "something extra" in Cajun French). Over a long weekend, thousands of people would clog the two-lane highway from Houma to sample the home-cooked gumbos, jambalayas, and shrimp boulettes (similar to crab cakes) on offer. One testimony to the cooking talents available: Myo Pellegrin, who got invited to cook his tasty jambalaya for the White House, was among the volunteer cooks, as was his wife, Imelda Pellegrin, who for a while ran a popular Chauvin Cajun restaurant, La Trouvaille (The Lucky Find), with her sister, Wylma Dusenbery. (I dined there several times. The menu sometimes included a tasty oyster gumbo.)

In fact, Lagniappe got so popular that it was eventually canceled by high church officials concerned about public safety (and perhaps the extravagant amount of beer that was being consumed there). Miss Imelda, as I affectionately called her, passed away about a year after I interviewed her for this book. Her husband, Myo, and sister, Wylma, had died before her. Their Lagniappe legacy lives on, however, since sales of beer and food, including a lot of gumbo, did pay off the church mortgage.

What about poule d'eau gumbo? When I'd inquired of friends still living in the Gumbo Belt, I'd gotten a mixed reaction. For the vast majority of people on earth, *poule d'eau* and *gourmet meal* would never appear in the same sentence.

The coot, sometimes called the mud hen, looks something like a diminutive black duck, but it's no duck. A member of the rail family that includes the marsh hen and tropical purple gallinule, it has a white face, a pointed beak, chickenlike legs and oversized feet with broad lobes that expand and contract. This gives it traction in the water and the ability to support its weight and scratch around like a chicken on marshy ground, though it far prefers the water to land. It often swims with ducks but doesn't quack. It grunts, croaks, and squawks. In fact, it pretty much never shuts up.

Still, it has four traits that Cajun hunters see as virtuous. It's plentiful, slow of wing, rather dull-witted, and easily skinned, avoiding the tedious and smelly plucking rituals for wild ducks. This all makes the poule d'eau a more popular and ubiquitous target for wing shooters than, say, the fleet blue-winged teal. Interestingly, Louisiana's hunting season allows for the taking of les poules d'eau cousins, the marsh hen and gallinule, but I've never heard of either of those being turned into gumbo. (Which doesn't mean they aren't.)

Maybe that's because coots are so much easier to find. A migratory species, they nest and summer in the northeast and winter in the South and along the Gulf Coast, in particular, traveling as far as Panama in Central America. In the Louisiana winter, coots often raft by the thousands with mixed groups of other waterfowl. This helps to explain why the state has the second largest population of migratory bald eagles in the United States. Like Gumbo Belt hunters, the eagles know an easy meal when they see one. The giant raptors diving to pluck slow-winged coots out of the air is a common sight. If eagles find poules d'eau delicious, their waterfowl friends don't think much of their company. The coot is a quarrelsome thief, often badgering ducks and geese out of their food.

If adventurous cooks in the in the rest of the country had an interest in cooking with coot, they'd have little problem. My Louisiana friends might be surprised to learn that I've seen them in places you might not expect: in New York City's Jacqueline Kennedy Onassis Reservoir in Central Park; in the ponds of San Francisco's Golden Gate Park; dabbling along the Lake Michigan waterfront in downtown Chicago; sparring with ducks in Lady Bird Lake in Austin, Texas; and swimming in saltwater ponds in Puerta Vallarta, Mexico. But while you can find literally thousands of recipes for duck on the web, the coot rings up no more than a dozen on Google, and half of them are framed by questions like, "Does anybody *really* eat coot?"

But if most of the rest of the world declines to dine on the lowly coot, among a subset of Cajun and Creole cookers (many of them of or near Henry's generation), poule d'eau gumbo is at the top of the gumbo chain, a delicacy that harkens back to a simpler, more rustic time. "I mean, there's nothing like this anywhere else," says Henry, a cheerful man with a wry, elfin grin, as he dips a ladle into the 20-quart Magnalite pot that he's been tending now for two-and-a-half hours. "But you've got to know how to cook them."

He's right. Even in the Gumbo Belt, poule d'eau gumbo is a little too gamey for the majority of modern palates. My mother cooked and ate duck gumbo but wouldn't touch a poule d'eau. Ditto for my dad, who would eat just about anything, including possum and raccoon. A cousin once told me, "Lips that touch a poule d'eau will never touch mine."

But today I've come to the right spot. The lowly poule d'eau is revered here.

The location is the thirty-six-acre compound and highly Cajunized man cave of Glynn Trahan, a bilingual entrepreneur who, among other things, farms alligators for a living. He's invited Henry and maybe a dozen other friends, most of them longtime gumbo and jambalaya chefs, to his digs to cook, drink, hang out, play a little Cajun music, and, when it moves them, speak Cajun French. The old tongue still gets a daily workout in these precincts.

"You're in the country now," says Chris Cenac, my Houma doctor/writer pal who's helped to organize the festivities, knowing of my poule d'eau gumbo interest. The Cenac and the Trahan families go back for generations. Chris, whose French baker forebear came to this area at the end of the Civil War and went on to become a prosperous land owner and farmer, can't stay for the gumbo. He's finishing research on the third in a series of richly detailed histories chronicling the settlement and early plantation and farming life of our bayou region. But he leaves me in good hands, and in an interesting place.

Trahan's man cave is a Spartan, aluminum-sided structure fronted by a roomy covered porch with a concrete floor. The porch has the requisite hunter-gatherer accoutrements, including a fish-cleaning station, a seafood-boiling stand, a commercial-sized freezer and tables and chairs for lounging, drinking, and dining. Inside, it's hard not to admire the oversized full-color Duck Dynasty poster with the bearded, ZZ Top–looking trio staring deep into your eyes. Nearby is a large Coors Light sign with a toothy gator chomping on a bottle of the brew. Various ducks frozen in flight by expensive taxidermy decorate the walls. A hefty green ornamental frog adorns a rusting wood stove. It holds a sign that says: "Mosquitos Wanted." And then there are the three live baby alligators crawling around in a stainless-steel sink. All this is surrounded by cooking equipment: multiple stoves, propane burners and refrigerators and coolers filled with food stuffs, beer, and liquor.

Trahan, sporting a camo ball cap, a turquoise tropical shirt, and khaki shorts, is built like a guy fond of his gumbos. "You know what we got here?" he says, welcoming me warmly. "The best cooks in this whole community."

Not to mention an interesting cast of characters. There's Russell Neil, known to all as "Mr. Pete," a nickname attached to a very long story in which he was originally called "Mr. Pit" or just plain "Pit." He's a fit-looking septuagenarian and former shrimp boat captain in jeans and a crisp blue shirt who once owned a seafood restaurant and still cooks commercially, mostly gumbos and jambalayas, for groups of up to 150 people. He sells his own line of Mr. Pete's Cajun Spices. He's cooking a seafood gumbo in parallel with Sou Henry's poule d'eau gumbo.

Henry, in a short-sleeve maroon golf shirt that reveals a dragon tattoo on his right forearm, is a former World War II and Korean War army combat veteran who in the old days trapped muskrats in the nearby marshes and then had a long career in the oil patch. The nickname "Sou" turns out to be rather common in the Cajun bayous. The term generally describes an antique French coin in circulation before the Louisiana Purchase, that is, before the French sold the Cajuns and Creoles out to the Americans. It was valued at five centimes or about one U.S. penny. The most famous Sou was the late gumbo-cooking U.S. senator Allen J. Ellender, who doubled down on the appellation by being known to close friends and family as "Sou-Sou."

There's also Joe Lyons, who commutes from Chauvin to Africa for his day job, in which he works a month on and month off. He's a convivial, bearded, bespectacled, big-boned man wearing a red company T-shirt and jeans shorts who has come to help out with the gumbo prep. He once captained 300-foot oil-field work vessels out of Nigeria and now docks supertankers. (And he tells me, cooks his gumbos wherever his work takes him.)

Trahan is a jack-of-all trades who owns and oversees a sprawl of 8,000 acres of duck-, poule d'eau-, and alligator-rich marshes beyond his compound. The alligators are the moneymakers. "We harvest alligator eggs, about six thousand a year," Trahan tells me. "The hatch rate is about 90 percent." Eighty-three percent of the hatchlings grow into adult gators that Trahan's enterprises harvest and sell for their skins and meat. Under a deal with state fish and game regulators, the remainder of the hatched gators are "put back in the wild after they reach four-feet long," says Trahan. "That's why the gator is doing so good these days." He's right. Overhunting had so decimated populations that in 1962, authorities closed the season for a decade. Today, Louisiana's gator population is estimated at two million—the largest of any state where alligators exist. (And, by the way, alligators *love* poule d'eau as much as some Cajun gumbo chefs do.)

"Check this out," says Trahan. He disappears and comes back clutching one of the foot-long gators I'd seen earlier.

"This one's about a year old. Want a picture?" he says.

The aromas of the competing gumbos fill the air. Pots clank as Mr. Pete and Sou Henry stir in their ingredients. The cookers and their coterie take their art seriously and freely offer up advice on ingredients and techniques. Many poule d'eau gumbo cookers use only the oversized gizzards of the bird, often combining them, as Henry has done this afternoon, with duck breasts and smoked sausage. Others use the whole coot minus head, beak, and feet and sometimes ladle in fresh oysters, which they feel complement the wild poule d'eau flavors. Otherwise, the base of the gumbo is cooked as most gumbos are, with a roux and the Trinity of onions, celery, and green peppers, with garlic often thrown in.

The talk turns to rice, the indispensable gumbo bowl filler. Is using a rice cooker, for example, better and easier than the old school way of covering the rice in a conventional pot with water equal to the thickness of the rice? (Opinion is divided.) Is parboiled rice—rice that has been soaked, steamed, and dried before milling—superior to conventional long-grain rice?

Tonight, the cooks are using Zatarain's parboiled rice but somebody pipes up, "Actually, the Walmart parboiled is the best."

A lot of Cajuns keep an open kitchen and that's true today. The batches being cooked are big and anyone who wants to drop by for a bite and a drink is welcome.

One of the visitors is Glynn Trahan's eighty-year-old father, Wilton Trahan, who lives nearby and has wandered in to check out the gumbo progress. Trahan introduces me. "Look at him," says Glynn, laughing. "He looks better than me." The senior Trahan smiles and firmly shakes my hand.

One of the things I'd observed throughout the Gumbo Belt is the pace of gumbo-cooking is perfect for reminiscing. It's slow, methodical, and takes place in stages. It allows ample time for the kind of storytelling that lubricates the reaffirmation of family and friends and the stories that bind them. Cook, talk, cook, talk, sample, eat, talk. Oh, and drink, too.

Glynn Trahan has a story.

"You wouldn't believe what we did in the old days," he says. The family trapped muskrat and nutria together, retiring each winter to a two-room cypress-and-tar-paper camp propped up on stilts in the marsh. "No electricity, no heat, not much of anything. . . . Momma would light a kerosene lamp at night and put it in a pan of water, 'cause we were afraid the camp would catch fire. We'd skin everything outside, but the fur would come inside with us at night."

The Trahan kids would take three months off school during the winter trapping season. That helps to explain why Glynn dropped out before graduating from high school and his dad only has a fifth-grade education.

Glynn looks at Wilton admiringly. There was a store across the lake that also served as a fur-trading hub where the family sold its catch. "Every three or four days, we'd go into the store and, seriously, for us it's like a kid going to Disneyland today."

Jokes and gumbo-cooking go well together, too, especially Boudreaux and Thibodeaux jokes. Gumbo Belt people know these jokes well, but for outsiders, a brief explanation. Boudreaux and Thibodeaux are lovable Cajun clowns who are usually the butts of their own jokes or, like the Road Runner cartoon character, end up outsmarting some version of Wile E. Coyote. A fair number of them are bawdy. These jokes all must be told in a thick Cajun accent (and that's not a hard thing to produce here since everybody has one). Mr. Pete has a million Boudreaux and Thibodeaux jokes.

"Did you hear the one about Detiveaux, Boudreaux, and Thibodeaux in the strip club?" he asks. People probably have, but etiquette absolutely requires that nobody ever stops anybody else from telling a Boudreaux and Thibodeaux joke, even if you've heard it a thousand times.

It goes like this. Basically, the trio is sitting at the bar and the stripper comes by, turning around to show off her, uh, charms. Impressed, Detiveaux takes out a fifty-dollar bill and puts it in her G-string. Boudreaux, not to be outdone, fetches a hundred and does the same thing. Thibodeaux, panicked that he has no cash, takes out his wallet and fetches his debit card. He runs the stripe along the stripper's butt crack—grabs the $150.00 and says to the dancer, "Here ya go."

I know some polite people will find the joke vulgar but it's just too goofy not to laugh at, and everybody does.

Trahan breaks off the hilarity long enough to tell Mr. Pete, ambling back over to supervise the seafood gumbo pot, "If you need more shrimp, I got 'em in that white cooler there."

"I could use some," he replies.

The seafood gumbo, which includes crab, is finished about the same time as Henry's poule d'eau gumbo. Mr. Pete's recipe is fairly conventional even though he adds a small can of Ro-Tel tomatoes to the batch. Most Cajuns don't cook with tomatoes. It's also heavy on the garlic. The gumbo is chock full of succulent, perfectly cooked shrimp. The roux is a shade of chestnut brown and the tomatoes give the dish an interesting reddish cast. People dig in, me included.

Oh, man. It's a killer.

As for Sou Henry's poule d'eau concoction, it's beautiful, rich, exotic—the roux a deep chocolate color, the aroma and flavor redolent of the nearby sea yet with a pleasing earthiness. I have two helpings.

This isn't my first poule d'eau gumbo, just the first one in decades. When I still lived in Houma in my twenties, I went duck hunting every season. And whenever I planned a hunt, my mother made this known to two maw-maws, elderly, widowed sisters who lived down at the end of the blue-collar suburban street where my parents moved after we quit the country.

I honestly never knew their real names because everyone on the street called them by their nicknames, Tante Dee-Dee and Tante Da-Da. They shared two passions with Bonnie, cooking gumbo and watching daytime soap operas. They were often found in the late afternoon on my mother's living room couch, discussing the soaps and plotting supper, often in Cajun French. And whenever my mother told them I was going duck hunting, one or the other would call me, pleading in their pleasing Cajun accents, "Ketch us a pool-doo for our gumbo, cher."

My mother loved Dee-Dee and Da-Da and we all had a warm familial relationship. Sometimes I would have fun with them on the phone when they called. They had among the most unusual Cajun accents I had ever heard.

"Who's this?" I'd say, pretending I hadn't heard properly.

"Dee-Dee."

"Are you sure? You sound like Da-Da to me."

"Ken, it's Dee-Dee."

"I dunno. I'm not convinced. Put Da-Da on the phone. You could be Dee-Dee posing as Da-Da. Or Da-Da posing as Dee-Dee."

Even though I did this several times there would always be a long silence, then: "Ken, you tellin' me I don't know who I am? You makin' me crazy, you know dat!"

And then we would both dissolve into hysterical laughter.

I usually was able to make Tante Dee-Dee and Da-Da happy. Even spooked poules d'eau go into a lumbering takeoff routine that requires them, in the manner of loons, to flap hard and run across the water for several yards before they get airborne. Once up, they are slow and have not learned, as have some ducks, evasive maneuvers. They make people who are average shots like me look like professional skeet shooters.

Of course, I was invited many times when Dee-Dee and Da-Da cooked gumbo from the poules d'eau I supplied but I dined on it just once, a bowlful being dropped off at my mother's house. I recall I found it more interesting than good. Even so, I'm now sorry I didn't think to ask for their recipes or even go over to watch them cook.

Tante Dee-Dee and Tante Da-Da are long gone, but, as it turned out, the elderly parents of Carla Jane Freeman, the significant other of my brother Chris Wells, are old school Cajun cooks, and poule d'eau gumbo has long been a family specialty. Even before getting the invite to Glynn Trahan's, the Freemans—Larry and Beverly but Mr. Peg and Miz Bev to their friends—had said I could come watch them cook. But our first date got canceled when Peg fell ill.

When they learned I would be back in Houma, they were happy to reschedule and warm up the gumbo pot. I was interested in a comparison with Sou Henry's gumbo because the Freeman recipe included oysters and they cooked with the whole poule d'eau, not just the breasts and gizzards. We gathered at the house that Chris and Carla Jane share in a lovely oak-filled neighborhood that, in the old days, was part of a Bayou Black sugar plantation. Chris had managed to get the poules d'eau from a friend named Barry who runs a sort of Ducks-R-Us operation down a local bayou. If you want wild game, call Barry and it arrives at your door the next day dressed and ready to cook.

Peg, on the cusp of his eighty-fifth birthday, had his roux going by the time I got there and was just about to toss in his onions. He's a gentle-spoken man with deep-set blue eyes behind wire-rim glasses. He's sporting a jaunty checked blue shirt and crisp khakis. It's only when he removes his blue Exxon ball cap that you realize he's balding. He got his name for his incessant playing of a child-hood knife-throwing game that most people know as mumblety peg. He's among the cooks who, even if they use the Trinity, stir in the onions first under the theory that they brown better that way and give the gumbo a more robust color. (Confession: I've since bor-rowed the technique.)

Bev, eighty-two, is a trim woman in a smart green dress accented by a gold cross and small diamond pendant. Her hair is impeccably coiffed. She's sitting nearby offering gentle advice. It wasn't hard to notice that the Freemans, soon to be married sixty-three years, often seemed to intuit each other's thoughts. As the gumbo starts to take shape and they ladle in a rich, café au lait–colored stock, Peg says, "I think I need to put a little more water in that."

She nods. "I know. But look, it's already pretty."

Talk turns to the oysters, which Carla Jane has acquired from a local supermarket. (My brother, who manages a nearby bed-and-breakfast and its brisk wedding business, is away at work on this day.) Bev reminds her husband, "We're not gonna need to put them in till about twenty minutes before the end. We'll just save the juice till later."

Peg nods. It's clear they have a gumbo plan. They cook with a kind of meticulous fondness for the dish and each other.

I ask them about their gumbo history and poule d'eau gumbo in particular.

Peg grew up poor on nearby Bayou Dularge, one of the many Cajun hamlets south of Houma, in a family of six kids. His parents divorced and his mom died young. Bev, whose maiden name was Jackson, was second of ten siblings. She grew up on a family farm on upper Bayou Black not that far from here. They met and married in 1950.

"I really didn't have the money to get married, but it was either get married or lose her," Peg recalls. He digresses. "I love gumbo," he says. "I could eat it three times a day."

He began cooking at his parents' hunting camp as a young-ster. Bev started early, too. "My parents liked to party," and cook-ing duties sometimes fell to the older kids. "I've been cooking since I was ten."

After Peg's parents divorced, the family fell on hard times. His mom, from a Cajun family, the Champagnes, did what she could to keep food on the table. What they couldn't catch they had to buy.

"We had a seafood place on the bayou," he recalls. "Momma would go to see what they had." The family was Catholic and observed the Catholic restriction of not eating meat on Fridays. It turns out the poule d'eau has an official Catholic Church exemption: It's considered seafood. "So, Momma would buy poules d'eau, mostly because they were cheap, maybe ten cents apiece. And that would be the gumbo. But I came to really like it. Back then, everybody ate it. Nowadays, people hardly fool with them."

Bev, listening intently to this, offers a shocking admission. She'll help direct the cooking of the poule d'eau gumbo today, but she won't eat it. "I used to love that but not anymore," she tells me.

She traces her aversion to a minor crisis in their marriage some years back and tells the story with great deadpan. Typically, Peg would hunt ducks and poules d'eau and she would do the plucking, cleaning, and dressing. Sometimes he'd dump as many as fifty ducks or poules d'eau on her at one time. Once, she was trying a new duck-plucking method using paraffin and plugged up the entire plumbing of the house when the melted paraffin got poured into the kitchen sink and congealed in the pipes.

Peg wasn't happy and, as the Cajuns say, raised hell.

"That was it for me," she says, laughing. "After years and years and years of cleaning all those ducks and poules d'eau, I said I'm never cooking, cleaning, or eating that again. That was the end of it."

Peg shrugs his shoulders, smiling sheepishly.

"He has a black lady who does it for him now," Bev says.

About an hour passes and the decision is made to ladle in the poules d'eau, which have been simmering in a succulent broth in a pot on the side. They are cooking with whole birds. All told, says Peg, you need about four hours to brown and tenderize them properly.

They also add garlic. "You don't want to do it too soon because you don't want it to brown," says Bev.

Peg stirs the pot and the Freemans turn to a tender topic, their deep love of their fishing camp on nearby Lake Decade which is getting harder and harder for them to visit and tend to as age and health issues take their toll.

"It's heaven out there," says Peg. "You don't have to worry about nothing."

A prosperity his family never knew made the camp possible. Like a lot of bayou Cajuns, he took a job in the oil patch back in the 1950s as the first offshore wells began to come in, working for the oil-field services firm Schlumberger.

"In fact, I worked on the very first one in the gulf. It was called Thunder Bay," he recalls. After fifteen years, he and a brother-in-law tried their hand at an offshore rig sandblasting business, but environmental issues doomed the technology. A car dealership followed and then for five years he owned and operated a popular sports-fishing marina at a place called Falgout Canal.

He sold that to build a supermarket, which he successfully ran for five years until a heart attack in 1980 and subsequent bypass surgery mandated a blunt talk with his doctor. The surgery was quite experimental back then and of three patients who underwent the procedure that day in New Orleans, "I was the only one who came back."

"The doctor told me, 'You better get out of that business or you won't be around for too much longer.'"

Happily, the supermarket location was in a still-thriving Houma business district and the Freemans have been able to rent it all these years, living off that and other retirement income.

Peg looks at his wife. "That camp—every other week we went fishing, usually with another couple. We'd leave on Sunday and come back on Thursday. We'd fish when nobody else was there. We'd go everywhere, all the way to the mouth of the gulf by Oyster Bayou. Oh, man. It was unbelievable. Lost Lake—you wouldn't believe the fish we pulled out of there."

Bev interjects. "You remember the time I told you, 'Let's go throw the cast net at Jug Lake?' Caw, we caught so many shrimp, they filled the bottom of the boat."

But then came what Peg calls his "heart wobble" and that ended the cast-net throwing. Then came a knee replacement. More recently, he's been diagnosed with chronic heart failure. Bev, it turns out, had fallen and broken her pelvis about two months before. She's just beginning to walk without a walker.

The fond reminiscences of their sojourns at the camp are leavened when Peg mentions a sad fact of contemporary life throughout the coastal Gumbo Belt. The state's marshes—by some estimates comprising the seventh largest wetland on earth—have for decades been eroding at an alarming rate, beset by a complex combination of natural and manmade forces: subsidence, sea-level rise, the decade-long diversion of marsh-building sediments caused by the leveeing of the Mississippi River following the Great Flood of 1927, and massive dredging of the marshes by the oil and gas industry.

"When we first bought the camp," says Peg, "there were nine football fields of marsh around it. Now, there's water under the camp. That land's all gone. It's a crime what they did to our marsh."

About an hour-and-a-half later, the gumbo is almost done. Some diced green onions have been added along the way. The oysters come out of the refrigerator. Peg spoons them in one at a time. They're huge. "Salty," says Carla Jane who has sampled one, but not overly so.

"Not too many," he tells me. "You don't want to overpower the gumbo. Plus, we'll add some oyster water for flavor."

He stirs them in and waits a couple minutes, then samples the gumbo. He nods. The poules d'eau are completely tenderized, so much so that the meat is falling off the scrawny leg bone.

"I guess we coulda taken off those legs," he says. "People don't want to fool with bones."

Carla Jane, who has been making the obligatory mayonnaise-based potato salad to go with the gumbo, chimes in. "It's poule d'eau gumbo, Daddy. You're supposed to spit the leg bones."

Time for me to sample. I think the addition of oysters is the ticket. It becomes a wholly other dish than Sou Henry's version. Still, I can concede that poule d'eau gumbo might be an acquired taste for people not overly fond of these bold, wild flavors (and spitting out leg bones). But I enjoyed every bite, and the company even more.

I help myself to two bowlsful and some of Carla Jane's tasty potato salad. Peg digs in, relishing every bite. I like his attitude. I feel the same way when I eat my own gumbo and know I've nailed it.

It's only when things are winding down that he updates his health issues, heart failure, in particular.

After insertion of stents, a heart valve replacement, and more recent vein therapy, "They really can't do anything more for me. The doctor says I could live a good long time or go tomorrow."

He takes another bite and shrugs. "I've enjoyed my life," he says.

It's nice that he did. For less than a year after our poule d'eau cooking session, Beverly Freeman passed away after a short battle with cancer. Peg died of heart failure a few months later.

{ 7 }

MOBY GUMBO

"Here comes the sausage," says Chef John Folse.

Chef has a penchant for understatement.

A 15-foot-high stainless steel robotic arm has just lifted and poured, into what Folse modestly calls a "kettle," the first batch of what will be 400 pounds of lightly smoked sausage.

Yes, pounds.

The sliced meat avalanches down the kettle's silvery sides, sliding into a light film of melted butter that prevents it from sticking. An ingenious system of mechanical paddles and blades keeps it moving. A second, third, and fourth bin shortly follow. Soon, the cavernous spaces of Folse's sprawling USDA-sanctioned factory fill with the delicious aroma of browning sausage.

It really does smell like your momma's kitchen if your momma is from South Louisiana, which is the effect Folse is trying for. "You know, that's how Louisianans talk about food," he says. "You go into somebody's house and they've got something great on the stove and you don't ask, 'What's cooking?' You say, 'It sure smells good in here.'"

The reason Folse needs 400 pounds of sausage is that he's making a 5,000-pound batch of chicken-and-sausage gumbo. No, that's not a misprint. We're talking 2.5 tons. Before this gumbo is done, about ninety minutes from now, Folse's factory team will add 400 pounds of chicken and vast mounds of onions, celery, and green peppers, not to mention okra, cayenne pepper, salt, granulated onion, and garlic plus a semisecret sauce. All of this is stirred into a slurry of dark-brown Cajun roux deep enough to swim in.

"Now you understand why I have to be able to make roux by the ton," says Folse, in his white chef's outfit, obligatory hairnet pulled down to his ears. "If we are going to create the flavors of the black iron pot coming out of your momma's kitchen, the dark brown roux is essential."

I knew people cooked gumbo in big batches for church fairs and cooking exhibits. In November 2015, for example, a team of Louisiana lawyers cooked a Guinness World Records 5,800-pound batch of gumbo for a competitive gumbo-eating contest in Larose, Louisiana. But I'd never imagined commercial gumbo on this scale until Folse invited me to tour his cavernous gumbo factory near the west bank of the Mississippi River about forty miles southeast of Baton Rouge. Folse makes far more than gumbo here. About 150 food products, including three styles of red beans, along with etouffees, jambalayas, and all manner of soups come out the plant, with most of it going to the retail frozen-prepared foods trade. Target, Walmart and Albertsons drug store chain are among his customers.

Folse also sells sauces and packaged roux to other food companies and restaurant chains, including a bourbon whiskey glaze used by the TGI Fridays restaurant group. And in a nod to his Cajun Catholic roots, during the Lenten season the plant makes forty-case batches of crawfish bisque that involve the stuffing of three thousand crawfish heads. The bisque is shipped in freezer bags to stores just before Good Friday. Any home cook who's taken on crawfish bisque knows how intricate and painstaking a dish it is to make. It's not the kind of thing you'd think could ever be done at factory scale.

Folse says the bisque-making isn't so much about moneymaking as it is a duty to keep this traditional Lenten Gumbo Belt dish alive and with it preserve an important food memory. Most contemporary home cooks find it too labor-intensive to undertake. But if bisque is available on supermarket shelves, people will buy it, eat it, and remember. "If I don't do this, it's gone," he says.

But gumbo is the big deal here and Folse has perfected doing it in a big way. "Behold, there is my black iron pot," he says as he leads me on a tour and points at the nearest in an array of four kettles. "And we can dump 10 tons of gumbo—10 tons—every forty-five minutes if they're all operating at the same time."

They're quite the pots. The stainless-steel, cylindrical, rounded bottom kettles sit on three-foot-high steel pilings and measure about four feet deep and perhaps twelve feet in diameter. They are equipped with all manner of state-of-the-art computer-controlled accessories: Steam injectors and a sophisticated pumping system that allows plant operators not just to cook these gigantic batches but to seamlessly transfer the gumbo to chillers and an automated pasteurized bagging operation. Special X-ray–type sensors scan every bag to make sure each has the exact amount of sausage, chicken, and other ingredients. That way, nobody who buys a bag gets short changed.

Today's 2.5-ton batch will result in 1,250 64-ounce freezer bags of gumbo ready to be shipped all over America and the world. The factory also produces gumbo in 28-ounce bags. The company doesn't disclose its wholesale prices, but you can order a 64-ounce (4-pound) bag of Folse Louisiana Chicken & Sausage Gumbo from CajunGrocer .com for $15.00 and change. The 28-ounce bags retail for $9.35. On average, the factory will cook and bag 65 tons of gumbo a week, alternating between four and five different varieties, including seafood. Retail, that's close to half-a-million bucks a week or about $25 million a year.

"These kettles cost me about $125,000.00 each so I've got about half-a-million dollars tied up in them," says Folse, laughing, amid the thrum of his gigantic, high-tech kitchen. "I've got to make a lot of gumbo."

And the tonnage, as Folse repeats over and over again like a mantra, isn't the real challenge. The real challenge is to scale gumbo up to these humongous batches yet retain the taste and texture captured in South Louisiana's home kitchens. "As I tell my team, we won't sell anything that Louisianans won't eat," says Folse. Probably half of the factory's output is sold in Louisiana to consumers happy to find authentic-tasting Cajun dishes they can grab from the freezer case at their local supermarket on days when they are too busy to cook for themselves.

But he also has his eye on a far more expansive market. "Our goal was to become the company that can make food like we make it at home and sell it to the world," he says. "Our goal is that if you're eating our gumbo in China it will taste like the gumbo that your grandma made in Houma."

To accomplish this, Folse and his team begin with a 5,000-gram recipe—a little more than five quarts of gumbo, and in a feat of extrapolation, figure out how to tweak it into a recipe that will hold up at 5,000 pounds and come out of a freezer bag looking and smelling like authentic gumbo. This is done in his test kitchen through a series of experiments using recipes out of the numerous cookbooks that the chef has produced over the years.

Folse learned, for example, that in order keep a consistent "natural chicken" flavor throughout these multi-ton batches requires mixing a puree of what he calls "liquid chicken" into the gumbo before adding the actual diced chicken. The real chicken can't be incorporated until near the end of the process lest the chicken overcook.

The plant makes and smokes its own sausage with a mixture of pecan and oak wood but jobs out the chicken processing to a Louisiana company "that cuts it to our specifications," Folse says. All the ingredients in Folse's factory, including shrimp for his seafood gumbos and spices and herbs, are Louisiana sourced.

If you spend much time with Folse, an upbeat, energetic, loquacious man, you can't help but understand that he's running a mission as much as a company. For him, the breakout of gumbo and South Louisiana cuisine onto a national and world stage is, pure and simple, a credit to the place and culture that produced it.

Paramount in this is the preservation of what the chef frames as "the glory of the black-iron pot" and the ingenuity and authenticity of the generations of home cooks who have kept the traditions alive. Everything that comes out of his factory is measured against this standard. "You don't want to put the culture or the cuisine into a museum," he says. "You want it to evolve but not in a way that is unrecognizable. We have been very proud and protective of our culture and the traditions that were handed down in full form in families for generations. That authenticity is what we need to make sure doesn't get lost."

That sentiment was the chief motivation in the founding of the Chef John Folse Culinary Institute at the Nicholls State University in 1995. Folse recalls hatching the idea a year or two earlier over bowls of gumbo at his Donaldsonville restaurant, Lafitte's Landing, with then Nicholls president Donald Ayo. (Ayo retired in 2002 after two decades at the Nicholls helm.) The overarching goal wasn't just to teach students to master the art of Cajun and Creole cooking, but to steep them in its lore and traditions while also encouraging them to do independent research into the region's deep and old foodways.

The institute, where Folse still teaches and serves as board chairman, has grown from a handful of students to an enrollment of three hundred. It recently moved into a state-of-the-art 33,000-square-foot building with teaching kitchens and a restaurant. Students can earn a four-year bachelor's degree in culinary arts at a cost of about $30,000. Two-year private cooking academies often cost twice that much.

Folse was clearly inspired by his roots. He was born in 1946 in the Mississippi River farming town of Vacherie and grew up nearby, absorbing the cadence of speech, pace of life, and cooking traditions of St. James Parish. Back then, Cajun French speakers were the majority. Vacherie was settled by Folse's Swiss-German pioneer forebears in the 1720s. The Germans readily accepted into their communities and lives the Cajuns who came four decades later. Intermarriage between the Germans and Cajun women was so common that sometime in the mid-1800s most of the Germans had given up their native tongue to speak Cajun French.

Folse (the original German surname may have been Voltz, Volz, or Folz) is a gleeful encyclopedia of the culinary serendipity of this mixing, the Germans bringing charcuterie and the smoked sausage into the food, the Cajuns bringing the roux, country French cooking influences, and knowledge of seafood soups. "The Germans loved to cook with pork and root vegetables," he says, "but the Cajuns had their own ideas about this." In the exchange of ideas, "that's how sauerkraut became smothered cabbage with andouille sausage" (in Folse's mind and mine, a great leap forward for cabbage).

Folse was one of eight kids. His mother, Therese Zeringue, died when he was seven years old. His father, Royley, was a fur trapper, moss picker, and logger who never remarried. After his mother's death, Folse's paternal grandparents moved in to help out. His maternal grandparents, the Zeringues, were a constant presence. Cajun French was the everyday language. Food, with gumbo at the center, was enormously important to his family and their tightly knit circle of Cajun and Cajunized-German friends.

"You began with the roux," recalls Folse. "Every mother taught her daughter how to cook roux at home and the sons learned how to make a roux at the hunting camp." His mentor was his maternal uncle, Paul Zeringue, who would round up the boys in the family from the time they could manage a kitchen knife and say, "C'mon, we're gonna make a gumbo." That was his favorite dish.

In Uncle Paul's world, "if you were old enough to chop an onion, you chopped the onions," says Folse. "Maybe you later got to do the green onions. Maybe next year you prepared the rabbit. The point is that every year you got a better station and you woke up one day realizing that, having watched and listened and helped, you not only could make a good roux, you were a pretty good chef."

Back then, it was a matter of great pride to both parents and kids when these lessons had been both taught and absorbed. "Children were praised by the qualities of their fricassees and courtbouillons and gumbos," recalls Folse. In the heavily Catholic community, "It was nice to have the priest praise your Latin, but the ultimate affirmation was when Uncle Paul put his arm around you and said, 'What a good gumbo.'"

Folse feels Uncle Paul's calling. "The greatest challenge today," he says, "is walking into my culinary classes and making my students disciples of the traditional—to make them aware we're stepping back three hundred years."

Though he knew cooking was his "life's DNA" he started out in hotel operations, not thinking he could actually earn a living as a chef. But a German chef, on Folse's training rotation in a hotel kitchen, saw his expansive home-hewed technique and the tasty concoctions he could whip up, and urged him to rethink his career. The rest is history. Folse and his wife, Laulie Bouchereau, started their first restaurant in Baton Rouge in 1974 and opened Lafitte's Landing four years later. His production company and plant, officially known as Chef John Folse & Company, opened in 1991 and in 2008 moved into its current facility.

And this operation is but part of a sprawling Folse food and media empire that includes a catering operation out of Folse's White Oak Plantation in Baton Rouge and a cookbook publishing and baking operation in Gonzales. His *The Encyclopedia of Cajun & Creole Cuisine* is in its fourteenth printing. And with star chef Rick Tramonto, Folse in 2012 opened a high-end New Orleans French Quarter restaurant called R'evolution. On the menu is his "Death by Gumbo"—roasted quail, andouille, and oysters finished off with a dash of filé and served over rice—that sells for $18.00 a bowl. Folse says that dish comes right out of the Cajun hunting camp gumbo tradition of his Uncle Paul.

Folse employs about 160 people in the factory here and 400 company-wide. "Everything here today," he says, gesturing around his plant, "came out of that restaurant business."

Beyond hard work and an ability to cook, Folse also had to gin up some old-fashioned Cajun ingenuity to get where he is today. There were no existing kettles to cook 2.5-ton batches of gumbo when he first conceived of the idea. He had to invent them.

For years, however, he was dissatisfied with his gumbo because he couldn't produce ample amounts of the dark brown roux he came to see as essential. He needed roux by the ton to make roux-rich gumbo by the ton but, like the cooking kettles before, nothing on that scale existed. So back to the drawing board he went.

"Here, you have to see this," he says as he leads me into his roux room. Inside are two of Folse's pride and joys, imposing black cast-iron, drum-shaped containers each capable of making 1,000 pounds of roux at a time. He gestures toward them like a proud father. "We use 500 pounds oil and 500 pounds of flour for each batch," he says. That's the fifty-fifty mixture used by my own mother and a vast majority of other gumbo cooks.

The design challenges were daunting. He had to figure out not only how thick the cooker walls had to be to hold the superhot roux but what size of drive and transmission apparatus you would need to push the paddles to keep a half-ton roux stirring so it doesn't scorch. "How would you heat it to maintain temperature? How do you push a roux that big? Everybody said it was impossible."

He ended up flying off to Germany after finding a company that could build the roux-cookers to his specifications. Roux suddenly became a business in itself. The factory these days produces dark, medium, and light oil-and-flour roux along with duck fat and butter roux that mostly get sold to other food companies.

Following Folse around his gumbo factory is a bit like following Willie Wonka in his chocolate factory. Everything is of grand scale and Folse sees magic being done everywhere. The smooth-functioning technology clearly delights him. He's effusive in praise of his team, to whom he is simply known as Chef. Otherwise everyone is on a first-name basis. As we watch the 5,000-pound batch of gumbo come together, Folse could be someone seeing it for the first time instead of the thousandth.

"Look at the color," he says as the kettle absorbs and stirs in the dark roux slurry that's just been poured it. "It's looking like gumbo now. That's beautiful. Wherever they eat this, they will be eating real gumbo."

"We're dumping in the chicken now," a plant worker tells the boss. That means the gumbo's getting close. They'll add a little more water, the secret sauce and then bring the batch up to 190 degrees F. and hold for fifteen minutes. Then, a little more salt and the gumbo will be ready for pumping.

We head back to Folse's conference room to continue the discussion and where he wants me to sample some factory gumbo. We talk as we go. He's a man of a thousand ideas and his latest one is the creation of a Bayou Studies Program within the Nicholls State Culinary Institute. It would be the "repository for all things bayou, instead of having every-thing go to LSU or Tulane." Folse says he's already got a $1 million pledge to that end. (The program, in fact, is already up and running.)

We also talk about a curiosity of mine, the disappearing Cajun accent. His eyes light up. "True, something's being lost." He tells of a star student of his whose parents and sister are both shrimpers, speak Cajun French and English with thick Cajun accents. But the daughter has gone off to study both abroad and in New York. "She sounds like she's from New York City—she could've come off Broadway," says Folse. "It's not that that's bad. But it's what's happening."

Folse, in fact, has among the more unusual Cajun accents I've encountered. It seems me to be somewhere between Brooklyn and the bayou. I ask him about it. He laughs. When as student at Nicholls he took a speech course, the prof called in a linguist to try to decode the accent. The verdict: Cajun with a mysterious mix of Bostonian brogue.

Chef remains mystified. "That's impossible," he says, laughing.

Folse has ordered up cups of the recently cooked megabatches of gumbo, but first wants me to sample his crawfish bisque. It comes, and I dig in.

I'm sorry, but nothing coming out of a factory kitchen should taste that good.

Next, the gumbos arrive. I take a bite of each and tell Folse what I'm required to tell everybody when I try their gumbo: "Well, it's not as good as my momma's."

But I honestly think that in a blind tasting with gumbos cooked in home kitchens, it would hold its own.

To be sure, it's not hard to find Cajun/Creole purists who will never in their lifetimes buy anybody's commercially made frozen gumbo from a website or supermarket shelf, even the stuff made by a chef with the Gumbo Belt credentials of John Folse. As I traveled the Gumbo Belt, I ran into a hard core of purists who turn up their noses at even restaurant gumbo, no matter the credentials or reputation of the restaurant. For these folks, gumbo was invented at home, is only cooked properly at home (by Momma), and should stay at home. The uprising over Disney's misfortunate incursion into gumbo-making is a manifestation of that.

I understand and even respect that opinion. It just doesn't happen to be mine. Nothing will ever taste better to me than my momma's gumbo. But my travels throughout South Louisiana, and to ramparts far removed where I found gumbo being cooked, revealed what I consider to be the glory and genius of the Gumbo Diaspora. Sure, Chef Folse makes a ton of money making gumbo by the ton. But anyone who's spent time with him, or the late Paul Prudhomme, or Tory McPhail at Commander's, or others who are passionate about gumbo, soon understands that the desire to expand gumbo's boundaries, markets, and diners has a deeply missionary component, an "envie," as the Cajuns would say, to share our creation with the world and spread the joy it brings. And what's wrong with that?

{ 8 }

READY, SET, COOK!

I'd missed the arrival of the Gumbo Police by fifteen minutes.

They'd come and gone by the time I stumbled, at 5:45 a.m., into the oversized white tent of Norris International Services on what will turn out to be a pristine Sunday morning. The Norris encampment is part of a sprawling, already bustling tent city that had sprung up over the weekend along a closed-off section of Main Street and into Bouligny Plaza on the banks of Bayou Teche in New Iberia.

Even people who have never set foot in Louisiana might know something about New Iberia in the southwest quadrant of the Gumbo Belt if they're fans of the best-selling mystery writer James Lee Burke. The New Iberia native has set most of his books in his hometown and his chief character, detective Dave Robicheaux, often eats his gumbo in Bon Creole, a New Iberia restaurant. (Bon Creole is a real place with a killer gumbo on the menu even if Dave and the killers he chases are fictional.)

It's October 2016 and the Greater Iberia Chamber of Commerce is putting on the twenty-seventh annual World Championship Gumbo Cookoff. Norris International is one of ninety-three teams competing. There are other competitions and festivals scattered throughout the Gumbo Belt, but New Iberia's is the only one that claims global stature. Over the years, teams have come from as far away Japan and Canada to compete.

I didn't want to just amble from tent to tent, watching. I wanted to help cook, be part of the action, so I'd requested through the chamber's Kelly Roark, vice president of operations, to be embedded with a team.

She steered me to Norris, a thriving, family-owned maker of specialty equipment and valves for the oil and gas industry. Norris has entered the contest for nine years running and has considerable gumbo-contest cred. It's a six-time finalist and its shrimp-and-duck gumbo won in its category in 2010 and 2013.

As I made my early morning entrance into the Norris tent, I was greeted robustly by Brad Norris, the bearded, energetic, loquacious thirty-two-year-old who will be running the show today. "Ken, you made it," says Brad as he flashes a smile as if to say, jovially, "Lightweight."

I'd met Brad the day before so that he could fill me in on how the contest works and how the Norris team, which is mostly gumbo-crazed family members, gumbo-crazed coworkers, and gumbo-crazed friends, maybe fifteen people in all, planned to get back atop the leader board. It's a two-day competition but Saturday is given over to a red beans and rice cookoff. Team Norris doesn't do beans, so Brad had plenty of time to give me the lowdown.

When he'd mentioned the involvement of the Gumbo Police—a squad appointed by contest organizers who come armed with their noses to make sure nobody starts cooking too early—I'd actually promised to arrive at 5:00 a.m. so as to catch them in action. But I was overnighting a half hour's drive away in Lafayette with my friends, the Mays. We'd gone out the previous evening to celebrate their wedding anniversary and, in the way that it often happens when we get together, overcelebrating is a risk.

So, I was arriving a little hungover and a little late.

"Well," says Brad. "You can still catch the cannon."

"The cannon?"

"Yeah, they shoot off a cannon. It's the signal to begin cooking." He points toward Main Street. "That way."

I start walking in that direction and "Kaboom!" The cannon thunders as if it might have exploded in my ear. I haven't had my coffee yet. Now I don't need any.

I stumble back to the Norris tent. Brad hands me a three-foot-long whisk. "Start stirring. We've got to get our roux on."

Suddenly, there's a whole lot of stirring going on as every team fires up their roux pots. Indeed, by 7:00 a.m., much of New Iberia, population thirty thousand, will be cloaked in a warm roux aroma. With each team cooking at least two gumbos, and many cooking three, that's more than two hundred roux pots in simultaneous action. And most teams cook their roux in pots separate from the much larger pots necessary to accommodate big batches of gumbo required by contest rules. This collective stirring, simmering, and boiling creates its own atmosphere.

Here's how the contest works. Anyone can enter. It's divided into youth, amateur, and professional chef divisions. Entrants may enter in three gumbo categories, the two classics, chicken-and-sausage and seafood, and a third called *mélange*, which is any gumbo that falls outside of the first two traditional styles by, say, mixing seafood with poultry. Norris's shrimp-and-duck gumbo will be entering the mélange category, Brad tells me, and "We're also cooking a chicken-and-sausage."

Each team must cook a minimum of sixty quarts of each style they enter. That's so the public, which gets in free, can have a reasonable chance of sampling lots of gumbos given that the Sunday crowds are thick with ravenous gumbo-eaters. The Chamber will estimate this year's crowd at about 27,000, down actually from previous years because of a slump in the regional economy caused by the oil and gas bust.

The gumbo isn't free. You pay four or five bucks a pop for an eight-ounce serving, with seafood and mélange usually being a buck more than chicken-and-sausage since they are more expensive to make. The gumbo is ladled into a disposable plastic white bowl over rice and eaten with a white plastic spoon. Savvy cookoff-goers often ask the servers to skip the rice, so they get more gumbo per cup. Half the money goes back to the teams to cover costs and the Chamber gets to keep the other half. These proceeds have paid off the Chamber's downtown office building and still raise a great deal of its annual budget. The contest has seen a surge in popularity since its first year, when only ten teams competed in a small downtown plaza.

You aren't allowed to use electric pots. All gumbos must be cooked over an open flame, which means over large propane burners. Teams are allowed to chop their vegetables, make stock, and marinate or otherwise prepare their poultry, game, seafood, or sausage in advance. But the roux must be cooked on the spot and all the ingredients combined on the day of the contest. Everyone knows that the longer you cook a gumbo and the longer you let it stand, the more flavorful it gets.

Technically, you don't have to cook with a roux but the feeling among this hard-core Cajun crowd is that a rouxless gumbo is going to get laughed off the judging table. A Norris team member gleefully tells the story of how a team came from Missouri a couple of years back and dumped cans of tomato paste into their rouxless gumbo. That recipe in this part of the Gumbo Belt? You've got to be kidding!

"Them poor guys had no idea what they were doing," he says. "It made an impression—the wrong kind."

The final rule is that all gumbos must be done by 11:00 a.m., when they are then ladled into six small cups, put on a tray with the team's name printed on a paper bag, and delivered to the judges. It's at that point that the teams can start selling to the gumbo-hungry crowds.

If you have a super-popular gumbo, you have to make sure you hold enough back so that if you're chosen as one of three finalists in each category, you have enough to send the judges another six-cup sample. It's from the second and final sample that first, second, and third places in the three categories are awarded.

This year, the judges, chosen by the Chamber for their gumbo knowledge and/or cooking experience, are holding forth in Clementine on Main, a cozy downtown seafood restaurant just a couple of blocks from the tent city. Everybody has both sympathy for—and deep reservations about—the judges. It's a tough job because most people will lose and nobody in Cajun country wants to be outcooked when it comes to gumbo. Lots of gumbo egos are on the line. To prevent the appearance of favoritism, the Chamber allows each team to nominate a judge for the category in which they are entering.

Brad explains his view of the judging dynamics: "We want to make the finals and we should make the finals but it's a crap shoot if you think about it. So, this year, what style of gumbo will they prefer? Thick, thin? Dark roux, light roux? It's all pretty subjective. You just have to hope your gumbo matches the preferences."

Making a supersized roux for sixty quarts of gumbo is certainly the most labor-intensive part of the process. Brad is manning the shrimp-and-duck gumbo roux pot. This is his recipe and he is the maestro. His younger brother, Brian Norris, twenty-nine, who like Brad works in the family business, is tag-teaming the chicken-and-sausage gumbo with longtime family friend, Butch Comeaux. It turns out Brad apprenticed under Butch and learned much of his gumbo method from him.

"Actually, Butch taught me everything I know but I'll never tell him that," says Brad. "See that hat on his head? It wouldn't fit him in the morning."

Butch, overhearing this, laughs.

As we take turns stirring the roux, we talk.

Butch, fifty-nine, is a plumber by trade but a serious gumbo chef on the side. He cooked his first gumbo, learning from his momma, at nineteen years old, and has been refining his technique ever since. He's the guy who talked the Norrises into joining the contest, agreeing to be their roux chef in 2007, the team's inaugural year.

"I was with another team but, seriously, it was crazy. They were supercompetitive and there would almost be fistfights over how much pepper to put in the seafood gumbo. That kind of thing. They thought they could make money doing this, but this can't be about the money. It's got to be about the fun."

He points to Brian and Brad. "These guys are fun."

I know the fun quotient is about to increase when somebody starts passing around whiskey-infused whipped-cream shots in those little paper cups that restaurants often serve ketchup in. It's not 6:25 a.m. yet. I feel like I have to try at least one or risk being written off as an actual lightweight. It's not bad. I'm offered another.

Well, OK.

A third comes around.

Hmm, I decide to pass it on (to the glee of the next person down the line, who scarfs it down).

Other teamies have broken out some Michelob Ultras or Bud Lights or Miller Lites. Brad's preference is for Crown Royal Canadian whisky that he mixes from a large cooler into an oversized water glass. There is a brief team discussion about why mixing Tanqueray gin and 7UP, which somebody is doing, is a bad idea: It goes down faster than water. Not that this is stopping the person doing the mixing.

On the other hand, gumbo-making and drinking have a long and honorable association. Marcelle Bienvenu fondly tells the story of her mother's roux-making technique. "How long did her roux take?" Bienvenu says. "Usually, two martinis. She saw it as her quiet time."

Brad's roux for the shrimp-and-duck gumbo will take almost an hour to complete. I've done some of the stirring, but his chief assistant is Butch's son, Jason Comeaux, thirty-nine. Jason remembers being a seven-year-old sitting on a stool next to his mom stirring a roux.

"That's when I learned that when you start your roux, you can't leave the pot," he says. "I needed to go to the bathroom. Momma said, 'You can't leave the pot for any reason.'" He's also picked up some gumbo tips from his father.

Butch and Brian, running the chicken-and-sausage roux pot, finish their roux in a crisp thirty minutes. It's a good-looking, deep chestnut brown roux. "They started before we did, and we finished first. Experience pays off," says Butch, laughing and making sure Brad can hear him. It means they are getting their gumbo on quicker so it will have longer to cook, potentially giving them a leg up.

Let the smack-talking begin.

"Five dollars we finish in the finals and you don't," says Brad. Butch waves the challenge off. He comes over to look at Brad's roux in progress. "You need more flour in there," he says.

Brad shakes his head. "You think so?"

"I know so."

"I don't think so."

Butch shrugs. "OK. I'm just trying to help you out. See? He won't listen."

Brad goes over to look at Butch's roux. Somebody starts roughhousing. Butch's green, broad-brim sporting hat flies off—and lands in the roux pot.

"Whoa!" says Butch. "My poor hat!"

Someone flicks it from the pot, part of the rim browned by smoldering roux but otherwise unscathed. That's a huge save, like spearing a would-be home run with your glove in the World Series. Paul Prudhomme once described roux as so hot that it could very well be napalm. Also, it's not lost on anyone that scorched-hat flavor in a chicken-and-sausage gumbo would not be a good thing.

This incident will *not* get reported to the either the Gumbo Police or the judges.

Not ten minutes later comes a second brush with disaster. Norris

Team member Rich Touchet, Brian's father-in-law, who is also helping out with the stirring, backs in too close to the propane burner under the chicken-and-sausage gumbo. A purple LSU cooking towel he's stuffed into his backpocket catches fire.

"Whoa, whoa, whoa! Fire in the hole! Fire in the hole!" yells Jason.

Rich doesn't quite know that his butt is pretty close to going up in flames. Somebody rushes over and beats out the fire with his hands. There's a moment when I fear the chicken-and-sausage gumbo pot itself will go over, too. Sixty quarts of hot gumbo flooding the tent would require a rapid evacuation.

"Hey, that's my damned towel!" Brian yells. The whole tent dissolves into laughter.

The team sponsored by Berard Transportation cooking in the next tent over gets a whiff of the fire and thinks for a moment that maybe Norris has ruined one of its gumbos.

"What y'all burning over there?" one of them yells.

Rich doesn't miss a beat. "My ass!"

More laughter.

"You probably liked being spanked, Rich," somebody else yells.

That brings down the house.

Brad declares his roux, an almost dark cherry color, done at 6:49 a.m. and we begin to use a commercial-sized spatula to transfer the roux into the superlarge cooking pot. Along the way he's offered a few clues as to what he thinks has made his shrimp-and-duck gumbo a winner in the past. "Hog lard," he says. "I don't use oil. I'm Old School."

He also marinates his ducks, twenty-five to thirty, acquired from a local butcher shop, for a couple of days before the contest. Ditto with his shrimp. The other ingredients are fairly standard: the Trinity of onions, bell pepper, and celery plus garlic, salt, pepper, cayenne, and a dash of tarragon. With all the ingredients now combined save for the shrimp, Brad's gumbo looks beautiful.

Butch comes over and Brad offers a sample.

Butch tastes it with a plastic spoon.

"You got no seasoning in there," he says.

"We got some but it's too early to put more," says Brad. "The shrimp go in last because you don't want to overcook them. And I can't fully season it until the shrimp go in. Plus, the shrimp will make a little water. You have to take that into account, too."

By 9:25 a.m., both gumbos seem to be coming along nicely. The talk now is about seasoning and consistency. Butch adds a little more roux to the chicken-and-sausage gumbo. "We thought it was a little too thin," he says.

Brad is worried about the appearance of his shrimp-and-duck gumbo. Cooking with lard releases a lot of oil. You don't want to deliver an overly oily gumbo to the judges. He shows me a technique I'd never thought of, floating sheets of white paper towels on the surface and snatching them up with tongs at the point that they've soaked up so much grease they start to sink. It's a lot faster and more efficient than skimming the oil off with a big spoon or ladle, especially for a gumbo of this size.

"It works great," he says. But then he recounts an occasion when it didn't. Someone he knows who uses the technique screwed up and used scented towels. That was the end of that gumbo.

At 10:11 a.m., Brad declares it's time to add the shrimp to his gumbo and ladle in the final tranche of seasonings. Butch has decided the chicken-and-sausage gumbo is done and seasoned pretty much the way it needs to be. He won't do much more fiddling.

There's a lot of sampling going on. My teamies keep passing me spoonfuls to try. I agree with Butch that his gumbo doesn't need anything else. Of course, that's based upon my preferences. It's salty without being overly so and has a nice little peppery kick in the back of my throat without being too hot on the tongue.

I think Brad is being a little conservative with his seasoning, but I've bought into his shrimp explanation and, anyway, it's a good gumbo. I like the novelty of the shrimp-and-duck combination. It's an unusual and completely memorable flavor. It's the kind of gumbo I'd like to eat after it sits overnight in the refrigerator just to confirm my initial impression. I'm betting by then it would be seasoned perfectly.

Butch, sampling Brad's says, "Ours is better."

Brad laughs. "You watch what happens at 11:00 when we can start selling. You watch and see where everybody will be lined up. My side!"

At about 10:50, the cooks begin to prepare the cups for the judges. I had not expected it to be so laborious but of course it would be. You want to create a bowl of art by ladling in the best-looking bits of chicken, sausage, duck, shrimp and you want to make sure that you have enough liquid so that the gumbo looks and tastes balanced.

Done, Jason advises me that we'll walk interference for Brad through the crowds as he carries the tray to Clementine for the judging. Being jostled by hungry gumbo revelers is a real possibility. "You can't take a chance on spilling," he says.

I check my watch. It's 11:00 a.m. I look up. Brad was right. There are fourteen people in line for his shrimp-and-duck gumbo and only one in line for Butch's chicken-and-sausage batch. Of course, I'm rooting for my team but I'm still a journalist. As we wend our way through the crowd to deliver our gumbo to the judges, I'm looking for signs that other teams are attracting similar crowds. They aren't. A few of the tents have two or three people in line but nothing like the lines forming at Norris for Brad's concoction.

We deliver the gumbo without incident and the waiting begins. We wait and we wait and we wait. I wander around some, checking out the competition along an aisle with a street sign that says Roux Row. Some teams have clearly spent time on their names. There's UnRouxly, the Roux & Broux Croux, the Tabasco Rascals and the Blue Flame Gang, among others. It's apparent that every team is cooking chicken-and-sausage. There also aren't as many exotic gumbos as I thought there might be. Rabbit-and-sausage, in the mélange category, is the only one that strikes my fancy. In all of my years of gumbo eating, I've never eaten rabbit in a gumbo. My mother would put rabbit in her sauce piquant but would never even think of putting it in her gumbo.

I later spend four dollars and try it. It's got a medium-thick, dark, reddish-tinted roux. I can't say that I recognize the rabbit as a distinctive flavor, but it's seasoned nicely and the sausage is yummy. If four stars were available, I would give it two-point-nine, maybe even a three.

I wander back to our tent and when noon has come and gone and we've had no word from the judges, the team begins to worry, all the more so when we hear cheers coming from other tents. This clearly means they've been chosen as finalists.

Finally, at Brad's urging, we decide to take matters into our own hands and seek out the judges. Jason and I walk the short two blocks to Clementine. We inquire from man at a table out front.

"What's the name of the team? Norris? I'll check," he says.

He goes in and returns in a minute or so. It's not looking good. The remaining finalists have been grouped on a table and Norris isn't in the batch. But he does say that a group of judges just departed to deliver news to some of the tents and maybe Norris is in that bunch.

Jason is bummed. We return to the tent and he delivers the news to Brad. It's pretty clear that if no one shows up in the next few minutes, we've been aced out.

No one does.

The irony for Team Norris is that there was such a run on their gumbo that they all but sold out the shrimp-and-duck batch in an hour, only holding back a tiny amount in expectation that they would make the finals and need to deliver more gumbo to the judges. Chicken-and-sausage went almost as quickly.

"Look around," says Brad. "See? Even teams who are finalists still have gumbo to sell. We've been cleaned out. How do you explain that?"

He answers his own question. "You can't. The people love our gumbo even if the judges didn't. If there was a People's Choice Award, we'd win it."

Butch says, "So you think we should change the recipe for next year?"

Brad replies, "Never. 'Cause, what, you change it in some way and then you might have judges who liked it the old way. You can't do that."

He pauses and says, "Really, whoever the judges were this year they need to go to gumbo school."

Butch laughs. "Did you say that about the judges when you won?"

Brad at first waves Butch off. But then he laughs.

"Of course not," he says.

CREOLE GETS ITS CAJUN ON

"At the very moment when America was embracing *nouvelle cuisine* what did my mother do? She hired Paul Prudhomme, who was the antithesis of nouvelle cuisine. Some people thought she was crazy."

The speaker is Ti Adelaide Martin, daughter of Ella Brennan, grande dame of the New Orleans restaurant scene but simply Miss Ella to friends, admirers, and legions of New Orleans foodies. We are seated at the family table in the bustling kitchen of Commander's Palace, one of this food-mad city's best-loved restaurants.

Ti (pronounced Tee) is with her first cousin, Lally Brennan. They are an energetic pair who have been coproprietors of the restaurant since Ella, ninety-one as of this writing, stepped aside a few years back for reasons of health and age. I've come to talk gumbo, which is inexorably tied to the Brennans' revival of one of the jewels of the New Orleans restaurant crown. The cousins offer Miss Ella's regrets. She'd normally love to discuss this topic, but she's been ailing of late and not making many appearances at the restaurant. (Alas, Miss Ella passed away in May 2018 at the age of ninety-two.)

Commander's has been a fixture of New Orleans' Garden District since 1893, when Emile Commander converted it from a popular corner saloon into a restaurant that began to attract the cream of the upper-crust neighborhood's society. But it had gone through several ownerships and had lost a great deal of its pizzazz by the time the Brennan family, already legendary New Orleans restaurateurs, took it over in 1969. A family schism five years later divided the Brennans. Ella and her siblings gave up ownership in the Royal Street Brennan's Restaurant, but gained Commander's.

The Brennans knew the restaurant business—some credit them with creating the modern-day New Orleans restaurant scene—and they painstakingly remodeled the Victorian-era building, painting it "Commander's Blue" and adding its trademark blue-and-white wraparound awning. But they got off to a rocky start. Commander's was, Ella would finally admit, stuck in a haute Creole cuisine rut, unable to much distinguish itself from a substantial list of other top New Orleans restaurants that for decades had been cooking a localized version of a classic French menu. The rub was that diners, some of them perhaps influenced by the nouvelle cuisine movement, were restive and looking for something beyond Trout Meunière and Escargots en Casserole.

Recall that the nouvelle cuisine fad of the 1970s began in Paris as an effort to pare down elaborate French cooking into a lighter fare of fresher foods and smaller portions, done with an eye toward elegant presentation. It spread to New York, California, and much of the rest of foodie America in the 1980s. At its best, it was a rebellion against three-hour, three-martini lunches and the rich food that accompanied them, and had sparked something in diners looking for a change.

New Orleans diners were looking for change, too, and Cajun presented itself as an earthy, spicy alternative to staid Creole fare. Cajun fare got its first toehold in the city in the form of the Bon Ton Café in the city's Central Business District. Some version of the Bon Ton has been around since its founding in 1877, making it the third-oldest existing restaurant in New Orleans. At one point, Bon Ton was owned and run as a fine-dining Creole restaurant by a member of the Commander family, who would open the original Commander's Palace.

But Bon Ton got a Cajun makeover starting in the 1950s when Al and Alzina Pierce pulled up stakes from the bayou lands southwest of New Orleans and started cooking roux-based gumbos, jambalayas, and hearty "bayou food": the spicier, earthier, roux-based dishes beloved by bayou Cajuns. By the time Ella Brennan was ready to change chefs, the Bon Ton was packing them in. Though the unpretentious restaurant wasn't competing with Commander's high-end demographic on paper, that means little in a city where food snobbery expresses itself in a wholly egalitarian fashion: If it's good, we're going there.

Prudhomme, after his decade-long cooking odyssey outside the Gumbo Belt that included stops in Las Vegas, San Francisco, and Denver, had returned to New Orleans in 1970. He eventually pitched up as the chef at the French Quarter's Maison Dupuy Hotel, cooking his revitalized version of Louisiana cuisine. Lines formed. People were starting to notice. He was making a name for himself and revving up the growing buzz around Cajun food.

As 1975 dawned, Commander's, Miss Ella concluded, needed its own buzz. She had already been through a succession of European chefs and was happy with none of them. "Mom kept saying, 'They don't get it,'" Ti recalls. "They don't understand the gutsy flavors we want even in Creole cuisine. They had no knowledge of Cajun."

Ti tells the story: One day, Ella lunched with an old friend, Terry Flettrich, a popular local TV news personality.

"Terry says, 'How's it going?' Mom's like, 'It's horrible. I need a chef.'"

Flettrich knew Prudhomme well and had approached him about starting a cooking school in her Bourbon Street home. "Terry told Mom, 'Look, you need to get this guy.'"

According to one account in an obituary following Prudhomme's death in 2015, the chef said he at first only agreed to work lunch. Commander's executive chef was away on vacation and when he returned, finding Prudhomme ensconced in his kitchen, resigned.

Ella and her brother Dick Brennan approached Prudhomme about taking the top job. He resisted, not sure he was the right fit and, anyway, he was happy where he was. Instead of saying no outright, "I asked for a huge salary—a ridiculous salary" thinking that would quash the deal. But it didn't.

"And as a result of that," says Ti, "it's just a fact that this is the first place where Cajun and Creole crashed together in the same kitchen in New Orleans."

It set off an explosion. It was also brilliant strategy for Commander's, catapulting the restaurant into one of the top ten highest-grossing restaurants in America. Most important to Miss Ella, it recaptured a spirit that had been missing. With Prudhomme, Commander's got its mojo back. Indeed, after Prudhomme departed in 1979, opening K-Paul's Louisiana Kitchen in the French Quarter, Commander's would haul in one star chef after another: Emeril Lagasse, Jamie Shannon, and most recently Tory McPhail, winner of the 2013 James Beard Award for Best Chef: South.

Commander's didn't exactly toss out its classic Creole menu, understanding that some loyal diners wanted the comfort of the food memories associated with dishes they'd tasted during that engagement dinner thirty years before, staples like Trout Amandine and Oysters Rockefeller. Indeed, Commander's Turtle Soup is based on a New Orleans Creole recipe probably unchanged in two hundred years. But forget the nouvelle cuisine food fad. Prudhomme brought bold Cajun spice to revivified recipes and a revamped menu. He sold Miss Ella on the virtue of showcasing the region's culinary gifts, the fresh seafood from the nearby Gulf, the crawfish from the swamp, the fresh produce and fruit from Louisiana gardens.

It's not like there weren't tensions. "Mom was very big on presentation," recalls Ti. "Paul never cared what the food looked like. Mom would say, 'Paul, that's too heavy. It looks horrible.' He would just say, 'Taste it, Ella. Taste it first.'"

"There were tugs of war," says Lally Brennan, "but it turned out wonderfully."

And central to this revolution was the elevation of gumbo, which had been kind of an afterthought in the old Commander's, something that seemed at best obligatory to the menu, not essential. Prudhomme made it essential, pushing the beloved dish front and center, bringing in the hearty chicken-and-andouille recipes of his birthplace in the southwest Cajun prairies and from time to time experimenting with game like duck, quail, and goose.

Of course, Miss Ella wouldn't let him forget where he was. Something about the gumbo had to have a Commander's flair. And that's still true today.

"It's probably accurate to say that today we're gumbo fanatics," says McPhail. With the kindly assent of Ti and Lally, he has invited me to spend a morning in Commander's kitchen to watch how the evolved version of Commander's gumbo comes together.

McPhail, a sandy-haired man with a ready smile and an amazingly laid-back manner given the pressures of his job, is explaining the rhythms of his job while sketching in his route here. His rise to the top post at the restaurant shows once again that Miss Ella and Ti and Lally have no fears of picking an unconventional chef if they feel the fit is right. McPhail grew up in the tiny town of Ferndale, Washington, near the Canadian border. He hunted, fished, and helped his parents and grandparents run their farms. Fresh meat, game, fish, and produce were mainstays of the McPhail family table. This spurred not just an interest in cooking, but an early passion for "all things natural,"

"But it's the Pacific Northwest," says McPhail with a wry smile. "God bless them—great salmon and halibut on the table but no bottles of hot sauce, not much spice."

After high school, McPhail enrolled in Seattle Community College and earned a degree in culinary science. Restless, he looked at a map of the United States and said to himself, "Where am I going to go? Ah, New Orleans."

McPhail knew New Orleans had Mardi Gras and he had some vague knowledge that the city had an interesting cooking scene but admits he was otherwise clueless. "I thought New Orleans was a beach town," he tells me, laughing. "I was thinking SCUBA every day but, no, New Orleans wasn't quite a beach town. I was a naive kid."

He arrived and quickly began to understand that he'd found a food nirvana. He got himself hired by Commander's then executive chef Jamie Shannon and, as he worked his way up the ladder through all twelve stations of Commander's kitchen, he began to explore New Orleans "one inexpensive meal at a time."

The shock for McPhail was how good the common cooking was, how a neighborhood poboy shack could craft a sandwich with so much pride and flavor that, in its own way, it could stand up to the elaborate fare coming out of kitchens like Commander's. It began to dawn on him that there was no other place like it. "The test of a community is how the less fortunate eat," he says. "When somebody can take an inexpensive thing like a poboy and turn it into a flavor memory you keep for a lifetime, to me that takes more talent than adding truffle oil to something."

His love of New Orleans aside, McPhail decided he needed to broaden his experience and left the city on a tour of several culinary hot spots, taking jobs at The Breakers in Palm Beach, the Michelin-starred L'Escargot in London and its sister restaurant, the Michelin two-star Picasso Room; and the Caribbean/Creole-intensive Mongoose Restaurant in the U.S. Virgin Islands. He returned to the Commander's family in spring 2000 as executive sous-chef at Commander's Palace Las Vegas and then got the call from the Brennan family in January 2002 that they wanted him to run the show here. "There are three or four of us in the kitchen here who have left to do other things, but we always keep coming back," he says.

Why?

"We want to be part of dynamic things that go on here," says McPhail.

Like the evolution of gumbo.

"Follow me," he says. "I have something cool to show you."

He opens the door to an electric roaster/smoker and a flood of warm aromas cascades out. Inside are racks holding a succulent whole chicken, freshly smoked andouille sausage and tasso, the lightly cured and smoked pork shoulder that is more and more today finding its way into gumbos, jambalayas, and other such dishes.

Today's gumbo will be a version of chicken-and-andouille and McPhail is pointing out how the various ingredients get cooked and/or prepped to the kitchen's specifications while he explains Commander's gumbo philosophy. No gumbo is started from scratch on the day it is served. Roux and stocks are laboriously prepared and fussed over by prep cooks who start their day at 5:30 a.m. The whole kitchen is attuned to the importance of how the gumbo turns out.

"Some restaurants that you go into, one guy makes the gumbo and that's all he does," says McPhail. "Here, there are twelve different folks who can make the gumbo. We think involving a kitchen full of talented chefs helps us be a little more creative."

The roux here spends at least some time in the oven where the desired color, from medium café au lait to dark chocolate, can be achieved without having to watch it so carefully and constantly. Chickens are roasted and andouille lightly smoked and sampled regularly to assure that they meet the desired taste profile.

"There's some form of gumbo in the pot 24 hours a day here 362 days a year," McPhail says. (Commander's is closed on Christmas, Mardi Gras Day, and for an annual staff dinner and party.) He guides me to two fifty-gallon stainless steel kettles filled to the rim and where succulent pieces of chicken and sausage and herbs float atop a rich, simmering stock.

"Smell that," he says, smiling.

I do. My stomach starts to growl.

"So here," McPhail says, "the idea is to create what we think of as a more balanced version of Cajun food. We want it so it's spicy, salty, and smoky, but we don't want our diners to be blown out by only a couple of taste sensations."

That leaves room, he says, to add "more luxury ingredients to our gumbo."

Such as?

"Follow me," he says.

We arrive at a twelve-quart sauce pan simmering on an electric burner. It's filled with a thickish, unfinished, pecan-colored gumbo base. Nearby is a pink cutting board atop a stainless-steel work table. A large kitchen knife and a scrum of small bowls holding spices clutter the board. McPhail comes up with a clear plastic bag.

He picks up the knife. "Some of the chicken you saw earlier," he says. He lays it out and dices it, putting it in the pot.

Then comes more andouille. The andouille that had gone into the pot earlier as "base flavor" has started to disintegrate, therefore the need to add fresh chunks. "You want to be able to see the nice pieces," he says.

The next two ingredients would have startled my mother.

"These are cognac-roasted peppers," he says. "They are well seasoned. Then we'll add some fresh oyster mushrooms." After they cook down a bit they'll add balance and flavor.

Then come two ingredients that are staples of many gumbos, green onions and cayenne pepper.

"You see some guys just dump in gallons of Worcestershire sauce and Louisiana hot sauce into their gumbos," says McPhail. "This one has a little of that in there, but I don't want to overdo it. I don't like it to be too acidic. We like it to be nice and round so we use more cayenne pepper than anything. We'll put a little black pepper on top of this."

Next comes an ingredient I would never have thought to put in gumbo. "A little brandy," he says. The rationale: Brandy has "a little bit of bitter quality to it and helps round things out."

"It's really starting to smell good," McPhail says.

He gets no argument from me.

The last ingredient is, well, mind-blowing.

"Foie gras trim," he says. "Everybody likes a little foie gras, right?"

McPhail scoops some generous lumps of foie gras out onto his cutting board and then smooths it out using a pestle to the consistency of peanut butter. "That way there are no little lumps when we add it to the gumbo. It'll blend in nicely."

He adds, "Some folks finish their gumbo with butter. We don't have to."

Luxury ingredients, indeed.

Later, McPhail sets a bowl down before me on the Commander's family table, paired with a French chardonnay. Commander's only serves its gumbo in appetizer sizes with no rice. "The richness of the recipe makes rice superfluous," says the chef.

As you might expect, the gumbo is beautiful, the color a luscious, almost chocolate-brown. Succulent pieces of chicken and andouille float amid a sprinkling of green sprigs of parsley.

The taste?

Richer than any gumbo I've ever eaten. The foie gras comes through but the flavor is subtle. Twinned with the smoky influence of the sausage, the balance is just right.

As you know, I'm required to give my mother's gumbo my top rating of four stars. This one gets three-point-eight.

Interestingly, later when I tell people about this gumbo I sometimes get incredulous responses from those who see themselves in the gumbo-purist camp. Basically, the reaction is, "that's too frou-frou to really be gumbo."

My response: This gumbo is within the spirit of gumbo's primal creation, a modern embodiment of the theory of the seven nations, i.e., food-centric acolytes experimenting and borrowing ideas, with the joy of the taste being the only test. I would eat this gumbo over and over again.

And why shouldn't we experiment with gumbo so long as it's done with a sense that perfecting gumbo in the future requires knowledge and homage to the past?

Our ancestors certainly did.

{ 10 }

GUMBO HUNTING IN TREME

You can't go gumbo-sampling in New Orleans without dining in the Treme. Sprawling roughly west and north of the French Quarter, Treme is the oldest African American neighborhood in America and the first place in the country where freed slaves and free people of color could own property. It's here, in the colorful shotgun houses that still line many streets, where generations of Creole cooks honed recipes that have greatly influenced the evolution of New Orleans cuisine. And it's also here where the city's first black-owned restaurants cropped up: Dooky Chase's, where Leah Chase's spirit still guides the kitchen, is one prominent example.

I've come on a pristine fall day to Li'l Dizzy's Cafe on the leafy ramparts of Esplanade Avenue to talk gumbo with Wayne Baquet Sr., Li'l Dizzy's laid-back founder, owner, and spiritual chef. Baquet hails from a storied New Orleans Creole family that traces its Crescent City roots back more than two hundred years. The Baquet family (pronounced bah-KAY) came, Wayne will tell me, with French colonials and free people of color fleeing the Haitian Revolution (1791–1804), an uprising in the French colony then known as Saint-Domingue.

"The free people of color and the French people had to get out or get killed," says Baquet, who has done serious research on the family's genealogy. The revolution culminated in the elimination of slavery and the creation of modern-day Haiti.

It inadvertently proved a gift to New Orleans. The Baquets stopped briefly in Cuba before settling permanently in the city, which has been richer for their presence. The first generations of New Orleans Baquets were cigar makers, cobblers, and carpenters but the family clearly carried a creative gene. Two of Wayne's great uncles, George and Achille Baquet, were among the founding gentry of New Orleans jazz. Accomplished clarinetists, George played with the likes of Louis Armstrong and Jelly Roll Morton.

Achille not only mastered the clarinet but, before moving out West and later to Europe to earn fame and fortune, was musical mentor to Sidney Bechet, the iconic jazz saxophonist whose bust earns a billing with Louis Armstrong's statue in Treme's Louis Armstrong Park. Meanwhile, other Baquets have found high posts in journalism. As of this writing, Dean Baquet, Wayne's brother, is executive editor of the *New York Times*, and Terry Baquet, another brother, is director of community engagement for the New Orleans *Times-Picayune*.

And then there are the notable Baquet cooks and restaurateurs. Wayne's aunt, Ada Baquet Gross, with her husband, Paul Gross, started an eatery in 1947 called the Paul Gross' Chicken Coop. It was the city's first twenty-four-hour fried chicken joint, Wayne tells me, "at a time when nobody else was really doing chicken." The Chicken Coop was regularly packed and its fried chicken recipes provided inspiration for the spicy fried chicken that is a signature dish, along with gumbo, red beans and rice, and Trout Baquet on the Li'l Dizzy's menu today.

Wayne's father, Eddie, was a onetime mail carrier who got the restaurant bug from Aunt Ada and who honed his skills working in her restaurant. In 1966, he went out on his own and opened the eponymously named Eddie's, a place that was both restaurant and home, Eddie having sold the previous family digs to finance the purchase of the property at 2119 Law Street. (The location is about a five-minute drive from Li'l Dizzy's current perch on Esplanade.)

Wayne, second of five brothers, recalls the family lived in cramped quarters in the back and ran the restaurant out of the front. In the early days, Eddie did the butchering, ordering, and generally ran the place while Wayne's mother, Myrtle Baquet, and an aunt, Anna Gibson, did the cooking. The kids pitched in. "My father fell in love with cooking over time and became an excellent cook," Wayne says.

Eddie's was a sensation, and not just because it got that Bill Cosby shout-out on *The Johnny Carson Show*. It attracted a racially mixed and demographically diverse crowd—a hallmark of Li'l Dizzy's today— but unusual at the time, especially during Eddie's early years. White cops, black civil rights workers, laborers, university professors, local and national politicians, celebrities and a certain kind of adventurous tourist, they all crowded in. If the food is good, people will come. And the food was paramount; but for some, Eddie's appeal was partly polit- ical. At the time he was still helping to run the Chicken Coop, Eddie had made a name as a civil rights activist, eventually receiving a small business award from the National Association for the Advancement of Colored People.

In the early 1960s, New Orleans blacks were picketing still- segregated white businesses along Canal Street, the storied com- mercial boulevard separating the French Quarter from the Central Business District. According to a 1991 *Times-Picayune* profile, Eddie made the Chicken Coop a kind of haven for the protestors, inviting them in to eat, discuss strategy, and store their picket signs—a stance at the time not just unpopular among some of the city's staunch segre- gationists but which carried personal risk in a racially tense city.

Baquet continued his activism upon opening Eddie's. The restaurant wasn't exactly a casual drop-by place. In a 1977 review, New Orleans food writer Richard Collin noted that Eddie's was in a neighborhood requiring caution to navigate and given its "decrepit exterior . . . you may even doubt that there is a restaurant behind that Falstaff (beer) sign." According to Collin, "This is one of the most gifted Creole kitchens in town and some of the best New Orleans dishes are served here in breathtaking versions."

Or as Brett Anderson wrote in a May 2014 piece for NOLA.com, titled "The Importance of Eddie's," in remembrance of the restaurant that shut its doors in 1999: "What Collin described is a model of what a huge swath of food enthusiasts today would consider the Holy Grail: An indigenous American restaurant on native soil, unsullied by trends or even influences beyond the community it serves."

Li'l Dizzy's came to be in 2005. Wayne, after a long apprenticeship in his father's kitchen, became a serial restaurateur, having by the time of Li'l Dizzy's debut opened ten restaurants in various parts of city. They all bore the Baquet trademark of relatively inexpensive but deliciously crafted Creole classics, and always with a Baquet twist. One example: a dish currently on the Li'l Dizzy's menu called the Great Jambalaya Omelet. It blends all the traditional ingredients of a Creole jambalaya—herbs, spices, celery, onion, garlic, bell pepper, chicken, and sausage minus the rice—into a savory egg dish.

Less than a year before, Baquet had sold his last creation, a well-regarded eatery called Zachary's. His family threw him a retirement party, but retirement didn't last long. Baquet grew restless and bored and stumbled upon his present location when he went to lunch at a faltering eatery called Big Shirley's. A waitress who had worked for Baquet previously complained, "We can't get anybody into this place."

Wayne looked around and thought, "Well, I bet I could." He felt the location, with its Treme cachet plus proximity to the tourist-magnet French Quarter just blocks away, was perfect for his next Baquet venture. He struck a deal to buy out Big Shirley's operations such as they were. One of his first calls was to his grandson, Zachary—the namesake of Zachary's—to tell him that he was opening up shop again. All that was lacking at that point was a name. Zachary, having inherited the Baquet family music gene, is an accomplished trumpet player. And when the talk turned to music Zachary let it slip to his grandfather that his bandmates in the group he then played in called him "Li'l Dizzy"—an honorific comparing him with trumpet bebop legend Dizzy Gillespie. "And that explains Li'l Dizzy's name," says Baquet.

The decor of Li'l Dizzy's epitomizes the studiously casual attitude of the classic New Orleans neighborhood restaurant. A Mardi Gras–green façade is augmented by a cheeky Mardi Gras–purple awning supporting white ceiling fans, all set off by a black-and-white Li'l Dizzy marquee that lets you know this is a "Baquet Family Restaurant." Simple industrial metal tables and chairs allow for sidewalk dining during good weather. A trio of large windows at the front let in commodious light.

Inside, a glance at some of the adorned tiles in the otherwise utilitarian drop ceiling immediately lets you know Baquet (like pretty much every other living person in the city) is a New Orleans Saints football fan. Soda cases crowd the floor near an upright Coca-Cola drinks cooler. Diners sit on wooden chairs with padded green seats at the restaurant's seventeen square laminated tables placed close together. Hot sauce, condiments, salt and pepper, and sweetener adorn the table centers.

The buffet stand forms an "L" with the open cooking station, where you can watch that jambalaya omelet ($13.99) come together for breakfast or see how the Trout Baquet ($15.99) is prepared for lunch. There are cheaper gumbo shacks in the city, but the portions are generous. (Li'l Dizzy's briefly served dinner but Baquet stopped when he felt the talent pool had become too stretched to cover three meals a day.

But he says he hasn't totally given up on the idea of restarting dinner service one day.)

Li'l Dizzy's brick and pink pastel walls are a testament to Baquet's music and political sensibilities, his pride in his family name and traditions, and the large number of honors the restaurant has garnered over the years. An imposing poster of Miles Davis gets equal billing with a portrait of Wayne's father, Eddie. A framed, signed tribute from President Barack Obama and Vice President Joe Biden fills up space, as does an autographed photo of President George W. Bush dining there with a clutch of New Orleans political bigshots. Another photo tells you Obama's attorney general Eric Holder dropped in one day.

The day I arrived for my first visit, Li'l Dizzy's was about half full but it was 11:00 a.m., a bit early for the lunch crowd, and it would be jammed by the time I left forty minutes later. The waitstaff really pushed the buffet and as tempting as it looked for $15.99, I was locked in on the gumbo. (Note: If you go on Trip Advisor and read the 293 reviews that cumulatively rate Li'l Dizzy's four-point-five out of five stars, the handful of negative ratings have less to do with the food than with complaints by some customers who felt they were being stampeded to the buffet line.)

My gumbo came promptly and was served in a simple white bowl. The broth, owing obviously to the roux, was a rich, dark-chocolate color with a subtle reddish tint (though Baquet uses the bell pepper, onion, and garlic as his Trinity and doesn't employ tomatoes in the recipe). Three succulent crab claws floated along the perimeter and generous portions of shrimp, ham, and hot sausage and smoked sausages welled up in the middle near an emerging island of white rice. Two slices of French bread balanced on the plate rim—an appetizing presentation with a pleasing, spicy aroma.

As for the taste? It was beautifully complex and the spiciness reminded me a bit in style of the Thai hot-and-sour seafood soups that I was fond of dining on when I still lived in New York City. It would rank in my personal "Top 5" of all the gumbos I sampled during the research for this book.

"That's the hot sausage coming through," Wayne tells me when I inquire about the spicy flavor. "That sausage—and we make it ourselves—is probably the most important ingredient in that gumbo. My wife and I created this recipe, I'm going to say, about thirty years ago when frankly we couldn't find anybody to supply us with consistent hot sausage. It's a blend, 50 percent beef and 50 percent pork. We take a whole batch and mix it all together with fresh ingredients and then we make patties out of it."

Baquet, who might pass for a college professor with his trimmed salt-and-pepper beard, studious-looking glasses, and resonant voice, pauses and smiles. Like many chefs, he's proud of his creations. "And I have to say, it *is* good," he says.

In fact, so many gumbo diners began complimenting the sausage that it begat something of a side business. These days, Baquet hires a company to process the sausage into links that sell briskly from Li'l Dizzy's cold case in five-pound packages for about three dollars a pound. "Seriously, during the holidays, people who used to live in New Orleans who are here visiting come in droves to get the hot sausage. They realize you can't find this stuff any other place. When I go visit my daughter in Atlanta, we bring our hot sausage—and our meat—for gumbos and red beans and rice."

I ask him about his roux, which he also bags in ten-ounce packages and sells for eight dollars a bag over the counter to customers wanting to attempt to replicate the Li'l Dizzy gumbo flavor. "I got the roux from my father," he says. "We do it in the oven. No oil. We just brown flour in one of those big roasting pans at 300 degrees. Now, we season the flour before we roast it. That's also different from the way a lot of people make their roux." His view is that the seasoned flour amps up the roux's taste.

As for cooking time: "Well, it depends on how dark we want the roux to be. The longer you roast it the darker it gets. The roux is one of the secrets of the consistency in our gumbo. The roux is always the same. Now, the way we do it is that, while the roux is in the oven, you can take a little butter and put it in the bottom of the pan and you can start browning some of your ingredients that take a longer time to cook. . . . Then you add the water and then you whisk in the roux so it won't lump up. Guess what? Then it's finished, you add some filé at the end and you've got gumbo."

This is the classic Li'l Dizzy's Creole Gumbo.

Baquet admired his father's talents in the kitchen, but confesses he learned basic cooking—including cooking his first gumbo—as a youngster from his mother, Myrtle, his aunt Anna Gibson, and his maternal grandmother, Eva Romano. "They cooked a mean gumbo," he recalls. These days he cedes the chef's duties at Li'l Dizzy's to his staff and spends his time managing the restaurant, doing the ordering and deciding what will go on the daily buffet menu. Always on the buffet menu: bread pudding, spicy fried chicken, and gumbo.

A fourth that appears quite often is Trout Baquet, a dish that symbolizes the utter Creoleness and creativity of Li'l Dizzy's kitchen. Locally sourced speckled trout, a saltwater species, is dredged in a garlic-and-black-pepper preparation, then pan-fried—seared, really—to a crusty finish. It's then topped with freshly picked crabmeat sautéed with onions, parsley, and a smidge more garlic, and served with a fresh lemon wedge.

I'd hazard to say that a large majority of Creoles and Cajuns count the mild, firm, white, flaky flesh of the speckled trout as the best-eating fish in the Gumbo Belt and it typically needs little adornment. My favorite recipe is to brush the filets with a little olive oil, sprinkle on some sea salt and coarse ground pepper, and flash-grill them over hot charcoals. Then I serve them with a simple white wine, lemon, and butter sauce on the side. Thus, I must admit that, when I first stumbled across the Trout Baquet recipe, I felt that it represented overkill—

there's no need for a tarted-up recipe for a fish that is killer-good with the simplest of preparation. Then I tried Trout Baquet and admit that I was wrong. It's a transformative dish.

Baquet also plays the all-important role of Creole raconteur and the public face of his restaurant. There's probably no one of consequence in all of New Orleans that Baquet doesn't know on a first-name basis. It's also clear that he loves, loves, loves his native city. "I think New Orleans is probably the most interesting city, along with New York, in the country. You can find everything here. Jazz was born here, we have better food than anybody. We just flat-out do. The culture is here. And I'm right in the middle of it."

When I ask Baquet what *he* loves most of all the dishes that come out of his kitchen, I'm expecting him to pick the gumbo. But he doesn't, as much as he says he loves it. "Red beans and rice with my hot sausage. I always said that if I were on death row and it was my last meal that's what I'd want. Throw in some French bread."

He says there's a secret to Li'l Dizzy's red beans and rice: "The key part is to soak the beans. Soak the beans overnight so that when you cook the beans and add your seasoning and everything, the beans cook to a light color, not dark. Dark beans don't look good. Juicy light beans over some steamed rice—some hot sausage on the side. Oh, boy."

I have one other stop to make in the Treme: Dooky Chase's, where the legendary Leah Chase still makes appearances in the kitchen now and then. On a stormy, rain-swept, spring afternoon, I'm steering my rental car along the bumpy ramparts of Orleans Avenue to the corner of Orleans and North Miro Street where Dooky Chase's brick façade and cheeky green awnings make for a cheery presence in an otherwise rather austere neighborhood. Friday is the only day the restaurant is open for dinner and having scoped out the weather, I calculated that if I got there at five o'clock, just as the doors opened, I should have no problem getting a seat. Surely, the lightning, thunder, and gully-washer rains would keep most sensible people away?

I'm totally wrong. The place is already packed, with a line of umbrella holders snaking out the entrance. I find a parking spot on the street and join them, in due time making my way inside to the hostess. She's a smiling and pleasant woman who greets me warmly, and then looking around at the full tables, says she doubts she can seat me.

I nod with a chastened expression. Then the hostess, peering over her reading glasses, surveys the dining room again and, perhaps feeling sympathy for me, or because a table for two in the very back of the restaurant was about to clear, announces that I was in luck after all. I take my seat maybe ten minutes later and a cheerful waiter who introduces herself as Martinique takes my gumbo order after I wave off the menu.

With the crush of diners, it takes a while for it to arrive, but when it does I can tell, without having yet taken a bite, that I'm getting my money's worth at $13.99 a bowl. Half a blue crab, a couple of crab claws, and heaps of shrimp and hot and smoked sausage emerge from a luscious, medium-thick, deep chestnut-brown roux, all surrounding a sculpted ball of white rice dusted with a little paprika and chives. It's another beautiful gumbo. (As for those crab claws, well, it's often indelicate but one method is to crack them open on the rim of your bowl with the handle of your knife and then pick out the gumbo-saturated meat with your fork.)

Taste? It's pretty much as good as it looks, with the seafood and sausage complementing each other, throwing off smoky and salty flavors, though I think it's little oversalted for my taste. But the hot sausage gives it the kind of peppery kick I like in my gumbo. One other small complaint: I feel it could have been served hotter. But all in all, it's a first-class gumbo and as a marker dish for Dooky Chase's I can understand why the restaurant has had such a long and successful run.

(I would've loved nothing more than to discuss these matters with Miss Leah and I tried, leaving voicemail messages with a publicist. After dining on the night I visited, I also left a detailed note for her with the kindly hostess about my project and my desire to interview her. The hostess said she would make sure Miss Leah saw it and perhaps she did. But I never heard from anyone.)

Like the Baquet family, the Chases have a storied, even iconic place in the food and sociopolitical history of the Treme, with the restaurant at the forefront. In 1939, Dooky Chase Sr. and his wife, Emily, opened a modest sandwich shop which by 1941 had morphed into lively neighborhood bar and restaurant, where black workers crowded in on Friday nights to cash paychecks that the white banks wouldn't touch. Meanwhile, Dooky's son, Dooky Jr., was carving out a name for himself as a gifted jazz musician, forming a sixteen-piece jazz band that performed to sold-out audiences all over the South.

In 1946, Dooky Jr. married Leah Lange and Miss Leah, as she would come to be called, lent her prolific gifts to the restaurant, transforming it over time from a kind of scruffy neighborhood joint into a fine-dining establishment that not only showcased high-style Creole cooking but African American art. Indeed, according to the restaurant's website, "Dooky Chase's Restaurant was the first art gallery for black artists in New Orleans," as well as among the first black-owned fine-dining restaurant in America.

From its founding through the civil rights movement of the 1960s, Dooky Chase's, like Eddie's, was also a place of gathering and support for New Orleans' African Americans and national civil rights leaders who were fighting to liberate New Orleans from its segregationist past. Among those who joined local civil rights activists for strategy meetings over food in Dooky's upstairs meeting rooms was Martin Luther King Jr. Since my visit, Dooky Jr., Leah's husband, has passed away, but Miss Leah remains a charismatic force in not just her restaurant but the New Orleans food scene.

The stormy night I visited I didn't expect to find Ms. Leah in the kitchen or in the lovely, high-style dining room that she has created (and she wasn't there). But her spirit certainly was. As was the spirit of my mother and my gumbo-cooking grandmother and, well, with all the lightning and thunder, perhaps the spirits of all the Creole and Cajun maw-maws who have cooked this dish so lovingly and passed it down so that we might understand what moved them.

Taste, pleasure, beauty, simplicity—a desire to make the people they loved happy. And feed them well.

11

MY GUMBO LIFE

It's 1959. The Wellses are country folk, settled into our small farm-stead on the banks of Bayou Black. Here's how chicken gumbo used to begin.

"Granny's gone out to murder a chicken. I can't look," my mother says to her sons gathered around the breakfast table on a balmy spring Saturday morning.

The Wells boys—Bill, the eldest, me, Pershing, Jerry, Chris, even Bobby the toddler—rise in unison and stampede out to the back porch of our farmhouse to watch.

Lora Ann Landers Wells, our paternal grandmother, and Pop—born William Henry Wells but Willie to his Arkansas family—live with us.

Granny can't be more than five feet tall and you will almost never hear her utter a cross word. She is soft-spoken and kindhearted and dotes on her grandsons. But though a gentle soul, her hardscrabble Arkansas upbringing required her to learn some tough skills. One of them: She knows how to pop a chicken neck with a skill and glee that makes us Wells boys sometime wonder if there's somebody else trapped in Granny's body.

She has a clever chicken-killing method. She stops at the chicken-yard gate just long enough to put a handful of feed corn in a pouch of the apron she wears as part of her chicken-killing uniform.

Then, when she spies the chicken she thinks is fat enough—always a hen; Granny, like my mother, won't eat a rooster—she'll approach it nice and slow. She'll "cluck, cluck, cluck" at it in her soft, gentle voice and then throw some of that corn down at her feet. When the chicken comes over and starts pecking, Granny pounces. She snatches it up just behind the head with a speed that always shocks us and—Pow!— whipsaws it so hard that it breaks its neck.

Then she flings the thing down and it does its chicken death dance for a minute or so, flopping around like something possessed of demons. It's horrifying to watch but it's impossible to look away. By the time the hen has died, Pop or Dad will have a big pot of water boiling on an outside fire, and Granny will pick that chicken up by its broken neck and dunk it a few times to scald it properly, otherwise it's next to impossible to pluck. Almost nothing smells worse than a scalded chicken, but Granny doesn't seem to mind the smell, or gutting the thing, either.

My mother stays out of sight while all this going on, and I can't say I blame her. But Bonnie does admit that farm-killed chickens taste a lot better in her gumbo than the packaged store-bought ones that have only just begun to be available in town. And Granny will always say, "Well, back in Arkansas, if we didn't kill a chicken, we didn't eat a chicken. Of course, who could afford a chicken? Only rich people had chicken back then."

And Bonnie will reply, "Well, Momma"—that would be our Maw-Maw Toups—"killed her own chickens when Daddy was still alive and worked for the sugar company as a blacksmith. That's when they lived in the country."

I know my mother, born in town, wishes most days we'd stayed there. But she's not going to let Granny Wells out-country her, at least when it comes to chicken talk.

We are here because my father, who had grown up roaming the wild river bottoms of east-central Arkansas, had tired of town life and his town job delivering mail for the post office. He also feared his six rambunctious sons getting into town mischief. So, he took a job with Southdown Sugars, a large area sugar mill, whose salary package included the rent-free, tidy planter's colonial we now lived in.

Its virtues include a front porch with a view of the bayou, six fertile acres of gardens and pastures, an old but serviceable barn, a corncrib to store seed corn and chicken feed, chicken coops, and even a pigpen. Most virtuous, in my father's view, is that there are six pastoral miles between us and town and the nearest neighbors are a quarter-mile away, thus out of hearing range of Wells boys' commotions. The house sits surrounded on three sides by a sprawl of sugarcane and corn-fields and beyond the fields on all sides lie deep woods, marshes, and swamps. Most of this land is owned by the sugar company and thus free to us to roam, hunt, fish, and trap.

Dad has died and gone to hunter-gatherer heaven. My brothers and I, though we liked our little house in town well enough, feel like we have been freed from prison.

There's only one off-note to this idyllic scene. My mother is thirty-three years old, a pretty, willowy, dark-eyed, softhearted, and often nervous woman from a loving but excitable family. She adores her six sons, all babies, most children, almost all old people, dancing, cooking gumbo, and on most days, I think, my father.

But Bonnie was raised by her overly protective mother in poor but proud circumstances in the cocoon of a sleepy small town. Many things about the country scare her. She comes from pioneering stock, an eighth generation Louisiana family, her Toups forebear immigrated from the German portion of Switzerland to France in 1719, and two years later sailed from France to the Louisiana wilderness with a wife and two young sons. Bonnie's parents and grandparents all grew up in the country before retreating to small-town life. But all of that somehow seems to have gotten wrung out of my mother.

And now she's gone from a nice quiet little place in town with a tidy yard full of roses and day lilies and lots of friendly neighbors to the far more feral ramparts of the country. Snakes *do* sometimes drape the trees here and creatures wild and surprising often patrol the farmyard at night.

It also doesn't help, from Bonnie's viewpoint, that we keep a kind of country zoo and only a small part of it dedicated to gumbo. We have thirteen dogs; countless feral barn cats, most without names, that live on rats, field mice, and birds; twenty-odd rabbits, mostly pink-eyed albinos, in a big wooden cage screened over with chicken wire; a pen full of quail; a pig named Petunia that thinks she's a dog and has become my pet (but will, one day, end up as sausage); about three dozen interbred chickens, including a vicious, turkey-sized, perpetually horny white rooster that we keep locked up in a cage. That's because he has been known to attack even Dad, his rooster spurs trussed up like a knight brandishing a lance.

And then there's our milk cow, Bessie, and her calf, Henrietta. The calf is a scrawny, skittish thing which Dad named after my mother, Henrietta being her formal name. Somehow, my mother is flattered by this. Granny Wells, who learned to milk cows back in Arkansas, milks Bessie every day and then boils the milk on the stove to pasteurize it. It doesn't taste like store-bought milk, but we drink it readily.

More recently we've added to this collection a monkey—yes, a monkey—gifted to us by Annie Miller, our friend who runs a snake- and reptile-collecting business a couple of miles up the bayou. Of Native American roots, Annie will go on to become Alligator Annie, a gator whisperer and pioneer in the Louisiana swamp-tour business.

She will also convince my father that he and his sons, with all those hands, would make excellent snake hunters for her live-snake collecting enterprise. She sells them to zoos, collectors, and biological research labs. She'll pay ten cents apiece for garter snakes and fifty cents a pound for all other snakes.

The money sounds great to Dad. I do my own calculation. We've taken up bowling at the VFW alley in town and games cost twenty-five cents each on Saturdays. One average-size snake could fetch enough money to spend an entire Saturday afternoon at the bowling alley.

I'm in. So are my brothers, or at least those of us old enough to tromp the woods and fields and run down live snakes and catch them with our hands.

My mother loves Annie Miller but hates the snake-hunting idea. If Dad wants to risk snake bite, so be it. "But why you want to take my boys?" my mother will ask.

"We'll only catch harmless snakes," Dad explains.

"Yeah? Which ones would those be?"

Bonnie adopts the Toups family view of snakes: All of them are poisonous or dangerous in some way. Remember the famous one in the Garden of Eden?

And she reacts to the monkey the way she reacts to all new critters: "Why we need that thing, Rex?" she'll say to my father. "Why we need another cat? Another dog? How come you want to keep that raccoon in a cage? I never heard of nobody who had a mink for a pet. Nobody."

Bonnie isn't lying. We do have a mink named Stinky for a pet if you are willing to stretch the definition of *pet*. The critter darted across the road in front of Dad's Jeep station wagon one early morning as he drove to one of his favorite fishing holes. He escaped the Jeep wheels but got a glancing blow from the boat trailer in tow.

Dad didn't normally mess with roadkill. But because he didn't squash him and since a mink hide could fetch maybe twenty dollars and Dad can skin anything that's ever lived, he braked and picked the mink up off the road and threw him in the boat. He figured he'd just skin the poor dead critter later, stashing his sleek body in a wire minnow trap.

But that mink surprised my dad and came to, and Dad said, using one of his Arkansas aphorisms, "I'll swan, boys, that mink's woke up on us! Y'all want to keep him?"

Of course we did!

The truth is that except for maybe the monkey part and the general critter overload, and maybe the snake collecting, we aren't that different than our Bayou Black neighbors. Like us, many kill their own chickens, slaughter their own pigs and cattle for pork chops, steaks, and the hot- and smoked-sausage that go into their gumbos; still milk cows and still grow a good many of the vegetables for their gumbo pots. Though a handful of Creole families live on Bayou Black, the menfolk working, as Dad does, for the sugar mill, this is overwhelmingly Cajun, not Creole, gumbo country. Pretty much everybody here who cooks gumbo cooks it with a roux.

A lot of the older people on Bayou Black still speak French, way more than did in our neighborhood in town. Maybe 250 families live along the narrow, winding twenty-mile long bayou from which the community takes its name, most in turn-of-the-century wooden farmhouses with tin roofs and porches, although the brick ranch house has just started to make an appearance. We have our own little country public school (first through eighth grade), our own recreational baseball team, and a clear identity as a community. Gibson, the bayou community up the road, is our fierce rival in baseball. It's also full of Protestants, many of whom came with the logging of the nearby Great Atchafalaya Swamp in the 1920s and stayed.

Bayou Black people don't have much truck with Gibson people. That's in part because probably 95 percent of all Bayou Black residents are Cajun and Catholic; some have been around for generations and they look with at least mild suspicion upon the Protestant interlopers. (They remember who kicked them out of Acadie.) Indeed, at the literal center of Bayou Black's elongated community is the St. Anthony of Padua Catholic Church and its lovely old cemetery with whitewashed, above-ground tombs. The church sits mid-bayou amidst a sprawl of sugarcane. Next door, perhaps not coincidentally, is Elmo's Bar & Grocery. It's but a short walk across a parking lot paved in clam shells from the pews after Sunday mass to the soothing dimness of Elmo's, where beer is a quarter and highballs fifty cents. God, beer, whiskey, and then home for gumbo on Sunday. Is there a better life?

A handful of the farms on Bayou Black are owned by well-to-do sugarcane farmers and landowners, but most are working-class people who farm small lots of cane or vegetables or raise cattle at least part-time and supplement their incomes and larders with jobs at the sugar mill or in town or by hunting, fishing, and trapping. A few have taken jobs in the oil field. Almost everybody has a pirogue, the Cajun version of the canoe, tethered to a dock in the bayou or stashed on the bayou banks or in their barns across the road from the bayou. If you want ducks or poules d'eau for your gumbo or turtle for your sauce piquant or French-fried frog legs for your cast-iron skillet, you need a pirogue.

By this time, Bonnie has gotten to know most of the people who live up and down the bayou—my parents are active in our little country school—and she is especially drawn to the Cajun French speakers. So, when we hop in the Jeep and *roder* (a Cajunism pronounced row-DAY, which means to idly roam or sightsee), my mother will have Dad stop here or there when she spies someone up on a porch or tending a bayouside garden with whom she can *parler français*. Dad doesn't mind as long as there is someone to talk hunting and fishing with in English.

Sometimes there isn't.

After Granny's murdered chicken is plucked and dressed, my mother and Granny will joust, mostly good-naturedly, about whether this will be fried chicken or chicken and dumplings, Granny Wells' favorite recipes that she's brought from Arkansas, or end up in Bonnie's chicken-on-the-bone gumbo.

If the Wells boys get to vote, gumbo it usually is.

Still, we do understand that we are doubly blessed in the cooking department. Granny is an excellent fry cook, turning out the best cornmeal-battered fried catfish we've ever eaten; tender, mouthwatering, milk-and-flour-dredged fried chicken; crispy fried young squirrel, not to mention squirrel stew with brown gravy and homemade dumplings. On the wild game front, she even has an exotic recipe for roasted raccoon involving Coca-Cola, suffused with various spices, as a marinade. Pop, however, is the only person in the family fond of this dish and thus it is cooked rarely.

Granny also whips up collard greens, tasty black-eyed peas, and silky smooth mashed potatoes with a brown gravy flavored by bacon drippings. She even fixes poke salad, a wild green she sautés in fatback from the leaves of the mildly poisonous poke weed that she and Pop harvest from fields on the edge of the woods behind our farm. She makes buttered toast in a cast-iron skillet that still transcends the taste of any toast I've had ever since. Her hand-kneaded fried apple fritters, dusted with a bit of brown or powdered sugar, are so good that Dad has to referee his sons' access to them when Granny puts a platter of them down on the table.

She also cooks a dish that goes down well with the Wells boys, Dad, and Pop, but which repulses my mother: fried squirrel brains. It might be the presentation that bothers Bonnie. Granny deep fries the skinned squirrel heads in hot oil and heaps them on a plate. They get passed around at the supper table, where everybody gets one. You basically crack them open by banging on the little skulls with your butter knife handle, then scooping out the milky-white brains onto your plate with a spoon. Done right (and assuming you can get beyond the aesthetics of it all), they're quite sweet, with a texture resembling firmly scrambled eggs. Dad is always trying to get my mother to try them, noting that lots of people he knew back in Arkansas ate them. Bonnie wrinkles her nose and says, "That sounds like a good reason to stay out of Arkansas."

What soothes my mother's country-phobia is her place as the star of her kitchen and the frequent and honest accolades that come from her husband, sons, and in-laws for what comes out of Bonnie's pots. She's frugal but inventive. With that murdered chicken, for example, nothing goes to waste. The gizzard and neck and any trimmed fat go into the stock pot. The chicken itself is butchered into eight pieces—Dad sometimes lends a hand with this chore since my mother isn't great with a knife—and browned and then put in the gumbo pot after my mother has married her Trinity and added the stock.

In my mind I can still trace the progress of my mother's gumbo by the slightly changing aromas wafting from the kitchen, which turns out to be another thing that Bonnie admits she likes about living in the country.

It's hardly the greatest kitchen in the world. The linoleum-covered floors slant and the appliances are old but it's roomy and light, with a place for a breakfast table, and it opens onto a small porch overlooking a side yard of fig and citrus trees that also holds our cypress cistern and clothesline. Best of all, it has a big window above the sink overlooking our chicken yard out back. It's from here that she can help Granny Wells spot candidates for the pot.

Beyond the fenced-in chicken yard is Bonnie's sprawling garden. Well, it's our garden but to her it's her garden because it supplies the green peppers, onions, shallots, and okra for her gumbos, the mirlitons and yellow squash for her squash casseroles, the hot peppers for the home-bottled pickled pepper vinegar condiment that sometimes gets sprinkled in our gumbos, the Creole tomatoes (a wildly popular Gumbo Belt cultivar) for her salads, at least some of the corn for her corn soup, the red potatoes for her otherworldly smothered potatoes, and the cantaloupes and honeydew and watermelons that in season spare her and Granny Wells from concocting desserts every night. (Bonnie could live without dessert, Granny can't.)

It's also the one outdoor space that she doesn't seem to mind. My mother, though fastidious, dirt-, bug-, and critter-phobic, seems to think that at least the dirt and bugs in the garden are do-gooders. So, she can often be seen in the spring, when we plant, elbow deep in a muddy row, helping us set out the tomato plants, which seem to do best if you start them in a stew of muddy goo. Bonnie's transformation in the garden always amazes me.

One thing Bonnie won't do in the garden, however, is pick okra. Her sons, to whom Rex has assigned all the okra-picking duties, don't blame her.

We plant two fifty-yard-long rows of okra each spring and by the time the stalks are head high and the pods mature, it's the heart of the sultry, soul-sucking Louisiana summer. It may sound strange, but okra seems to have an aversion to being picked. The tiny hairs on the pods and milky-white secretions from the stems, released when you cut the okra from the stalk with a knife, are extremely acidic and can cause serious itching. Some people claim that the dance craze, "The Twist," was a musical acting out of okra itch.

Therefore, okra-picking precautions must be taken. You don't approach the okra patch without a long-sleeve shirt, gloves, cap, and kerchief wrapped around your neck. Sunglasses or goggles are also advisable. If errant okra juice finds your eyes, you're in for deep pain and maybe even a trip to the eye doctor. Try that outfit in 98-degree temperatures with 100 percent humidity, which is what okra grows best in, and you'll see why the Wells boys would rather go to the dentist than pick okra. This is also why my father, when he feels the need to discipline his sometimes rowdy sons, will send us out to the okra patch at high noon. As a result, misbehavior goes way down during okra-picking season.

Okra, however, is forgiven in my mother's kitchen. There's Bonnie at the stove, two colanders overflowing with fresh-picked, diced pods on a counter nearby. She has two large pots on the front burners with about an inch of vegetable oil in each. When the oil begins to smoke, Bonnie stirs in her okra and in a matter of moments the kitchen is filled with an aromatic sizzle. This technique also cures okra of another of its negative reputations—sliminess.

One batch is going to be transformed into okra stew—okra; fresh, blanched, and diced, garden tomatoes; and caramelized onions—and served over white rice. While Bonnie wouldn't dream of putting tomatoes in her gumbo, she loves them in her okra stew (and we do, too). Her explanation: "Okra stew doesn't have a roux like gumbo does."

The second batch of okra will go into a seafood gumbo she's making for supper. We know many Cajun families that go off gumbo in the summer and they have good reasons. The air conditioner is still a thing of the future for most people living on Bayou Black. Maybe a rich farmer or two has a window unit, and if they do, it's placed in a bedroom to make sleeping possible on those ninety-degree, windless, humid summer nights. We simply sweat it out.

We love our gumbo because it's the one dish more than any other that, if cooked in sufficient quantities, can get us through two or even three meals. So, heat be damned, we eat our gumbo at least once a week year-round.

We can take breakfast or lunch in our laps on the couch in the den, but we are required by my parents to eat supper at the table, the same as Pop is required to recite grace every night. Pop, like Dad, has had a fitful religious upbringing. Both are non-attending Baptists who, if they believe in God at all, would place their bets on finding Him hanging out in the woods.

But Granny insists on grace and the unspoken acknowledgment is that we delegate grace to Pop because he says it fast, in under ten seconds, in a mumbling voice that nobody, not even Granny Wells, who often interprets his mumbles, can understand. It always sounds to me as if grace ends in the phrase "Pardon our peas in geez it's a shame, amen," though it begs the question of how our peas might have sinned. It may be that he is actually saying, "Pardon us, please, in Jesus' name, amen" but nobody ever gets around to asking him. And given that we're a family of healthy appetites, nobody wants grace to get in the way of getting to our food.

The table is also the place to observe my mother in her comfort zone. The gumbo pot is in the middle of the table, the obligatory rice in a large bowl next to it. We pass around the gumbo bowls, Dad doing the honors—rice, gumbo, rice, gumbo.

Then Dad, having filled the last bowl, says, "Eat up, boys."

We don't dig in, we dive in. The clanking of spoons in bowls sets up a racket.

And sometimes I just watch Bonnie, her face aglow. She declines to take a bite until someone says, "Ma, this is the best one yet."

And then my mother smiles and says, "You think so? I was little worried about my roux."

"Ma, it's amazing."

And only then will Bonnie take a bite. Usually, she will say, "It's OK," and then look around the table with a serenity and satisfaction absent from the ordinary day. So, what of the spiders, the snakes, the crazy monkey, the way-too-many dogs and cats and rabbits, the wild unpredictability of the country life. In this moment, all that fades and my mother is at peace, totally certain she has created something that flies so close to love that it must be love itself.

12

THE GLORY OF GUMBO'S PANTRY

And what we don't harvest from our garden, we take from Gumbo's Pantry, for we live in the Pantry's lap.

Bayou Black, forming a handsome alluvial ridge running roughly east-west for some twenty miles, is but a tiny part of a vast mosaic of woodland ridges, waterways, marshes, swamps and barrier islands that make up the Louisiana estuary. At 3.2 million acres, it dwarfs in size the far better known Florida Everglades and its 1.5 million acres. It stretches the width of the Louisiana coast and more than one hundred and twenty miles inland to the upper portions of the Atchafalaya Basin. At 1,800 square miles, the Atchafalaya holds the largest contiguous cypress swamp in North America.

The Louisiana estuary comprises about 40 percent of all of America's wetlands. The state's waters and wetlands underpin a commercial seafood industry—shrimp, crab, oysters, and fish—that generates about $2.4 billion a year in wages and sales. It produces almost a quarter of the seafood catch in the contiguous United States. Only Alaska, owing to its huge salmon run, has a bigger seafood industry.

It's also a far more interesting and diverse estuary than the Everglades, with mighty rivers like the Atchafalaya meandering through vast, wildlife-rich swamps that feed scenic freshwater lakes flowing to brackish lakes and bays. And this fertile brackish mixing zone, the great incubator of the system, gives way itself to a sprawl of saltwater marshes, bays, and barrier islands fronting the Gulf of Mexico. It's one giant fish, crab, and oyster hatchery and one reason why almost 250 species of birds call it home and more than five million migratory birds use it as a stopover.

It also could be—should be—called the Cajun Glades, for this is the land that the Cajuns, more than any other people, made their own, their lives and lifestyles over time becoming inseparable from the low country that nourished them. They began arriving at a time when some parts of the estuary remained not simply untouched, but unexplored. They would settle the high ground along bayou banks, Bayou Black being an example, created by millennia of natural floods, or on the alluvial islands, called cheniers, that dot the great marshscape above the Gulf of Mexico.

For Chef Folse, who grew up on edge of the swamp like I did, the miracle of the Cajun Glades is in seemingly inexhaustible bounty of its Pantry. For in this vast, incredibly fertile, deltaic plain with its warm, subtropical climate and long growing season, a seed planted on high ground grew and a net or seine cast into a bayou or bay by a skilled fisherman often produced fish, shrimp, and crabs by the bushel. It's where oysters by the thousands could be harvested at low tide or tonged up from shallow reefs; where ducks and geese filled the sky in unimaginable numbers, and upland game like rabbit, squirrel, raccoon and deer provided an easy bounty for gumbo pots; where muskrats and other fur-bearing animals roamed the marshes and swamps in such abundance that, before the coming of oil, gifted muskrat trappers were among the wealthiest of all Cajuns.

Folse and others make the persuasive argument that the intricate bounty of the Pantry has been as indispensable to the evolution of gumbo as have the people who inhabited it; that only in this seren-dipitous meeting of geography, ecosystem, and cultures could gumbo have flourished.

In the old days on Bayou Black, and throughout the Gumbo Belt, the Pantry was sometimes the *only* source of sustenance for the Cajuns and Creoles, who had little or no access to stores and depended on farming, fishing, and hunting to survive. By the time we moved there in 1957, a supermarket had opened in Houma. But money was tight. We had a lot of mouths to feed and in some seasons the Pantry saved our family from hunger. The woods, fields, bayous, and swamps, along with our garden, probably provided half of everything we ate and helped to fill the gumbo pot.

The bounty was everywhere around us. We had a family taste for French-fried frog legs and bullfrogs thrived in vast numbers. One balmy spring night, my father and I paddling our pirogue through marshes not five miles from our farm—and using only our hands to catch with—came back with 113 bullfrogs for my mother's cast-iron skillet.

As Granny Wells' chicken-harvesting method demonstrates, Gumbo Life isn't for the queasy. My older brother Bill and I, deemed by Dad old enough to properly wield a hatchet, often man the frog chopping block. It's a well-worn stump out by our old cypress garage which mostly serves as our skinning shed. Heads removed, the frogs then go to Dad, who skins them out with catfish pliers and then throws their shimmering, milky white bodies into a big pot.

All that skinning produces a lot of frog heads, frog skin, and frog guts. But nothing is wasted. Stinky the Mink, who lives in a roomy cage out by the cypress garage, eats well after our frog hunts. Any surplus goes into the bayou where the wading birds, turtles, and gar happily dispose of leftovers. The truth is, our chickens love to peck on fish and frog leavings. Most people would be surprised what chickens will eat. I always am.

Skinning animals or cleaning fish or frogs is never pleasant—in fact, it's often extremely unpleasant—but you accept it as a feature of the Gumbo Life. It's a connection to the old ways and also part of my father's strict conservationist ethic. You only kill it or catch it if you intend to eat it, sell it, or share it with somebody else who's hungry (or keep it for a pet).

Once we caught a twenty-five-pound snapping turtle on a baited line. Bonnie would turn it into a delicious turtle sauce piquant, a dish akin to a stew and featuring tenderized, sautéed turtle meat cooked for hours in a tomato base—sauce fired up by black pepper and hot sauce. (Fans, of which I am one, compare turtle meat favorably to pork. People who don't like it so much have said it tastes more like goat.)

But first my father had to dress the turtle. He shot the beast in the head with a .22 rifle, lopped off the head with a hatchet, and stuck a garden hose into the neck cavity to flush out the blood. Then he flipped the turtle over and cut into the shell with a hatchet to retrieve the edible meat, mainly from the legs and haunches. The viscera, including the heart, went into a bucket for later disposal. Somehow the bucket got forgotten about and two hours or so later, when we remembered our duty, we returned.

The turtle's heart was still beating.

We rushed the bucket to the bayou and cast the heart and entrails into the water where it's entirely possible another turtle did the honor of disposing of them.

You learn to be efficient at skinning because it cuts down on the time you're exposed to the blood, guts, and the stench. Pop and Dad are speed skinners. Pop, using something called the "stomp and pull" method that he learned in Arkansas, can skin two squirrels in under a minute if he wants to show off. Dad can take off a coon's hide in ten minutes without ever nicking the hide, which would diminish its value to the fur buyers. He skins surgically, so as to leave the fat on the coon carcass.

Dad, besides selling the hides, does a brisk business in coon-meat among the Southdown factory and field hands. He delivers the skinned and dressed coon whole, leaving on the right rear foot and a bit of hide so that the buyer knows that it was a coon. He's brought this quality-control method from Arkansas where some people apparently passed off skinned dogs as skinned coons, the two looking almost indistinguishable once their hides are peeled away. (This did not go over well when the fraud was discovered.)

I've learned to be a proficient skinner, not as gifted and Dad and Pop, but I don't make many mistakes. I can lop off frog heads with one chop which, all things considered, is best for the frogs. My coon hides come out looking pretty good. We cure them by using straightened coat-hanger wire and thin bamboo stakes to transform the pelts into an almost perfect rectangle, employing a method Pop calls the Arkansas Stretch. We then tack them up to the sunny side of the old cypress garage to dry in the sun awaiting the fur buyer from town. Some years, the garage looks like it's covered in a coonskin coat. By the time we would move from Bayou Black, I had skinned so many coons that I'm 100 percent positive that I could still skin one, maybe even blindfolded, all these decades later.

Do I want to?

No.

Though my mother usually cedes the frying duties to Granny Wells, she makes an exception for frog legs. She dredges them first in a spicy batter of flour and cornmeal made with a bit of vegetable oil, some eggs, cayenne, Tabasco, salt, pepper, and who knows what else. Then she tosses them into a superhot cast-iron skillet where they fry up nice, golden, and crispy.

It is true, by the way, that the fast-twitch muscles of frogs remain in the on position for some time after they have been skinned. Once—

seriously—a headless, skinned frog hopped right out of my mother's skillet when it hit the hot grease, causing Bonnie to declare she was done with frog-leg frying. (She wasn't.) Anyway, that night we had a French-fried frog leg feast, with steaming bowls of seafood gumbo as the appetizer.

The bounty of the Pantry then astonishes me even now. While that might have been an exceptional frog hunt, we commonly came back with fifty frogs. On fishing trips for sac-a-lait (known elsewhere as the crappie) and bream, we'd fill up croker sacks with a hundred or more fish, eating what we needed and passing the rest on to friends, relatives, and Dad's coworkers at the sugar mill. On one coon hunt to a beautiful oak ridge called the Mauvais Bois, we bagged twenty-one coons in an afternoon, so many that I thought we might sink the little johnboat we had arrived in. On a family crawfishing trip to a small swamp off a nearby slough called the Hayfield Canal, we came back with more than one hundred pounds of the mudbugs after just two or three hours of fishing with hand-rigged crawfish nets.

If we journeyed down to the saltwater, it was nothing to fill up an eighty-four-quart cooler with redfish and speckled trout or catch twenty-five pounds of jumbo shrimp by simply throwing a cast net. Crabs? Once, fishing with my youngest brother, Bob, at a saltwater dam near the Cajun Hamlet of Montegut and using nothing more than chicken necks tied to twine, we caught twelve dozen fat, succulent blue crabs in about two hours. There were at least a dozen other crabbers there that day, and they all caught as many or more crabs than we did.

Most of ours got boiled; some went into Bonnie's seafood gumbo. Nothing pleases my mother more, in fact, than when we come home with the goods like all those fat blue crabs.

Bonnie is fastidious about her seafood gumbo: Crabs go in quartered, claws separated, and enough claws so that one or two floats in each bowl that gets served. The claws are as much ornamental as they are part of the flavor. Appearance is important.

Bonnie is fussy about her shrimp, insisting on medium-sized ones for her gumbo. Jumbo shrimp, in her opinion, are inappropriate for gumbo because they have a sharp taste absent from smaller shrimp.

Bonnie wouldn't dream of making her seafood gumbo without okra and she wouldn't dream of putting okra in her chicken-and-sausage gumbo. When I ask her why, she explains, "That's how I learned to do it."

Bonnie has other ironclad gumbo rules The only wild game allowed is duck—no squirrel, no raccoon, no rabbit, no deer. No sausage in seafood gumbo, ever, and no seafood in chicken-and-sausage gumbo, ever.

Oh, wait, she will sometimes bend her no-seafood-in-chicken gumbo rule if fresh oysters were available. "You can put oysters in your chicken-and-sausage gumbo but not shrimp or crab, and never fish. Never. No fish in any kind of gumbo. Not even in seafood gumbo."

It's been years since I've found anyone who puts oysters in their chicken-and-sausage gumbo, not even me, since I've mainly cooked gumbo for my wife and two daughters who are not nearly as fond of oysters as I am. But I recall it as scrumptious. Her trick was to add the oysters toward the end so that they stayed plump but still imparted a complementary oyster flavor.

One reason you don't find oysters in gumbo much anymore is that these days they are an expensive indulgence. During our Bayou Black days, they were often free. We simply took them from the Pantry.

Dad finally saves enough money to buy a seventeen-foot sportfishing boat with a forty-horsepower Johnson motor—big enough to accommodate all Wells boys who want to go fishing. With a wooden lapstrake hull, it's heavy and slow. But it saves a lot of arguments over who gets to go with Dad in the two-person pirogue.

It's a chilly day in January under a pristine blue sky and we're fishing for reds and speckled trout in the saltwater marsh below the Cajun hamlet of Dulac. What my mother calls a "coup nord"—a cutting north wind, in proper French "couper le vent du nord"—has blown through earlier, exposing sandbars and mudflats for as far as the eye can see.

The fish aren't biting but Dad sees opportunity: the coup nord has exposed literally miles of oyster reefs chock-a-block with huge clumps of oysters. These aren't anyone's oyster beds but God's.

We motor carefully toward the bank, the Johnson kicking up mud in the shallows, and begin to pluck oysters with our gloved hands. We always keep a burlap gunny sack in the boat (you never know what you might catch or harvest) and in a half hour we have a bulging sack of oysters.

Dad travels with an oyster knife—a specialty tool with a stout wooden handle and blade thin enough to slip through a clinched oyster shell yet strong enough to pry it open at the hinge.

"Anybody hungry?" Dad says.

All six Wells boys are aboard. That's not even a serious question. We're always hungry.

These oysters are some of the biggest we've ever seen. Dad does some math to include himself, figuring six apiece should take the edge off.

Dad reached into the sack and begins shucking them and passing them around. We slurp them right out of the shells, casting the empties overboard. They are fat, juicy, salty—perfect, so good that we don't miss the homemade hot sauce-and-vinegar concoction we usually dip them in.

Dad seems to agree. He starts shucking again and pretty soon everybody's slurped down a dozen oysters. It's entirely possible, had Dad not been there to supervise, we would've consumed the whole sack.

But Dad wants to make my mother happy. Back home, the afternoon having warmed up, he mounts the front porch and shucks the oysters into a bowl my mother has provided, tossing the shells into a bucket. The shells won't be wasted. We'll hose them down and use them to fill in potholes in our clam-and-oyster-shell paved driveway.

Interestingly, Bonnie isn't fond of raw oysters, she doesn't like the texture. But once she gets them in the pot, she transforms them to her liking.

About a quarter of these will go into her next gumbo. The rest will be rendered this very evening in Bonnie's Oyster Spaghetti.

After gumbo, nothing pleases Rex and his sons more than that dish, which begins with sautéed onions, garlic, and celery into which my mother stirs tomato paste, chopped tomatoes, and a complex of seasonings—some of which she declines to reveal—that every single time transfigures this into God's own version of pasta sauce. One trick I've observed: the oyster juice goes into the sauce well before the oysters. And the timing of the oysters is critical because they naturally shrink during the cooking process. You can't put them in too soon because you'll have tough, shriveled oysters or put them in too late because you'll rob the sauce of that divine oyster flavor.

It was on these occasions that I saw that the Gumbo Life was about more than just gumbo, that we lived in the midst of something both simple and extraordinary. My dad, brothers, and I harvested the gifts of the Pantry and my mother took them and rendered them into dishes that fed not just appetites but our hearts as well. Our Jeep was battered and old, our farmhouse creaky, our bank account often depleted.

And yet, when we gathered nightly around the family table we felt, if not rich, extremely lucky to be where and who we were.

13

GUMBO AS DESTINY

The breathless, serendipitous courtship of my parents was stoked by my father's first encounter with gumbo.

Henrietta Kathleen Toups, born in 1926, was the baby and frost blossom of her family, "a December surprise" as she was always saying. One of seven surviving children, she never knew her father, Louis "Lulu" Toups, who died at age fifty-two when she was but a year old. Maw-Maw Toups became a forty-year-old widow and never remarried.

Lulu had by turns been a blacksmith, woodworker, and coffin-maker, but poor health exacerbated by a fondness for whiskey meant he'd worked only fitfully in his final few years and thus left his family more or less penniless. Two years later, the Depression would only deepen their poverty.

Eighteen years separated Bonnie from her eldest brother. By the time she was twelve years old, half her siblings had married and moved out of the cramped rental house they shared on West Tenth Street, although they all remained in Thibodaux and still lived, in a way, as one big extended family. Her only sister, Heloise, thirteen years her senior, was during that time as much of a second mother as an older sister.

Bonnie attended a free Catholic school where her most vivid memory wasn't learning her ABCs or math but how the nuns once washed out her mouth with soap when she was overheard speaking Cajun French on the school grounds. The sisters were in league with the "Americain" establishment that now ran Louisiana. The state's modified constitution of 1921 specified that the "general exercise in the public schools . . . be conducted in the English language," a dictum that was widely interpreted as prohibiting kids from speaking French at school. This was part of the push to "mainstream" the French-speaking Cajuns and Creoles by eradicating their native tongue.

Bonnie quit school at the end of seventh grade, a decision that was made easier by this gross act of cultural cleansing, but mostly out of dire necessity. The entire Toups clan, like the vast majority of their neighbors, was struggling to survive. Jobs had evaporated. The older Toups men had learned carpentry and woodworking from their father, but the sugarcane economy which had propped up Thibodaux for decades was itself in a deep swoon. No one was building houses or remodeling kitchens or bathrooms. There was no welfare safety net.

My mother, on the cusp of thirteen, took a job in a nearby shrimp-processing factory where she peeled raw shrimp eight hours a day, six days a week, for pennies a pound. She recalls coming home exhausted and sometimes falling asleep, too tired to be awakened for supper. She would sometimes dream of peeling shrimp. She discovered during this time that she was mildly allergic to being pricked by the sharp points emanating from a shrimp's head and spine and her hands would itch and swell. But she couldn't afford to stop working.

In missing supper, she wasn't missing much. The ingredients for the delicious gumbos Maw-Maw Toups had cooked in better times, especially chicken and sausage, were no longer affordable except to the rich. Supper, on many nights, was a bologna sandwich on white bread bought from a neighborhood grocery store. My mother at least had the small comforts of town and the support of her big, close-knit family.

Meanwhile, Rex was growing up in the woods, literally.

He was born in 1920 in rural central Arkansas on the banks of Bayou Des Arc at the junction of the White River. A doctor came by horse and buggy across frozen, muddy roads to deliver him on an early December day. He would be an only child; a sibling, a girl, had earlier died at birth.

At seven years old, Pop gave Rex his first hunting rifle and he bagged his first squirrel the same year. By the time he was ten, he rambled, sometimes alone and with ease, through the vast river bottoms of old growth forests surrounding their shack. Rex would sometimes stay out all night hunting coons with Pop, a carbide lantern and the Arkansas moon to light the way, the bawling of black-and-tan hounds for company.

Town, such as it was, was a tiring ten-mile wagon ride away. Home was a tarpaper shack with a dirt floor, windows without screens and an outhouse out back. Water came from a well that had to be thawed by fire in the coldest part of the winter. He reached the one-room school he attended by mule-drawn wagon and did homework by a coal-oil lantern.

There was no gumbo in my father's life then—on some days, not much food at all. A hard tack biscuit with a slice of fatback was considered a great breakfast. Lunch was a small bowl of grits. Supper sometimes came and went without any food at all.

Pop came from a family of four siblings, my grandmother from a family of nine. They were hardscrabble farm folk who picked up whatever menial work they could manage on the side, barely eking out a living. Pop's father, Rufus Wells, is listed in the 1880 U.S. Census as an eighteen-year-old "itinerant laborer." He died penniless at thirty-nine when Pop was nine. Rufus, descending from generations of farmers who had lived their lives in southern Virginia as far back as the 1730s, had been orphaned as a teen. He had moved from Virginia to Arkansas with his sister and her husband sometime after the death of his father in 1875. When Pop came of age, he wanted nothing to do with farming. He learned some carpentering. He became a master woodsman. He took up moonshining and bootlegging and hunted and fished for a great deal of what they ate, selling the surplus when he could.

And then there was a bright period of hope and prosperity. An executive of a real estate company in Little Rock, about sixty miles away, drove up one day. The company owned the land my family lived on and hundreds of acres around it. It wanted to open a fishing camp for well-to-do sportsmen and proposed deeding my grandfather ten acres surrounding their shack if Pop would build some rental cabins and run the camp.

He agreed and by 1928 the camp was doing so well that Pop went out and bought a shiny new Model A Ford. On the Fourth of July of that year there were so many cars in the camp's parking lot that my dad, who helped fishermen lug their gear to the cabins for tips, had to be carried to bed, he was so exhausted from his labors.

But October brought catastrophe: Black Thursday, the stock market crash that rung in the start of the Great Depression. Business literally vanished overnight. The Wellses settled uneasily into what became a subsistence existence, waiting, like millions of others, for the Depression to end.

In January 1936, they'd had enough. My father was a sickly fifteen-year-old, runty and suffering from malnutrition. They'd all tired of a frontier diet of coon, squirrel, hardtack biscuits, grits, and not much else. The Wellses pulled up stakes and moved to New Orleans, packing the Model A with such provisions as they could carry and leaving the rest behind and the shack unlocked. Pop had been led to believe by a sister, who'd moved to Louisiana with her liquor-selling husband, that there were jobs in New Orleans. They arrived to bitter disappointment. There were almost no jobs at all except the one that Granny Wells got sewing on buttons at the Tulane Shirt Factory for fifteen cents an hour, nine hours a day, six days a week.

Pop, despite his jack-of-all-trades skill set, couldn't seem to find any work; backwoods abilities were not in high demand and with Prohibition repealed, moonshining and bootlegging were out. So, he took to caddying for sparse tips at a nearby golf course. Dad pitched in, delivering groceries for $1.75 a week, plus a free daily poboy sandwich (the Cajun version of the submarine) from the grocery store down the street. The poboy was the best meal of the day. Their lodgings mirrored their economic fortunes: a rat-infested, four-room, ten-dollar-a-month shotgun rental house on St. Peter Street.

Trading Dog Patch poverty for city poverty hadn't exactly been the goal and everybody was miserable. But by the time they thought about going back, a notice came in the U.S. mail that the house and property had been seized for taxes.

A year into their urban poverty, an invitation by a high school chum of Rex's changed their lives. My father didn't know it, but gumbo was on the near horizon.

Dad, whose runty frame, country ways, and Arkansas aphorisms often earned him ridicule among his worldly New Orleans classmates, had made one true friend—an affable Cajun kid named Gene Authement (O-tuh-mohn). Gene came from a big French-speaking family from Houma and he and Rex bonded over their mutual love of hunting and fishing. It was Christmas break and Gene was going down to Houma to visit grandparents, who owned a fishing camp near the Gulf of Mexico. He asked Rex to come along. The plan was to overnight in town and then take his grandparents' oyster boat down to the camp.

Dad jumped at the chance though he had never heard of Houma and had no idea there was anything but marshland, swamp, and open water south of New Orleans. Their car trip was a journey to another world. They crossed the Mississippi River by ferry and watched the urban scrum of New Orleans give way to vast glades of sugarcane being picked over by legions of black men wielding cane knives; to sleepy towns with French names like Boutte, Paradis, and Des Allemands; towns where mossy cypresses clung to reedy bayou banks. They motored slowly along a winding, potholed narrow river of asphalt, improbably named Federal Highway 90, that turtlebacked through freshwater marshlands and only regained a semblance of high ground at a small sugar farming town named Raceland on the banks of Bayou Lafourche. The marshes, stretching as far as the eye could see, reminded Rex of the rice fields of Arkansas. There were plenty of alligators in that marsh, Gene told my dad.

Finally, they arrived in Houma, with its pretty turn-of-the-century downtown, its impressive brick Catholic Church awash in stained glass, its town square lined with century-old, moss-draped Spanish oaks flanking a nineteenth-century brick courthouse. Rex was astonished to find that about half the people he encountered, including Gene's grandparents, preferred to speak Cajun French over English, or didn't speak English at all.

They spent Christmas day at the Authement family home and then headed for the fishing camp, boarding a flat-bottomed, broad-beamed boat known as an oyster lugger, which the family moored in a waterway called Bayou Terrebonne. Hand-hewed, the flat-bottom lugger is purposely built for running in shallow water with heavy loads of oysters. Like tractors, luggers are built for power, not speed.

This was Rex's first close-up view of the Pantry. He loved what he saw. The lugger chugged slowly south toward the Gulf thirty miles distant, past postcard pretty cypress swamps that dripped mystery and limitless alligator-grass prairies that stretched out in the sun, golden as flax. It made its way into the great sprawling saltwater estuary that lay, at that time, basically pristine and unbroken from the Mississippi River clear to the Texas border, a watery jigsaw of meandering bayous, sprawling marshes and low-slung oak islands known as cheniers.

They cruised past colonies of hand-hewn shrimp boats tied to rickety docks and manned by sun-darkened men who shouted to each other in French; past houses and shacks up on stilts where shrimpers sat on porches weaving trawls and cast nets. Rex for the first time smelled the singular, warm-muck aroma of saltwater flats and marshes and caught the salty scent of the sea.

No matter that the Authement fishing camp was little more than a weathered cypress hut on pilings leaning precariously toward the lake. To him it was paradise.

Rex and Gene spent four delirious days on this remote Cajun seashore, beachcombing and fishing. Dad landed his first redfish, a species that fought with far more speed and power than any fish he'd caught back in Arkansas. He tasted raw oysters, shrimp jambalaya, and best of all, gumbo, for the first time. Something suddenly clicked for my father.

This was a wild, exotic landscape that little resembled the untrammeled hardwood river bottoms of Arkansas he'd once roamed, but to this place he felt an instant kinship. Strange as it may sound, he decided then and there he was never going back to Arkansas to live. It was on that trip, he would later tell me, that for the first time he understood the connection between the land, the people, and, more particularly, the cooking. Cajuns cooked with a simplicity, enthusiasm, spice, and skill that, Granny Wells' talents in the kitchen notwithstanding, simply didn't exist in most of the home kitchens of Arkansas. Rex decided then and there that if were ever to marry, he'd marry into a Cajun family if he could find one that would have him. It was that improbable teenage resolve that indeed would steer him toward my mother years later.

Rex left Houma but not before noting that the foundations for a new courthouse had just been staked out in the town center. He suddenly had a plan. Pop was handy with a hammer and a new courthouse needed carpenters. He would convince his parents that they'd all be happier in Houma, a friendly small town that also happened to be the gateway to the wild lands they all missed.

It took a year to quit New Orleans—Dad spent three months in Charity Hospital with anemia—but Pop finally landed a carpenter's job working on the courthouse and on Thanksgiving Day 1937, they moved into a small rental house on Peach Street on Houma's east side. Pop's job lasted for two years, and on the side he cooked up various enterprises which Granny Wells and my father basically ran: a restaurant; a shooting gallery; a boarding house. None made serious money, but the Wellses had at least climbed to the lower rungs of the middle class.

In June 1940, Dad graduated from Terrebonne High School, a matter of great joy to Granny Wells since the exigencies of poverty had required her and Pop to quit school after seventh grade. (Pop never liked school and was indifferent to its importance.) Then, in September, Rex shocked his parents. He told them he was enlisting in the U.S. Marine Corps.

Pop actually laughed at the whole notion and predicted my father would flunk his physical and, if not, never make it through the Marine's notoriously tough boot camp. True, the three-square-meals-a-day of their more prosperous Houma lifestyle had lifted him from runt status. In his senior year Rex had sprouted up a full six inches. He was now six-feet-tall, but he weighed 134 pounds—not exactly Marine Corps Poster Boy material.

But Dad surprised his father (and himself) by not just passing his physical but by becoming a model Marine, so good that after boot camp, his commanding officer offered him an appointment to Annapolis under a program that set aside seats for the top 1 percent of all Marine recruits. Rex agonized but reluctantly turned it down. The Naval Academy at its heart was an engineering school and Rex believed that his hillbilly education and subpar math skills would only lead to failure. He would be embarrassed if he washed out.

But he did win an assignment he wanted—sea school. It was considered then to be not just a place where the sharpest Marines often landed, but could mean a relatively cushy job as a captain's aide aboard the navy's mightiest war ships. Sure, there were faraway rumblings of war but the United States as a whole was in an isolationist mood. In peacetime, Rex saw this assignment as a portal to the travel and adventure he now craved.

My father aced sea school and, boy, did he get an amazing assignment. He would serve the captain aboard the Naval heavy cruiser USS *Chicago* stationed in an idyllic Hawaiian port called Pearl Harbor. In a few months, he was sailing around the world on a cruise that was one part goodwill mission, another part to signal to the Japanese, who were already marauding in the Pacific, that the United States would back its friends in a fight.

The *Chicago* landed in Fiji, Samoa, the Solomon Islands, and other exotic South Pacific ports of call. In Australia, Rex found himself with shore leave, drinking in bars where women bought him beers and lit the cigarettes he'd begun to smoke. Most of Australia's young men were already away fighting the Germans alongside the British in Europe. So, Rex, who could scarcely get a date in high school, found himself being greeted and treated like a rock star.

Then the world crashed for the second time in his life: December 7, 1941—the Japanese sneak attack on Pearl Harbor. The *Chicago* had providentially steamed from port three days before on a mission to deliver supplies to the U.S. contingent on Wake Island. It returned to find a sizable chunk of the U.S. Navy at the bottom of the sea.

Rex would spend three and a half years in more or less constant combat, fighting in some of the deadliest conflicts in the Pacific, both aboard ship and later with Marines who stormed ashore from landing craft to battle the Japanese on vigorously defended islands. The Battle of the Coral Sea; the Battle of Savo Island and Iron Bottom Sound; Engebi and Parry Islands; Guadalcanal and Guam—all were on my father's war record. In January 1945, he pitched up at sick bay on the hellhole of Guadalcanal, where he'd been transferred to walk sniper patrol after a harrowing landing on Guam. He was pretty certain he had dysentery. He'd lost a ton of weight. He was also unable to hold a cup of coffee in his hands. Marines he knew were dying around him every day. The doctor took one look at his physical condition and long combat record and his said, "You're going home for a while. You need a break and some medical attention."

The protocol was to ship you to the U.S. Navy hospital nearest your hometown. Rex couldn't believe it—he was heading to New Orleans. It took six weeks, via a hospital ship from Guadalcanal and a long cross-country train ride, to get home. On the ship, he was the only "patient" not locked up in psychiatric wards under armed Marine guards. The rest were Marines who had cracked up under combat and been diagnosed as psychotics. Dad still had the shakes but his hands and mind were steady enough to break the bank on a succession of poker games with the Marine guards, and he landed in San Francisco with six hundred dollars in his pockets. This was a fortune for a Marine making twenty dollars a month, including combat pay.

He reached New Orleans by train in March, checking into the New Orleans Naval Hospital for what the services then called combat fatigue. They treated his various ailments. They fixed his nose, which he'd broken as a kid. They gave him drugs for his shaky hands. He began to calm down. On his first leave, he took most of his shipboard winnings and went to a used car lot and bought a black 1939 Buick convertible with a white top that he'd seen on his way to the hospital.

With weekend hospital passes and gasoline ration cards he got by swapping his military cigarette allotments, Rex was suddenly a man of leisure and liberty. He would put on his dress blues and drive down to Houma to see his parents, then drive around town with the convertible's top down, hoping to meet women. He wanted to live a little.

Girls who had paid him no mind in high school now flirted with him. The local paper ran a story about his combat exploits on Guam. He spoke to the Houma Rotary Club. In June, he went, dashing in his dress blues, to a Cajun dance in nearby Thibodaux. Rex didn't dance but he knew pretty Cajun women liked to. And he'd never forgotten his teenage vow that, should he ever marry, he wanted to marry into a gumbo-cooking Cajun family.

And there was my mother. She was beautiful, trim, dark-eyed, and she could dance. She was in the company of her best friend and also chaperoned by her mother, Anna Virginia, who doted over her and watched her as fiercely as a lioness.

Rex and Bonnie struck up a conversation and could not be parted for the rest of the evening. After the dance, Dad drove Bonnie and her mother home in the convertible to the little, sparsely furnished rental house on West Tenth Street. About a month later, he proposed, though they never really dated. He just started showing up at the house every day and hanging around.

Maw-Maw Toups was honestly shocked, taking the not unreasonable view that my mother and father actually knew so little about each other, how could they possibly think about marriage? Moreover, Rex, though he was polite, well-spoken, and kind to my mother, was a backwoods Protestant, even though not a churchgoer. And the Toups family, like the vast majority of South Louisiana residents at that time, were staunchly Catholic. It was simply taboo in those days to marry outside your religion.

Bonnie wasn't shocked by their whirlwind romance. The minute she saw my father, she'd nudged a friend and said, "There goes the man I'm going to marry." (I met my mother's friend years and years later and she tells the story the same way.)

Bonnie was eighteen years old. It was wartime, after all.

By then, Rex had been discharged from the hospital and had gotten orders to report on August 15 to Philadelphia for reassignment. He knew he was heading back to combat. The war in Europe was over but Japan, despite being routed in the Pacific and bombed relentlessly at home, was still holding out. A massive assault on Japan and its home islands seemed inevitable. An invasion of that scale would be bigger than D-Day and military planners were already projecting as many as a million casualties if the Japanese fought to the bitter end, as everyone expected they would. Rex honestly believed he wouldn't survive another beach landing; he'd already dodged too many bullets that should have killed him. He would go, but fully expected to return in a box.

He confided this to my mother and in the emotional crucible of the times, this was all the more reason for my mother to marry him. Whatever fate would bring, they would at least have a few days together. They set a wedding date for August 11, 1945.

Talk about fate. On August 6th, President Harry S Truman ordered the first atomic bomb attack on Japan; on August 9, the second bomb fell.

Rex and Bonnie went ahead with their wedding. In the pictures, my mother, in her chiffon dress, looks at turns scared and delighted. Rex is smiling in his full-dress Marine Corps uniform, his impressive black-brimmed white hat cocked jauntily on his head. What's missing from the photos is Bonnie's family. When the Catholic priest in Thibodaux refused to marry them because Rex wouldn't convert, they chose a Baptist minister from Granny Wells' church in Houma. The Toupses didn't attend the wedding, a hurt my mother nursed for years.

They drove away in the convertible for a quick honeymoon in New Orleans. Fever got the best of them and they never even made it over the Huey P. Long Bridge into the city, settling instead for a cheap motel in the shadow of the bridge on the west bank of the Mississippi River. There's a good chance my older brother Bill was conceived that night.

Three days later, the war was over. Dad wouldn't have to report to Philadelphia after all. He got assigned as a guard at the Naval Air Station in Houma from which reconnaissance blimps were still being launched to scour the Gulf of Mexico for enemy submarines.

In a matter of weeks, he applied for discharge and got it. He was a civilian again.

I can only imagine my parents waking up one day not long afterward realizing Maw-Maw Toups was right. They knew so little of each other.

That they were quite different people with divergent views of what constituted the good life was already apparent by the time we moved to Bayou Black. Our sojourn there would ever more starkly frame these differences.

It's entirely possible—well, almost certain—that gumbo, which in a way precipitated their marriage, also saved it.

{ 14 }

SERPENTS ON THE ROUX BAYOU

By the time that monkey comes into our lives, we are in our second full-time summer in the country. The way my mother sees it, we've gone from being a more or less normal family with a small beige house in town and two dogs in a tidy yard filled with flowers, to keepers of a small zoo on a six-acre farm that we don't actually own.

We've become friends with a lady snake collector of whom my mother is quite fond but who has given us a nasty, horrible monkey, which Dad says it would be impolite to give back.

Why does my mother hate the monkey? His name is Peanut but it could have been FrankenMonkey. One day when we let him out of his cage, he climbed our tangerine tree fronting the porch and began plucking off the immature, golf ball–sized fruit. He then proceeded to pummel every Wells boy who attempted to climb the tree to coax him back into his cage with these green tangerine missiles. (I got a nice welt under my eye before retreating.) Another time, he ambushed our favorite dog, King, an affable black Lab mix, hopping onto to his back and riding the poor, terrified pooch around the yard like some tiny, manic rodeo cowboy. (The monkey eventually fell off; poor King ran terrified into the cane fields and didn't return for hours.)

And now, this snake business. Alligator Annie has also enlisted my father and the Wells boys to become live snake-catchers for her. What could possibly go wrong there?

The snakes are giving Bonnie the heebie-jeebies.

My parents' marriage has already survived a few shocks. The first was that their courtship was so fast and unexpected that my father actually never asked a critical question: "You can cook gumbo, right?"

The answer: My mother couldn't boil water.

Dad, according to my mother, sulked for a week and then they both agreed upon a plan. Bonnie would learn to cook gumbo and other things the way I did. She would appeal to her own mother to show her the gumbo way.

Upon return from their overnight honeymoon, Bonnie very soon learned she was pregnant, a fact that she disclosed at first only to her husband and Maw-Maw Toups. My grandmother, having participated in the wedding boycott, was now repentant. No way was a Protestant wedding going to get in the way of her relationship with her baby daughter and her coming grandchild. She was over all that. And she told the family to get over it, too. (And they did, for the most part.)

As for cooking, my father would drive Bonnie to Thibodaux, sometimes dropping her off for the day, and she and Maw-Maw Toups would cook together. It was informal. "You want to see how I make that roux, cher? You want to see how I stir in the vegetables when the roux's the right color?'" That sort of thing.

Anna Virginia's family, the Kellers, were, like the Toupses, French-speaking German Coasters. She was one of ten siblings. By the time I came along, only a few of those siblings were left. The most memorable of them was Great Aunt Eve, who was three years older than Maw-Maw Toups. Among the Toupses she was called Tante T'Eve (pronounced Taunt Tev). She lived outside of Thibodaux but often visited with Maw-Maw Toups, who lived with Uncle Pershing and his kindly wife.

Tante T'Eve was a small, thin, stern-looking woman who I never saw dressed in anything but black. She seldom spoke and when she did it was in Cajun French. She looked like she belonged in some grainy black-and-white movie set in an eighteenth-century French village. She also had a glass eye—her right eye, as I recall—and no matter which way she was looking, you always felt the glass eye was staring at you.

Also unsettling was that sometimes, in our presence, she would swipe the glass eye out with a handkerchief she always clutched, clean it off, and pop it back in. Once, she fumbled the eye, and it rolled across the wooden floor toward my cousins and me. We fled the room screaming, which embarrassed my mother (not the eye popping out but our reaction to it).

My mother, however, had great affection for Tante T'Eve, and credited her with playing a role in my mother's transformation into a great cook. She would attend these cooking sessions and give bits of wisdom in her solemn French.

The first thing Bonnie learned to make was Maw-Maw Toups' chicken-and-sausage gumbo, later graduating to seafood. And then she did what all good cooks tend to do, she began adapting her mother's recipes to the tastes of her own family. Dad liked his gumbo spicier than Maw-Maw Toups' gumbo and so did the Wells boys. So Bonnie would ladle in a little cayenne atop the black pepper and shake in a couple of drops of Tabasco Sauce.

Another difference: Maw-Maw Toups' Trinity was always finely diced and by the time the gumbo was fully cooked the veggies had pretty much melded into the pot. My mother's Trinity of celery, onions, and bell peppers was coarse. It turned out, as Bonnie later confessed, that this wasn't by choice. She just wasn't very good with a knife, had no patience for sharpening a knife, and also no patience for the extra time it took to finely dice everything. I also later realized that she never actually owned a good knife. Dad might spend luxuriously on a high-quality skinning knife to help him relieve coons and squirrels of their hides, but he thought any knife was good enough for kitchen duty.

Over time, however, I began to take notice that my mother's accidentally coarse vegetables gave her gumbo, in my opinion, more body and character and hint more of the veggie flavoring than Maw-Maw Toups' gumbos and I came to like it. So though I have a very good kitchen knife, I coarse-chop my Trinity the way my mother did. Also, Bonnie only used green bell peppers. Now peppers come not just in green but in red and yellow as well. I mix and match. I like the way they add color. The coarsely chopped peppers rise in a mosaic to the top when cooked. They make for a pretty gumbo. Does this change the flavor of my mother's gumbo recipe? Probably a bit.

But I'm just doing what my mother did. My wife, Lisa, and daughters, Sara and Becca, who have eaten most of the gumbo I've cooked in my life, love the coarse vegetables. If Lisa had her way, I would be required to double the amount of peppers in every gumbo. I resist because I feel too many peppers would unbalance the flavor and steer the gumbo farther away from Bonnie's flavor.

The other major difference between Bonnie's chicken-and-sausage gumbo and her mother's was that Maw-Maw Toups, for whatever reason, didn't bother to skim the oil from the top of her gumbo. Perhaps she liked the taste. But if you cook with lard, or even vegetable or peanut oil, and also use bone-in, skin-on chicken and fatty sausages, you will get lots and lots of oil. Bonnie taught me the importance of ladling this surplus off before serving; it was a big deal to her. (Some cooks even freeze this oil and recycle it into the next roux, contending it gives the roux more body. But my mother never did and thus I don't either.)

One day, while we were still living on Bayou Black and my mother was at the gumbo pot, she pulled me aside to tell me what she said was a secret that I could never tell anyone else. Ever. But it was something that so bothered her that she had to tell somebody.

I was prepared for some dark Toups family horror to spill out— some tale of abuse or a great moral lapse. But instead she said, "I love Momma's gumbo, cher, but I find it too greasy."

I actually laughed in relief, but have kept the secret until now. For, indeed, Maw-Maw Toups would've been deeply upset—wounded— that her baby girl to whom she had lovingly passed on her gumbo ways had anything but praise for her gumbo.

Despite the rapprochement after the Wells grandsons began arriving, and the fact that we sometimes seemed to be living as one big extended Wells-Toups family, there were still some intrafamily tensions. Those live snakes we started to catch for Alligator Annie Miller were the main friction point.

Though the Toupses like my father well enough and enjoy swapping stories with him over beer, they consider him more than a little odd. The Toups men, in birth order Louis (nicknamed Boy), Norman (nicknamed Man), Pershing (nicknamed Perch) and Huey (nicknamed Tiny, pronounced, in the Cajun, ty-NEE), all share my mother's aversion to anything lying outside the city limits. So, does my mother's older sister, Heloise (nicknamed Nanny). The three eldest, Uncle Boy, Uncle Man, and Nanny, could all reca.ll living in the country in the early 1900s when Papa Toups was alive and working as a blacksmith for Southdown Sugars, the very mill Dad went to work for on Bayou Black. But they were all more than happy to abandon the rustic life for the manicured spaces of town.

They've never hunted, fished, tromped the woods, set foot in a swamp, or owned a boat or a gun, nor have they ever wanted to. They love the Cajunized Thibodaux town life. They like proximity. For a while, Louis, Norman, and Pershing and their families resided next door to one another in a triangular cluster of modest, impeccably kept houses in a working-class neighborhood. They loved to gather over gumbo, talk French, and gossip. (When Uncle Pershing sold his little house in the cluster and built a new home a few miles away, Aunt Heloise bought it and kept the clustering tradition going.)

After supper on the weekends, they often set up card tables and play raucous games of bourré (booray), essentially Cajun poker, made ever more lively by the exuberant consumption of beer and Old Crow whiskey. Nothing pleased my mother more than being invited to these bourré sessions. (Dad would drop her off but not stay to play.) She often brought gumbo she'd cooked at home or cooked helped cook a batch in whoever's house held the bourré game.

For the Toups men, the sporting life means donning nice shirts, starched slacks, and polished shoes, slicking in some aromatic hair tonic, and ambling on Saturday afternoons the long block to the College Inn. This is a rambling and wildly popular bar that on weekends draws large, hard-drinking crowds who come from as far as thirty miles away for the live music, mostly swamp pop (think Fats Domino) and rhythm & blues. There, the Toups men belly up to the long bar; flirt with the women servers (then called "barmaids"); knock back a few cans of Jax Beer, their favorite brew; or sip a few highballs and watch the party scene unfold.

Rex will occasionally join them on these College Inn rambles, but it's not his thing. This makes him, in the Toups male worldview, a strange cat. His pleasures befuddle them.

What kind of person *purposely* walks the woods at night?

What kind of man paddles around in a swamp in the dark actually *looking* for alligators instead of trying to avoid them?

Who would want to spend a day tracking and shooting coons, and then skinning them?

Why would you want to skin *anything* when you could now easily get the chickens for your gumbo pre-plucked at the supermarket?

What sort of man insists that squirrel be served at his supper table?

As for squirrel brains? *Mais la!* (This is a Cajun idiom meaning more or less, "Holy cow, no!" Or "Geez, you can't be serious!")

If all that isn't enough, there are these new and, in Toups thinking, disturbing reports trickling from Bayou Black to Thibodaux. Rex has been trafficking in live serpents and enlisting his sons in this effort. The Toupses are mildly superstitious. Snakes aren't just dangerous; they could bring bad luck and disgrace.

The reports of the snake trade, of course, come from my mother, who later confesses to me that she shared it with her mother with the reluctance that she might have shared the news that she was divorcing my father or had become an alcoholic. It was a hard thing to admit because Bonnie knew this would be taken as another reason for her family to doubt the wisdom of her marrying Rex in the first place. But having exhausted her pleas to my father to stop the snake trade, she felt like she needed help.

This may help explain why we spent far more time in Thibodaux visiting the Toupses than they spent visiting us on Bayou Black. My mother has also let it slip that there have been snakes in our house.

Well, one snake in particular.

We usually keep our captive snakes no longer than it takes to transport them to Annie's for sale. But sometimes, if we get in late from a hunt, we stow them overnight in wood-and-wire cages out on the back porch. Rex also now and then will allow us to keep a particularly interesting snake for a pet, though never a poisonous one. Speckled kingsnakes are popular because they are extremely docile, don't mind being handled, and will lie coiled around your neck all day if you want them to.

In deference to my mother and her snake phobias, Dad has instituted an ironclad rule that we are never to bring snakes into the house.

But boys will be boys. Once, when my parents were away, we freed a baby rat snake, not more than eighteen inches long, from its cage and brought it in to watch it slither around crazily on the linoleum kitchen floor. And then, in some lapse of attention, the snake disappeared.

We figured that, with the kitchen door being our main exit to our chicken yard and pasture, the snake had simply slipped through a crack in the screen when we weren't looking.

Except that Bonnie, making a bed in the Wells boys' dorm a few days later, encountered what she thought was a pencil or stiff piece of rope as she groped under a mattress to fit a sheet.

I can still hear the shriek that came from the bedroom that afternoon when she discovered that she held our missing rat snake. (She threw it against the wall, knocking it unconscious. But my brothers and I picked it up and managed to revive it before letting it go into the nearby fields.)

My mother grilled us, but no boy was going to confess. Surely, we told Bonnie, the snake must have crawled in through an open door.

My mother gave Dad an earful when he got home from the sugar mill but surprisingly, he didn't interrogate us over our version of events, though I knew he was skeptical. Maybe he knew browbeating a confession out of us would only mean trouble for him as well.

I have an inkling we are headed for a snake crisis when I overhear Maw-Maw Toups, in a guarded conversation with my mother during a visit to Thibodaux, declare in her Cajun accent, "Ai-yi-yi, snakes! My poor grandchildren. My poor, poor grandchildren!"

And so it is one Saturday morning, with my father off at the mill, that Maw-Maw Toups mysteriously appears in our clamshell driveway, driven to the farm by Uncle Perch. My mother, looking out of our front screen door, feigns surprise, and then proceeds to order all of her sons out onto the front porch. She's fidgety.

We've just acquired a marvel—our first television—and discovered Roy Rogers, the Lone Ranger, and Saturday morning cartoons. Thus, my mother's orders for us to assemble on the porch are met with much grousing. Once on the porch, Bonnie further annoys us by requiring us to line up side by side in descending order by age.

We turn to look at Maw-Maw Toups, emerging slowing from Uncle Perch's car. She's getting out awkwardly, clutching what appears to be a metal pitcher of some kind. Our uncle sits in the driver's seat, staring straight ahead, not even looking at us. This is highly unusual. Uncle Perch, along with Uncle Huey, ranks as the sweetest of all of our uncles.

We wave at him and our grandmother, but they decline to wave back.

Maw-Maw Toups walks slowly but steadily toward the porch, her eyes glued to the pitcher. She reaches the steps, ascending as if in some kind of trance, and only when she reaches the first Wells boy does she look up.

With great solemnity, she dips her fingers into the pitcher and begins flicking each boy with water, making the sign of the cross as she plods her way down the line, muttering some unintelligible prayer.

I take a spray of water in my eyes and try to wipe it away.

"It's holy water!" my mother whispers fiercely. "She got it from the priest at St. Joseph's in Thibodaux. Be still!"

When Maw-Maw Toups reaches Bobby, the youngest, she completes her mission with an exaggerated flourish of her sprinkling hand and declares, "Them snakes not gonna get y'all now, chers!"

We all stare speechless at my mother, who is smiling with a mixture of embarrassment and relief.

She whispers to me again, less urgently this time, "Don't tell your father."

There's an upside to this (besides being saved from Satan's slithering masses).

Bonnie and Maw-Maw Toups retire to the kitchen. It's early summer and the blackberries and dewberries are plentiful this season. We've picked quarts and quarts of them from the thickets that grow along the sugarcane field ditches behind the farm, the bounty of the Pantry once again.

The berries sit in open containers on the kitchen counter. Bonnie gets out a large aluminum baking pan and while she coats the surface with oil, Maw-Maw Toups goes to work on her favorite dish, blackberry dumplings.

Out comes flour, cornstarch, baking powder, butter, milk and buttermilk, sugar (both powdered and granulated), lemon, and who knows what else. Maw-Maw Toups is known to improvise when she makes her blackberry dumplings. She transfers the berries into a saucepan with some water, fires up a burner on our rickety stove and, as the berries begin to heat and simmer, stirs in some lemon juice and sugar. The berries basically cook into a sticky compote which she then pours into the baking pan to a depth of two or three inches.

She then makes her dumplings in a separate bowl—whisking together flour, water, baking powder, salt, and cinnamon (or sometimes nutmeg if my mother has any). When she's satisfied that the dough is of the right consistency, she uses a large spoon to fashion her dumplings, dropping them in, maybe two inches apart, into the berry mixture so they form little white islands in a mixture of purple. All this then goes into the oven for about half an hour.

The aroma—otherworldly.

The taste? The cobblerlike dish ranks, in Wells boy appreciation, up there with Granny Wells' fried apple fritters.

The dumplings on, Maw-Maw puts on a big pot of strong French roast coffee, making it in the pot that Bonnie keeps for her. We use a simple drip aluminum pot, but Maw-Maw won't use such a pot. It's not how proper Cajun coffee is made, in her opinion. Hers is a tall blue-and-white speckled porcelain pot, shaped more like a tea kettle. The drip basket atop is open and doesn't have a cover.

Maw-Maw puts a pot of water to boil and then scoops in heaping teaspoons of the dark roast coffee, a popular brand called Community, tamping down each scoop so as to compact it. As the water starts to boil, Maw-Maw eschews pouring it over the grounds as we do. Instead, she begins ladling it in, a tablespoon at a time. It takes forever for her to make this pot of coffee, but the result is what I can only describe as amazingly strong and delicious Cajun espresso (an observation I can only make now since, back then, I'd never heard of espresso). The aroma is so powerful that it wafts from the kitchen clear out to the front porch.

The coffee done, Bonnie, with Maw-Maw Toups' help, starts preparing a chicken-and-sausage gumbo. With my grandmother's snake-protection mission accomplished and having been assured by my mother there are no snakes in the house, she and Uncle Perch have agreed to stay for lunch (the meal that we, and most Cajun families, refer to as dinner. And what much of the world calls dinner, we call supper). They will sip coffee, cook, and talk. It's the gumbo way.

My brothers and I are out in the yard when Dad, arriving on his lunch break, drives up in the Jeep wagon. About the same time, Bonnie emerges on the porch to summon everyone in.

"The gumbo is ready. Maw-Maw's dumplings are dessert."

There is something of the herd mentality among a family of brothers and we stampede up the wooden porch steps.

Bonnie says what she always says, "Boys! Ya'll slow down and wash up first. No dirty hands at my table."

Since we have only one bathroom, this takes a while and meantime

Dad has come in to find Maw-Maw Toups and Uncle Perch seated at the dining room table, which has been expanded by an extra leaf to accommodate the extra diners. Although we keep an open house like most Cajun families, we overhear Dad expressing mild surprise.

"Hey, good to see y'all. What brings y'all out today? Bonnie didn't say y'all were comin'."

There's an unusually long silence and then Uncle Perch speaks. "Aw, nuttin' in particular. Momma just felt like takin' a ride. Sometimes she likes to *roder*. You know. We haven't seen ya'll in a while."

"Well, good," Dad says. "Y'all are always welcome."

Then he says what he always says when my mother fires up the gumbo pot. "Boy, it sure smells good in here."

My mother fetches the gumbo pot from the stove and sets it at the center of the table. Uncle Perch helps with the rice. Everyone gathers round and Pop says his usual ten-second grace. My mother is, as usual, the last to be seated.

I wonder if we'll get through this whole meal without a revelation of Maw-Maw Toups' real mission on this day and I worry what the consequences might be. Will Dad be amused? Angry about what he might well see as superstitious nonsense? Dad is pretty even-tempered, but it could go either way.

But in fact, Dad will only learn of the holy water incident years later (and laugh like crazy when he does). On this day, it never comes up, partly, I'm convinced, because the gumbo is so good (and Maw-Maw's blackberry dumplings so divinely scrumptious) that the food seems to compel only the happiest of chatter.

Gumbo to the rescue again.

BAYOU BLACK TODAY

My family's Bayou Black sojourn ended in 1968, eleven years after we moved there. Dad would change jobs and buy a tract house in a subdivision on the north side of Houma. My Gumbo Life would continue, anchored by the indelible impression the place made upon me—the culture, landscape, people, food, the rootedness of it all. Moving—and eventually moving away from Louisiana—would allow me to see that time with a clarity and perspective that I likely would never have seen had I stayed.

My chief observation is that if Bayou Black hadn't changed much in the hundred years before we got there, it would change one hundred years' worth by the time we left.

I'm not reflexively against change and change isn't always bad. The potholed, often dusty clamshell road that we lived on got a coat of blacktop. "City water" and "city gas" arrived to replace aging cypress cisterns and butane tanks, all vast improvements in the quality of life.

But Southdown Sugars began to wind down its operations, eventually closing the mill and shipping the entire thing to Guatemala. Dad needed to find a new job and did so, leveraging his hunting and fishing knowledge to score a job as the sporting goods manager for the Sears, Roebuck & Company store that was about to open at the brand-new mall not far from our new home. The mall (I'm not exaggerating) was greeted with unrestrained awe. Our once sleepy town, in the midst of its oil boom, was growing and growing up!

That, in turn, spurred a demand for new housing. Southdown would soon begin to sell off its land and soon enough subdivisions, strip shopping centers, trailer parks, and even a car lot would eventually crop up on Bayou Black acres that once held sugar canefields and cow pastures. Some of the woods, including several hundred acres behind our farm, were logged heavily, ruining the hunting.

One small-time developer carved out a trailer park on former Southdown land, and bulldozed a stunning grove of old-growth water oaks to put in a sewer pond to serve his development. It was a place, when Southdown owned the land, that the Wellses hunted every opening day of the fall squirrel season. I called that grove the God Trees. Even if the hunting was slow, we'd stop on those often foggy October mornings and just stare up at the majesty of the sun cascading through the moss-draped branches and azure light. (The sewer pond overflowed several times and was abandoned in a few years when the parish government installed proper sewer drains. The trees, of course, never grew back.)

More and more oil field installations infringed upon the marshes, swamps, and fields. These days, there are virtually no public places to hunt along Bayou Black; the "No Trespassing" sign is the rule, not the exception. Cane fields still sprawl, notably on the south side of the bayou, but the number of farms and farmers has shrunk as many of the mom-and-pop farmers sold out to bigger players. The old French speakers have pretty much all died out.

Among the charms of Old Bayou Black were three graceful green one-lane wrought-iron bridges that provided passage over the bayou every few miles. Two have been demolished and replaced with drab utilitarian concrete structures. The last one has been condemned and no doubt will be torn down soon as well. Madison County may love and preserve its old bridges, but Terrebonne Parish, the governmental jurisdiction there, not so much.

Still, parts of Bayou Black retain their pastoral charms. I drive the old roads on every visit. One farmer still keeps cows. You can pass hand-lettered signs hawking okra or "rabbits 4 sale." A handful of beautiful plantation homes still grace the south side of the bayou, standing on immaculate, sprawling lawns of St. Augustine grass set beneath century-old live oak trees.

And not all of the old Southdown land got locked away from the public. Back in 1996, due to the generosity of a rich Houma lawyer, the U.S. Fish & Wildlife Service was able to acquire more than four thousand acres of prime Bayou Black wetlands to create the Mandalay National Wildlife Refuge. While most of it is only accessible by boat, there is a lovely, mile-long hiking trail, not too distant from our old farmstead, that meanders through some of the very marshes and swamps where the Wellses filled up sacks of live snakes for Alligator Annie. I walk it at least once on every visit.

As for our farmhouse—it's gone.

Upon Southdown's decision to close its mill, the company offered its houses for sale to the occupant/employees. Dad could have bought our spread for $7,000, but he turned it down. My parents had already offered on the house near the magic mall. They had no money for a second place. Over a secession of owners, the house fell into disrepair and was torn down in 2017. The last owner, showing his generosity, offered my brothers who still live nearby a tour of the old place before the demolition. They shot a video, which is all that's left to us, except for pictures that I've taken over the years on my drives by during my frequent visits home.

Elmo's Bar & Grocery closed long ago. Still, proof that Bayou Black hews to its gumbo traditions, a restaurant named the Bayou

Delight sits mid-bayou on the highway side, serving up a pretty righteous chicken-and-sausage gumbo. The diners are a mix of locals and tourists who have come off a swamp tour run by my old bayou childhood friend, Jimmy Bonvillain. He's Alligator Annie's son and took over her business shortly before she passed away in 2004 at the age of eighty-nine.

This was a lesson for me. The aesthetics and demographics of the Gumbo Belt may be changing, but gumbo transcends these changes. If anything, its hold grows stronger than ever, serving as it does as a fond reminder and symbol of the not-too-distant bucolic past from which it came. I'm always thinking I'm tasting and experiencing a bit of the old ways in every gumbo I eat.

As Bev and Peg Freeman, the since departed poule d'eau gumbo cookers, noted about the sinking marsh around their fishing camp, the health of Gumbo's Pantry itself, deserves some attention. The Bayou Black ridge, with an elevation of six to ten feet above sea level, is still high ground for this part of the world and, so far, mostly immune to the flooding that has ravaged other parts of Terrebonne Parish and South Louisiana in general.

But not so far south and east, the great, once unbroken swath of marshes that helped to protect our coast—a watery plain that rivaled the open ranges of the West—is eroding at an alarming rate. An anti-saltwater intrusion lock now sits at the intersection of the Bayou Black waterway and a southward-running channel called Minor's Canal. It's not unusual these days for it to be closed several times a year to block damaging saltwater tides from polluting the local drinking water supply.

The sprawl of development that has changed the character of Bayou Black is merely a reflection of the mall sprawl that is changing the aesthetics of much of the Gumbo Belt. The spread of malls and chain stores has obliterated or diminished many turn-of-the-century downtowns, including Houma's. While disconcerting (if your instincts are preservationist), this pales in comparison to the peril facing the wild coast. There is a palpable sense of angst about the future of the Cajun Glades and the health of the Pantry.

Since the 1930s, Louisiana has lost a swath of marshland equivalent to the size of the state of Delaware and each year about fifteen thousand additional acres vanish. Some of this is the result of natural forces like geological subsidence and sea rise. The specter of climate change exacerbating these losses looms over everything. But the vast majority of wetlands loss to date is due to man-made causes, notably the channelizing of the Mississippi River for flood protection and the collateral impacts of oil and gas exploration and production.

Following the devastating floods of 1927, the United States undertook an ambitious levee-construction program that essentially put the Mighty Mississippi in a straitjacket. While this drastically reduced flooding, and saved New Orleans more than once from catastrophe, it has had a huge unintended negative consequence. It was the river's silt that over the millennia built much of the Louisiana delta as the river meandered through the marshes, often changing course as it did. Now that silt falls into the deep waters of the Gulf where it only serves as a pollutant, creating a massive "dead zone" in the Gulf.

That itself, however, doesn't fully explain why a delta built over eight to ten thousand years has shrunk so much in the past eight decades. Dredging by the oil and gas industry is the other part of the equation. Between 1901, when drilling began in Louisiana, and the 1980s, the industry laid tens of thousands of miles of pipelines and dredged more than 9,300 miles of canals in one of the largest industrial invasions of an estuary in history.

These beeline canals were largely constructed to barge in drilling rigs to remote marsh locations and provide production crews access after the wells were completed. Atop that, the industry, aided by the U.S. Army Corps of Engineers, promoted the dredging of numerous navigation canals allowing ship-scale traffic to move more quickly from inland ports, like Houma, to the oil rigs in the Gulf of Mexico. The cost savings for the industry have been huge. The damage to the ecosystem, almost incalculable.

For all of this was done with no regard as to how this dredging would disrupt the delicate interface between upland marshes and saltwater wetlands by opening the fresh- and brackish-water buffer to massive saltwater intrusion. Saltwater poisons freshwater marshes and swamps, causing them to die and sink. Meanwhile, the vast majority of these canals and shipping channels were also built without erosion control; the battering of the soft marsh banks over time due to tides, storms, and boat traffic has taken another big bite out of our wetlands.

And this is hardly just a matter of the loss of valuable wildlife and seafood habitat. The presence of a badly eroded navigation channel called the Mississippi River Gulf Outlet (MRGO) is a prime example. A tidal surge enabled and magnified by "MR.GO" (as it is known) very likely helped turn Katrina from what should have been a moderately damaging storm into a $161 billion catastrophe. In 2009, four years after the storm, the MRGO was fitted with a permanent surge barrier and closed to maritime shipping.

In my old stomping grounds, a shipping channel called the Houma Navigation Canal, dredged in 1962 to provide oil industry workboats with a beeline straight to the Gulf of Mexico from Houma, is also finally being fitted with a saltwater lock and storm barrier at a cost of tens of millions of dollars. After it was widened at the urging of the oil industry in 1974, the channel has since been blamed for killing off thousands of acres of freshwater marsh by funneling lethal saltwater tides into the freshwater estuary and nearby cypress swamps. The widening occurred over vigorous objections of local commercial fishermen who in fact prophesied the harm it would do. (I covered the sometimes raucous hearing over the channel when I still reported for the Houma paper.)

That said, I remain cautiously optimistic as to the long-term fate of our coast. I have two reasons. One is that Louisiana's officialdom and citizenry have finally woken up and acknowledged this unfolding catastrophe, and for the first time in my adult life, there exists a practical plan—and at least some of the money—to launch a meaningful coastal restoration program.

We'll never turn the clock back eighty years and undo the full scale of losses, but it's entirely possible to stem the losses and in some cases substantially rebuild eroded marshes and barrier islands, expensive though that proposition is. In 2005, in the aftermath of Katrina, the state formed the Coastal Protection and Restoration Authority. It has since floated an ambitious $50 billion, fifty-year marsh and barrier-island rebuilding program has tied to hurricane protection. Some of this will be paid for by a $20 billion fund set up by BP after its disastrous Gulf of Mexico oil spill in 2010. The cost of doing nothing at all would be a disaster not just for Louisiana but the nation as a whole. Among other things, the Louisiana estuary also holds and protects close to $1 trillion in oil and gas infrastructure.

Closer to the heart: I think what will save our coast is the grit and resilience of the people of the Pantry—the Cajuns, Creoles, French Indians like the Verdin family, the Isleños of St. Bernard Parish, and others who have depended upon it for centuries to sustain them; and the people of New Orleans, natives and transplants, who intuit and treasure the city's singular place in the American experiment and strive every day to preserve it. For there is for the first time a recognition that the fates of the coast and the fates of our Gumbo Belt culture are inextricably linked. And as the gritty post-Katrina recovery of New Orleans and neighboring St. Bernard and Plaquemines parishes shows, nobody is giving up.

The experience of Ricky Robin, an indefatigable shrimp boat captain from the St. Bernard fishing hamlet of Yscloskey, is illustrative. I met Captain Robin in 2005. I was reporting on Katrina's aftermath for the *Wall Street Journal* and had flagged a ride from the Baton Rouge airport aboard a Coast Guard helicopter into the literal heart of darkness: the Katrina-ravaged ramparts of Chalmette, the St. Bernard Parish seat, where literally every habitable structure had been ruinously flooded. (All roads there were still under several feet of water.)

The first person I met upon landing was Ricky, standing alone in his white shrimper boots, soiled jeans, and a T-shirt. He'd been through a series of ordeals that might have easily defeated others. He had the means and opportunity to evacuate. But there he was, drawn to the one place, a makeshift command center, where there were generators and hope, dim as it was at that moment, that the monumental effort to claw a way back from this disaster might begin. He wanted to help out.

He'd already done quite a bit. Drawing upon decades of seamanship and the experiences of his father and grandfathers in storms past, Ricky had ridden out Katrina aboard his homemade fifty-six-foot steel trawler. When the killing waters came, Ricky not only saved his boat; he and other shrimp boat captains, hunkered down in a harbor called Violet Canal, saved hundreds of people who had been literally washed from their houses by the fulminating storm tides.

I had my doubts about St. Bernard Parish recovering in any material way. The day I met him, Ricky drove me around the few navigable parish roads in his van saved when his wife, fleeing for her life from the water, gunned it up to the top of a Mississippi River levee. The depth and breadth of destruction, particularly south in the fishing communities like Yscloskey, reminded me of bombed-out war zones I'd seen in Africa and the Middle East.

But as Ricky said to me, after a few days of thinking things over: a bayou guy—chaser of shrimp, master of tides, navigator by the stars; cooker of gumbo; a man whose father, grandfather, and generations of great-grandfathers lived and died in these ramparts building boats and harvesting the bounty of the sea—that guy wasn't moving to Arkansas or Mississippi or even to north Louisiana.

Ricky knows his roots. His Cajun ancestor, Gils Robin, settled in the St. Bernard lowlands sometime before 1776 as part of the Acadian Diaspora. The Robins intermarried into families of those Spanish pioneers, the Isleños, who began arriving in St. Bernard in 1777. That's coming up upon 250 years of families in the same place. Ricky is convinced that the seafood gumbo he cooks, chock full of shrimp and crabs pulled directly from his nets, comes from recipes going back centuries.

"We're staying put," Ricky told me.

And like tens of thousands of others, Ricky stayed: through the gutting and rebuilding of his Yscloskey home; through open-heart surgery; the sporadic overhauls of the *Li'l Rick*, his beloved shrimp boat; the calamity of the 2010 BP oil spill which, for a while, seemed an existential threat to his very livelihood as a shrimper and, indeed, to the equilibrium of the Pantry itself. Ricky pitched in, renting out the *Li'l Rick* as part of the massive, multibillion dollar oil-spill cleanup operation.

Hope these days has replaced despair. While the spill zone of the Gulf of Mexico hasn't fully recovered— the long-term effects on deep sea creatures like whales, sea turtles and dolphins are still unknown— other intertidal species like redfish, speckled trout, white and brown shrimp, blue crabs, and oysters have made a remarkable comeback, according to a 2015 report by the Harte Research Institute for Gulf of Mexico Studies at Texas A&M University.

Ricky Robin will vouch for that. Just go on his Facebook page these days and check out the iPhone videos of tons—yes, tons—of glistening shrimp that Ricky often pulls up in his trawl. Now, true, as he is constantly telling me, the shrimp price often sucks because of that very overabundance, but that's a different story. The point is this: His gumbo pot, once half empty, is now pretty much full all the time.

New Orleans is back, too, tucked in behind levees vastly improved from the sorry ones that failed under Katrina's onslaught. Tourism is up, the economy has seldom been better and, because tourism and the economy are thriving, the restaurant scene is lively and inventive, perhaps never more so in the city's storied culinary history.

I spent about four and a half months in and around New Orleans directly after Katrina and I literally saw it come back from the dead. Some people prophesied that it wouldn't; some even wondered if it *should* be resurrected. A Columbia University geophysicist, in a *Washington Post* essay a month after the August 2005 storm, wrote, "The direction of public discourse in the wake of Katrina goes like this: First we save lives and provide some basic assistance to the victims. Then we clean up New Orleans. And then we rebuild the city. Most will rightly agree on the first two. But should we rebuild New Orleans, ten feet below sea level, just so it can be wiped out again?"

That drew bristles and derision from the inhabitants of New Orleans and the Gumbo Belt at large. Did the *Washington Post* suggest San Francisco and Los Angeles be abandoned or relocated in the wake of devastating earthquakes in 1989 and 1994? Of course not.

And perhaps, unsurprisingly, in the vanguard of the city's recovery were some of New Orleans' chefs and restaurant owners—John Besh, Donald Link, the Brennans, among them—who understood how important it was to get the city eating again. They weren't just trying to save businesses they'd spent fortunes and years building, but they honestly wanted to help heal the soul of a place in deep mourning and uncertain what the next day would bring. Bringing back the food—real Nawlins food—would be a start.

You had to be there in those early days after landfall to understand what was at stake: 80 percent of New Orleans lying in a black lagoon of putrefying waters; no lights, drinking water, amenities. Dead people unrecovered in flooded houses. Shocked people trapped in the Superdome and the Convention Center with no actual timetable or good plan for evacuation. The French Quarter had fortuitously been spared flooding, but it was a ghost town, eerily dark at night. One bar, Johnny White's, had remained open through the storm and served warm beer by candlelight. Ice would be days in coming.

Everything else was dead. The storm came with Labor Day weekend looming, so all of the Quarter's restaurants and bars had loaded up with provisions. The post-Katrina weather turned unbearably hot. Thousands of pounds of shrimp, crabs, steak, and vegetables lay putrefying in commercial-sized refrigerators. Cops, National Guardsmen, and raw-ribbed stray dogs patrolled the streets. I would wander the Quarter with a flashlight, looking for other signs of life. You'd come upon an alley and hear a sound—the drone of a generator. It was cheering. Somebody was there. Maybe they'd stayed. Maybe they'd come back. But there was a human presence.

And then, on October 9, just six weeks after the storm, a miracle occurred. I was walking down Bourbon Street, amid the heat, flies, and festering mounds of garbage, past the people in white hazmat suits charged with decontaminating all the sad, dead restaurants, when I saw people gathered in a line. It was around lunchtime—normally joyous in New Orleans but not at this juncture. Since Katrina smashed in, everyone who had made it back to the Quarter, either to help out or to try to recover their homes, had been existing almost entirely on Kat Food—a post-Katrina diet of military MREs or Salvation Army food boxes.

It turned out that the line was in front of the Desire Oyster Bar. It was open, it had real Nawlins food. It had gumbo! In a town that takes its eating far more seriously than its politics, this was the best possible news. I joined the queue. The buffet was $21.00; the plates, knives, and forks plastic; the napkins paper, but so what. It included blackened prime rib; sautéed snapper topped with a savory but not overpowering crawfish sauce; and, the city's staple, red beans and rice with smoked sausage. The gumbo, meanwhile, was an exquisitely rich seafood gumbo made with shrimp and crab in a dark, chocolate-colored roux.

I went back for seconds. Then thirds. I returned the next day, gumbo as my beacon.

Gumbo was helping the city to come alive again.

Gumbo helped to save it.

While my long career in journalism has taken me far from Gumbo Belt and created a desire to spend at least part of my year in a big city—these days it's Chicago and before that New York, San Francisco, London, and Miami—this fight to save our coast remains personal to me. My brothers and some of my best friends in life still live there. I visit so often that some people are of the impression that I do live there. After a beer or two (or three), my accent returns. I *sound* like I live there.

And the pattern of these visits is always the same. After a day or two saying my obligatory hellos and sampling some good gumbo (A-Bear's Cafe is a favorite), I find myself in a boat speeding through the low country that my parents taught me to love, fishing pole in hand, camera slung around my neck. Catching fish is a bonus. Being out there is the payoff.

Most often I'm in the company of my youngest brother, Bob, who had what I considered to be, if not a dream job, a dream schedule. A registered nurse, he put in four ten-hour days a week at a local hospital and had three days off. Or, to be more succinct, he worked four and fished three, pretty much every week of the year weather permitting and owing to the fact that he is (a) a fishing fanatic and (b) has an indulgent wife.

Bob has a penchant for catching trophy speckled trout. And since he's out there pretty much all the time year-round, he knows what's biting and where. If Bob isn't catching fish that simply means the fishing sucks and you should just stay home. When I get to Louisiana, all I do is arrive at Bob's house and say, "Let's go." And off we go, most often to Lake Decade.

The lake is reachable from Bob's house on the outskirts of Houma by launching his dinged-up sixteen-foot aluminum johnboat at Canon's, a landing not much more than a mile up the bayou from our old place on Bayou Black. Twenty-five minutes later, zipping along the man-made channel called Minor's Canal, we're drifting the bank, blind-casting for specks, reds, and sometimes the occasional flounder.

Seen from the air, Lake Decade doesn't look all that impressive. It's a shallow, brown, brackish water body, angling southwest and maybe five miles long and half that wide, hemmed in by transitional marsh, its banks lined here and there with shell reefs. It also sits amid one of the places on the coast which has experienced some of the most serious wetland losses in recent decades. And yet, demonstrating the resilience of the system and how the Pantry is still amazingly full, it's also one of the most astonishing fish factories I've ever experienced. It's seasonally full of shrimp, crabs, and often giant schools of mullet, shad, and minnows that cruise its many shell reefs and tidal flats and thereby attract vast schools of game fish, speckled trout and reds particularly.

So there I am on a recent warm spring day, Bob manning the trolling motor at the bow and his best fishing buddy, Dr. Richard Brooke, a Houma pediatrician, in the middle seat as I cast off stern. Bob and the Doc, as they are known to their friends, carry on a good-natured rivalry and a running commentary as we float along.

Doc gets a hit and misses the fish.

"You suck, Doc," Bob says. "Who taught you to fish?"

Bob misses the next one. "A baby coulda caught that fish, Bob. What's wrong with you?"

You get the picture. They're Felix and Oscar of speckled trout fishing. I keep thinking they'll get a reality show one day.

On this day, fishing starts slow, and then explodes. Specks are everywhere. Maybe six drifts later, we stop counting after catching and releasing three hundred speckled trout. That's not a misprint. Most are "schoolies" in the two-pound range but a few weigh in at three and four pounds. Bob's taken some seven-plus-pound monsters out of here.

Tired of catching specks, we switch to top water baits and flog the banks for redfish that often prowl the shallows. This technique doesn't normally produce a lot of fish, but the fish it produces are always memorable. I'm slowly retrieving a Heddon Zara Spook lure when a red explodes on the bait with such ferocity that it actually rattles me. Ten minutes later, after a several line-ripping runs, I have a twelve-pounder in the net. We take its picture and let it go. My fish comes well after Bob and Doc have hooked up on several reds that size or bigger.

My brothers and I came here as kids with Dad, sometimes to fish, sometimes to duck hunt. I remember a beautiful, pristine, Indian summer day at low tide, shell reefs showing. Dad baited my hook with a piece of shrimp and cast it toward a small stream—what the Cajuns call a *trainasse*—coming out of the marsh. He handed me the rod and a redfish struck with such power that it almost jerked the rod from my hands.

I landed it—seven pounds of fury, my first "big" red. I was maybe ten years old and the happiest boy on earth.

We have to save the Pantry. Because I want to fish this place with my grandkids one day.

{ 16 }

THE GUMBO HIGHWAY AND GUMBO LIFE CONVERGE

The beauty of Gumbo Life is that the conviviality of it is portable, transferrable, and renewable.

After months on and off the Gumbo Highway, I'm taking a writing break. It's the fifth of July and we arrive at our sweet little log cabin on the shores of Little Tunk Pond, in the area known as Downeast Maine. My wife and I bought the cabin in 2014 when we still lived in New York City. The drive up from there was about eight hours. From our apartment in Chicago, it's a two-day slog.

But then, there you are, waking up the first morning to an azure sky, sun on the lake, loons calling, birds darting everywhere, the air sweetened in pine and cedar, the water a mirrored flat jewel catching the image of the rounded contours of Schoodic Mountain rising in evergreen splendor across the way.

I've come to our little slice of paradise with a mission. I've been inspired during my wanderings in the Gumbo Belt by just how creative people have become with their recipes. Again, I could never have imagined a gumbo finished off with foie gras. I want to go back and try the whelk gumbo recipe that Judge Timmy Ellender mentioned to me. I keep thinking somebody somewhere must be cooking a Tex-Mex gumbo, using chorizo and jalapeños instead of andouille and hot sauce, cumin and chili powder instead of thyme and filé. I make a note to try this one day but it's not the gumbo I want to cook here.

My inspiration comes about a week into our Maine sojourn from my pal Mark Robichaux, a fellow Cajun from Lecompte, Louisiana, who worked with me for years at the *Wall Street Journal* in New York. He grew up in the northern ramparts of the Gumbo Belt eating gumbo and hunting and fishing, as I did. He makes his home these days with his family in Stamford, Connecticut. I'm pretty sure he has the biggest gumbo pot and deep-fat fryer in all of Stamford (maybe all of Connecticut). He can deep-fry anything, and you'll go, "No, this can't be that good." He's got a jerky-making machine and does stuff with venison that I keep saying he should commercialize.

And if you put Cajuns anywhere near where they can fish, they will fish. So, for years while I still lived in Manhattan, we were partners in the *Bayou Belle*, a kitted-out nineteen-foot Key West fishing boat that we kept in Stamford Harbor and from which we chased striped bass and bluefish in Long Island Sound.

Since my arrival in Maine, Mark and I had been emailing back and forth. He has company coming and wonders whether I ran across a recipe on the Gumbo Highway that would be a showstopper. I send him Pat Mould's smoked-duck-and-andouille-sausage recipe, knowing Mark likes to cook with game. (He will cook the recipe to raves, but can't find duck so substitutes chicken.) Meanwhile, I want his advice because I want to buy a smoker to expand my cooking repertoire and Mark has owned several over the years. Here we do what we can't do in Chicago, which is grill outdoors almost every day, weather permitting: fish, chicken, sausage, all manner of veggies, asparagus, and bell peppers, in particular. I even grill the bacon for Sunday breakfast.

But I'm intrigued by smoking and the possibilities a smoker could add to my gumbo. In theory, on a chore day you could crank up the smoker, put on a whole plump chicken and let it cook slowly without having to bother with it too much. (The concept, actually, isn't all that different from gumbo chefs who make their roux in the oven.) Ditto with vegetables that could be eaten as side dishes or go into pastas or salads. People smoke cheeses on superlow heat, a process called cold smoking. I'm thinking I could get into that.

But what happens is that I get to the hardware stores in our "shopping town" of Ellsworth, thirty-five minutes away, and I'm paralyzed by the choices. Mark's advice finally leads me to the RiverGrille Cattleman 29", a wood-fired offset model in which the firebox is separate from the smoking chamber. I like the price: $129.00 plus tax, even though that's unassembled.

I get it home. Five hours later, on the hottest day of the Maine summer so far, I'm amid a sprawl of parts in the backyard, sweating like a Louisiana okra-picker in August, and still assembling the RiverGrille (uttering unprintable expletives and wondering if Klingons had written the instruction manual). But it finally comes together.

I'll need a few test runs of the RiverGrille but what I ultimately have in mind is a smoked-chicken-and-double-smoked-turkey sausage gumbo with proper homage to Chef Mould.

I start out conservatively. Chicken, good. Veggies, a mixed bag. The bell peppers are terrific, especially if you put them in pasta sauce. The eggplant, not so great, smoky but tough and stringy. It probably needed time in the oven before going in the smoker.

I then try salmon. "It looks and smells like smoked trout to me," says Lisa, who finds it overpowering. "Not my thing."

Not mine, either. But, no worries, Mom! Salmon will never find its way into my gumbo pot.

≋

Experimental gumbo requires confidence and willing guinea pigs.

It's about a month later and our Bostonian friends, Jim and Jane Levitt, are at Tunk, ensconced in their rambling log home just up the lake. Jim works in conservation and travels the globe lecturing on how to finance large-scale conservation projects; Jane has an active volunteer life. Their infatuation with this place is, if anything, even longer and deeper than ours. They love to hike, swim, kayak, boat, and eat well. Sometimes they feel like we feel—that it's just enough to *be* here.

They hold an annual event they call Lobsterpalooza which is kind of like a Cajun crawfish boil, except they serve the crawfish's giant first cousin. They'll steam up a couple of dozen lobsters acquired from a little lobster shack up on the highway called Tracey's. They spread the crustaceans out on a huge outdoor stone table and everyone just digs in. The Levitts have also installed an outdoor wood-fired pizza oven, out of which come creations you might expect to find in some out-of-the-way place in Tuscany. That's especially true when their son, Willie, a foodie who lives in New York City, is around and manning the fire.

These are my kind of people, Cajuns in spirit.

Their daughter Laura, just back from a college sojourn in Mexico, is visiting them, as is Jane's father, the indefatigable Bert Berkley, who lives in Kansas City. Bert will soon be turning ninety-three and remains active in his family's fourth-generation envelope business. After he leaves here, he's going off to fly-fish for salmon in Canada. Jane's sister, Janet, and her husband, Dan, are also in from Kansas City.

We're going to repay the Levitts' hospitality just as those prototypical Creoles did in New Orleans in 1764 by "giving a gombeau." I'll be serving my never-before-cooked recipe: smoked-chicken-and-double-smoked-sausage gumbo.

I buy five large boneless skinless chicken breasts and two pack-ages of Hillshire Farm smoked turkey sausage from Shaw's, our go-to supermarket in Ellsworth. Lisa won't eat pork or beef sausage (or pork or beef of any kind, making an exception for bacon), so I've been sub-bing turkey for a long time now. Of course, I'd prefer to use real Cajun pork andouille and I could order it from the website CajunGrocer.com. I've also found a supermarket brand, Aidells, made by a Northern Cal-ifornia company, that's not quite Louisiana andouille but it sails pretty close to the home-state variety. But I don't want to make a gumbo only I would eat.

I fire up the smoker, which I've placed next to my gas grill in a nook off the screened porch, with hickory chips. By this time, I know some tricks to get the fire going really smoky. I baste the breasts with a light sheen of olive oil and sprinkle on a little sea salt, freshly milled coarse black pepper, and garlic powder. I do nothing to the sausages except cut them into four twelve-inch links. I arrange everything on the smoker, close the lid, open the damper and let her smoke. I'm aiming for a temperature of about 160 degrees. About 190 degrees is considered ideal but I want lots of smoky flavor without overcooking the breasts.

I check in every thirty to forty-five minutes, but five hours later the breasts have browned up so beautifully that I want to call *Gourmet* magazine to come photograph them. (But since it is no longer pub-lished, I shoot the pictures instead.) The sausages have also taken on a deep, deep brown patina.

I tong everything onto a platter and head for the kitchen, where my standard "naked" gumbo awaits. I've hewed to my mother's basic recipe: flour-and-oil roux, chicken stock, the Trinity but with green, yellow, and red bell peppers for color, and a little fresh garlic for zest. To this I've added my spices: salt, black pepper, some Tony Chachere's Creole Seasoning, a dash of Tabasco and cayenne, plus quarter tea-spoons of thyme, oregano, and paprika.

I felt that with the smoky flavor I was trying to achieve, I needed a darker than normal roux to stand up to it. So, I'd kept my roux going until it was closer to deep chestnut brown than pecan. With my tri-color peppers floating on the surface, it's an attractive gumbo. I've now become a strong believer that with gumbos, visuals are important.

The biggest surprise, though, is when I slice into the chicken breasts on the cutting board. They are as succulent on the inside, with still a hint of pink, as they are browned on the outside. That's perfect. I'll cut the breasts into cubes. I'll get the naked gumbo up to simmer and ladle them in and they'll finish cooking in the gumbo but remain tender and plump.

And then, there's the aroma. I love smoke and these smell like they've just come out of Tennessee smokehouse. Ditto for the sausage, which have also plumped up nicely. I'll slice them thin and put a handful of slices in with the chicken to start imparting some smoky-sausage flavor. But I'll hold the big batch back until the gumbo is almost done. Otherwise, you risk overcooking the sausage.

At that moment, I think of my mom. If she were here she'd be very happy for she'd know I listened very carefully to her gumbo-making advice.

I can't wait to see how it all melds together.

The Levitt entourage comes in good spirits at the anointed time of six o'clock. It's a beautiful, balmy Maine summer evening. We dine on our screened porch. We pour wine and chat; it's help yourself to the gumbo, which sits on the kitchen stove next to the pot of rice I've cooked. There's sourdough bread and salad. An hour passes. Jim's on his third helping, me too. I can't help it if I like my own gumbo. My mother taught me that, as well. She liked to eat her own cooking.

We retire to the living room. Jim convinces me to pick up my guitar and play a few tunes. Wine, gumbo, and good fellowship will loosen a guy up. Moment of truth: The gumbo was way better than the performance. Still, what's important is that our guests leave full and happy, just like those Cajuns C. C. Robin saw in 1804 after they ate their sunrise bowls of gumbo. Two hundred and twelve years after one of its first mentions in print, gumbo is still making people feel good.

Even if I did cook it.

Thanksgiving arrives and we're back in Chicago. Our kids have flown in. Our eldest, Sara, and her husband, Iain Lake, have come from San Francisco; our younger daughter, Becca, from Austin, Texas. Given where they live, their busy lives, and the fact that air travel is such a drag, Lisa and I are overjoyed that they still want to hang out with us.

Sara, who took a magazine route into journalism, spent several years as a health and nutrition editor for *Self* magazine in New York City. Since moving to California three years ago, she's been involved in numerous web startups that in some fashion are trying to bring nutrition and fitness to the masses.

Iain works for the West Coast operations of a high-end art and antique shipping and storage business. If you live in L.A. but buy that Warhol at auction in New York, he's the guy who can get it packed up, insured, and shipped to you. He'll even hang it on your wall.

Becca is a kindergarten teacher who moved to Austin from the mall-lands of North Carolina a little more than a year ago, looking for a place with a somewhat livelier cultural and young people's scene. We're as thrilled as she is that she's found it there in that artsy, music-mad, food-mad, central Texas college town.

Sara and Iain have come toting the latest joy in their lives and ours, our first and (so far) only grandchild, Zoe Eileen Wells Lake. Zoe is now eighteen months old, walking, laughing, and saying a smattering of identifiable words while babbling on in some secret toddler language. Her facial expressions, as she toddler-talks some obviously serious point she's trying to make, crack us up. She's quite transformed from the tiny two-month-old we rocked to sleep when they visited us in Maine summer before last.

Among other things, I love to watch her eat. Such gusto! She's definitely my kin.

My girls want gumbo before they fly back home. Typically, I would make a turkey gumbo on the day after Thanksgiving with the leavings of the holiday bird. My mother did this and it's done all over the Gumbo Belt. But turkey dinner this year is at Lisa's sister's home and I'm not sure there will be leftovers. So the girls and I make a plan. I'll cook a chicken-and-turkey-sausage gumbo on Thanksgiving morning before we head out and we'll have it for dinner the next night. Even better, the girls want to help out. In 2012, when Lisa and I still lived in Manhattan, I gave Sara and Becca their first gumbo-cooking lesson. They seemed intrigued by the process but so far neither of them has cooked a solo gumbo.

The girls ran cross-country in high school and they continue to run today, as does Sara's husband, Iain. (In fact, they met at a running club in New York's Central Park.) They all rise early on Thanksgiving to run the annual Turkey Trot, an eight-kilometer race more or less along our lakeshore. I stay behind to do the gumbo prep and look after Zoe, who will be napping most of the time they're gone.

I'm hewing to my usual recipe with one tiny wrinkle. I'm going to use two types of sausage, the smoked-turkey that I typically use and a brand of chicken andouille that I discovered not too long ago at the Jewel supermarket where we shop. While not an honest substitute for authentic Cajun andouille, it nonetheless is pretty tasty. It's more peppery and smoky than the turkey sausage and I'm thinking it will help amp up the flavor a bit.

We gather in the kitchen around noon. Everything's ready. I have a stock pot simmering, using both skinless chicken thighs and a bit of store-bought bouillon stirred in and seasoned lightly with a bit of salt and pepper, a quarter stalk of celery, a bay leaf, and a chunk or two of the sausage.

The Trinity sits diced in two separate colanders, one for the onions, another for the celery and green and red bell peppers. I'm going to try a technique I observed in my gumbo travels, stirring the onions into the roux first and letting them brown before putting in the other veg-etables. Everyone who does that swears it gives gumbo a little more color and oomph.

I've measured out a cup of oil and a cup of flour and I find myself channeling my mother when I say, "First, we make our roux."

I take everything slow. I try to explain some of the intricacies; for example, how you know your oil is hot enough when it first begins to throw off just a hint of smoke. It's at that point when I stir in the flour and then usually turn the heat down to medium to make sure the roux doesn't run away from me and scorch.

"Ready?"

The girls nod.

I have Becca pour in the flour. It fulminates the way it should. I have Sara start to stir the roux with my wooden gumbo roux spoon, admonishing her not let any flour stick to the bottom. Becca later takes over the stirring. We keep watching the color mutate. I take a turn when Becca declares her arm is getting tired.

I laugh. "Who knew gumbo making was an aerobic sport," I say.

We stir and watch. About thirty minutes into the process, I like the color. "See, a nice deep shade of pecan. That's what you want. OK, now the onions."

Sara dumps them in and stirs like crazy. The pot squalls and sizzles, just like it should.

"We'll watch these until the onions start to brown," I tell them, "then we stir in the rest. You want everything to get coated with roux.

The funny thing that happens is that the moment you throw in the vegetables, your roux stops browning. The idea now, after all the vegetables are in, is to let them cook until they begin to caramelize and what I call 'cry' or 'sweat.' You'll see what I mean after a while."

Becca takes over the stirring. I always turn up the heat to high at this point. It gets the roux and the vegetables married more quickly. We stir on and off for about ten minutes and I have them take a good look.

"See what I mean by 'crying,'" I say. "There's a thin sheen of water on the vegetables and they've browned up and softened. We're ready for the stock."

Sara does the honors and Becca stirs everything together.

"The color will deepen a bit as we cook it more," I say. "But this is looking good. Now the chicken and just two or three slices of the sausage."

Though I've got thighs simmering in the stock, I've again been using mostly boneless chicken breasts, bowing to the tastes of Lisa and my girls. I've browned them in the oven but left them pink on the inside. They'll finish cooking in the gumbo.

Then I have them add the seasonings I've measured out and stir them all in. Our gumbo at this point is thicker than I want it to be and so we'll make some more stock from chicken bouillon cubes and add that after this has cooked for a bit.

About an hour into the process, we have a pot of gumbo, minus the sausage, that we're about to bring to a full boil. Some cooks I observed boil the heck out of their gumbos, particularly if they're cooking with things like duck or poule d'eau which require tenderizing. I don't. I bring my gumbo to a full boil for a couple of minutes and then ratchet it down to a very slow boil and then to a simmer.

"OK," I say. "We'll let this go for another 15 to 20 minutes, put in the sausage, bring it to a boil one more time, then shut it down and cover it. The sausage will plump up that way but not get overcooked and dried out. And since this is standing overnight in the fridge, we'll simmer it again tomorrow when we take it out for dinner."

We complete those steps and before shutting the gumbo off, we all take turns tasting it.

"Need anything?" I ask.

Our consensus is no. It's plenty salty and actually a little more peppery than my usual gumbo. I'm thinking this is because of the addition of the chicken andouille.

"And you know," I tell them, "that gumbo always tastes better the second day than the first. Some of the magic happens in the refrigerator."

The next evening, we have a full table for our team-cooked gumbo, which is how I like my gumbo suppers. Lisa's dad, Jim Newmark is here, as are her sisters, Debbie and Judy, and their significant others, Peter Norman and Tony Medici. Almost everyone at the table has eaten my gumbo before but this one is, of course, special because of Sara's and Becca's hand in the pot.

And for another reason as well.

There's someone at the table who's never eaten gumbo: Zoe.

I've tasted it again and it's good but I'm a little worried about the stronger-than-normal peppery kick. If anything, it's intensified overnight. I'm now regretting subbing that chicken andouille. Will it be too spicy for Zoe?

Her dad, Iain, does the honors, ladling the gumbo, and some tender chunks of the chicken, into her toddler bowl over rice. He offers her the first bite. She takes it, seeming a bit puzzled. Then she takes another bite and another. And then she wants the spoon herself.

Zoe Eileen Wells Lake demolishes that entire bowl of gumbo.

It's all Papa Ken can do to keep from crying with joy.

The kids fly home on Saturday. Lisa and I put away the inflatable bed, Zoe's books, Zoe's toys, Zoe's changing table, high chair, and portable crib. Order restored, though it feels a little deflating.

But then Sara texts me on Sunday.

"Dad, I'm gonna make gumbo!"

She wants some reminders of the recipe—proportions mostly—and the process and we text back and forth. I'm over the moon.

She texts again. "You'd be so proud! I'm using bone-in breasts (cooking in oven now) and making the stock with drumsticks."

That's my girl!

She's making her roux and worried she's scorched it. Seems her fire got too hot.

She texts me a picture of it. She's right. But before I can offer my opinion, she texts back: "I'm starting over."

She dumps it out and begins anew. It's the right move.

Later, she texts pictures of her new roux and her version of the naked gumbo, after marrying the Trinity and stock but before adding the chicken.

"Looks beautiful," I text back. And it does.

Sara, Iain, and Miss Zoe dine on Sara's first solo gumbo that evening. I text to see how it was.

She texts me back and says what I always said to my mother when I reported on the gumbos I'd cooked from afar: "It's OK but not as good as yours."

I'm betting it probably was as good, but it's a lovely answer and one that makes her dad smile.

My parents are gone. Dad died in 2000 while mowing his lawn—an Old Marine still trying to do his duty. Bonnie lost her long battle with emphysema in 1995. I can't remember the last gumbo she cooked for me, but I'll never forget the first one I cooked at her side when I drove home from graduate school.

Maybe Sara and Becca will remember this Thanksgiving Day

gumbo similarly. And maybe they will remind Zoe one day of how she gobbled it down so enthusiastically.

Maybe it will be on that day, down the road in a kitchen who knows where, when Sara says to Zoe: "First, cher, you make a roux."

RECIPES

BONNIE'S CLASSIC BONE-IN CHICKEN-AND-SAUSAGE GUMBO

This is my mother's original recipe.

SERVES 8 TO 10

2 pounds smoked sausage links, preferably Cajun andouille

Two 2½- to 3-pound hens

Salt to taste

Black pepper to taste

2 tablespoons Tony Chachere's Original Creole Seasoning

1 cup vegetable or olive oil

1 cup flour

2 large onions, chopped

5 bell peppers, chopped coarsely

5 celery stalks, chopped

2 garlic cloves, minced

2 quarts chicken stock

¼ teaspoon dried thyme
¼ teaspoon paprika
½ teaspoon Tabasco Sauce
1 bay leaf
About 1 tablespoon filé powder
Hot white rice for serving

1. Cut the sausage into half-inch slices. Set aside.

2. Cut each chicken into eight pieces, removing the wings, neck, and gizzard. Make a stock by placing the wings, necks, and gizzards in an 8-quart stock pot with 6 quarts water. Bring to a boil. Season with salt, pepper, and 1 tablespoon of the Creole Seasoning. Reduce the heat and add four to six slices of the sausage for flavor, Simmer for about 1 hour.

3. Heat 2 tablespoons of the oil in a skillet. In the hot oil, brown the thighs, breasts, and drumsticks. Set them aside on a separate plate.

4. Make a roux in a 6-quart saucepan with the flour and the remaining oil, bringing it to a deep chestnut brown. Add the onions, bell pepper, celery, and garlic, and stir briskly until caramelized, about 15 minutes. Pour in the chicken stock through a strainer, removing the wings, necks, gizzards, and sausage. Bring to a boil and then reduce to a simmer.

5. Add the browned chicken.

6. Add the remaining 1 tablespoon of Creole Seasoning, thyme, paprika, and Tabasco.

7. Cook for at least 45 minutes on low boil.

8. Add the remaining sausage and bay leaf. Bring to a full boil, then turn off heat, and cover the pot.

9. Let the gumbo sit for at least 1 hour.

10. Add filé powder to taste and serve over white rice.

Courtesy of the author.

LEAH CHASE'S GUMBO Z'HERBES

Leah Chase, the iconic Creole chef and mainstay of Dooky Chase's Restaurant, grew up in Madisonville, Louisiana, across Lake Pontchartrain from New Orleans. "Green gumbo," as gumbo z'herbes is also known, was a Lenten mainstay in her family. The dish—a gumbo blowout before the start of Lent— was cooked on Holy Thursday and laded up with all manner of meat that could be consumed before fasting began on Good Friday. This recipe is a slightly amended post–Katrina version that Leah cooked up in 2013 with Sara Roahen of the Southern Foodways Alliance.

SERVES 12

> 2 ham shanks
>
> 1 gallon water
>
> 6 to 8 pounds of 7 to 11 mixed greens of your choice (collard, mustard, turnip, spinach, cabbage, carrot tops, beet tops, arugula, parsley, green onions, watercress, romaine, curly endive, kale, radish tops, and/or pepper grass)
>
> 3 medium onions, roughly chopped
>
> 8 garlic cloves, peeled
>
> 2 pounds fresh hot sausage
>
> 1 pound chicken drumettes
>
> 1 pound andouille sausage, cut into ½-inch slices
>
> 1 pound smoked pork sausage, cut into ½-inch slices
>
> 1 pound beef stew meat, cut into ½-inch pieces
>
> 8 ounces ham, cut into ½-inch pieces
>
> 1 cup flour
>
> Vegetable oil as needed
>
> 3 teaspoons dried thyme
>
> 2 teaspoons cayenne pepper
>
> 3 bay leaves

2 teaspoons salt

½ teaspoons filé powder (optional)

Hot white rice for serving

1. Place the ham shanks and water in a large pot. Bring to a boil over high heat, reduce the heat to medium-low, and let simmer until needed.

2. Wash all of the greens thoroughly in salted water, being sure to remove any grit, discolored outer leaves, and tough stems. Rinse in a bath of fresh water. (A double sink works well for this.) Drain the greens in a colander. Place the greens, onion, and garlic in a very large stockpot and cover with water. (If all of the vegetables don't fit in the pot, cook them in batches, using the same cooking liquid for each batch.) Bring to a boil, reduce the heat, and simmer until the greens are very tender, about 45 minutes. Use a slotted spoon to transfer the cooked greens into a large bowl and let cool for a few minutes. Pour the cooking liquid into a second large bowl and set it aside. Working in batches, puree the greens in a food processor or by running them through a meat grinder. Use a little cooking liquid to loosen the puree, if needed. Transfer the pureed greens into a large bowl and set aside.

3. Cook the fresh hot sausage in a large skillet over medium heat to render the fat and moisture, breaking up the sausage with the side of a spoon. Transfer the sausage with a slotted spoon to a large bowl and set aside. Brown the chicken in the rendered sausage fat over medium-high heat and transfer it with a slotted spoon to the bowl with the cooked sausage. (The chicken will cook more later, so it does not need to be fully cooked at this point.) Set the skillet and the drippings aside.

4. Remove the ham shanks from their cooking liquid, reserving the liquid to use as stock. When cool enough to handle, pull the meat from the bones. Chop the meat into bite-size pieces and add it

to the bowl with the sausage and chicken. Discard the bones and the fat. Pour the ham stock into a large bowl and set it aside.

5. Return the vegetable puree to the large stock pot. Add the hot sausage, chicken, andouille sausage, smoked pork sausage, ham shank meat, beef stew meat, and chopped ham. (If it doesn't all fit in one pot, divide it between two pots.) Cover with equal parts of the ham stock and greens cooking liquid and bring to a simmer over medium-high heat.

6. To make the roux, place the skillet containing the hot sausage pan drippings over medium-high heat. Sprinkle the flour over the drippings and stir well with a wooden spoon. If the mixture is dry and crumbly, stir in enough vegetable oil to make a smooth, thick paste. Cook, stirring constantly, slowly, and intently until the roux turns light brown. (This isn't a dark roux, but the flour should be cooked.) Drop tablespoons of roux into the simmering gumbo, stirring well after each addition.

7. Stir in the thyme, cayenne, bay leaves, and salt. Simmer the gumbo until the stew meat is tender and the chicken is cooked through, about 1 hour. Stir often to prevent scorching. If the gumbo gets too thick to stir, add more stock or water.

8. Slowly add the filé at the end of cooking, if using. (It will lump if you don't stir it carefully.) Serve hot over hot white rice.

Courtesy of the Southern Foodways Alliance from *The Southern Foodways Alliance Community Cookbook* (UGA Press 2010, edited by Sara Roahen and John T. Edge).

SENATOR ALLEN ELLENDER'S
SHRIMP AND CRAB GUMBO

Born in the small Cajun hamlet of Montegut, Louisiana, Allen J. Ellender went on to a long career in the U.S. Senate, rising to the Senate's president pro-tempore—putting him third in line for the presidency. Ellender (some say with an assist from a longtime secretary) cooked this dish in Washington to the delight of presidents, senatorial colleagues, and political bigwigs of all stripes, and in this way did his part to further the Gumbo Diaspora.

SERVES 4 TO 6

7 tablespoons fat (vegetable oil or smoked bacon fat)

1 rounded tablespoon flour

2 pounds onions, chopped fine

3 celery stalks, chopped fine

1 medium bell pepper, chopped fine

Zest of 1 lemon

1 lemon (same as used for the zest), white membrane removed and
lemon cut in pieces

3 garlic cloves, minced

Dash of dried thyme

2 bay leaves

Dash of Tabasco Sauce

Dash of Worcestershire sauce

Dash of McCormick Season-All Seasoned Salt

Salt to taste

2½ pounds fresh okra

3 pounds peeled shrimp tails

1 pound crabmeat

1 pint oysters

Hot white rice for serving

Chopped parsley for garnishing

Chopped green onions for garnishing

1. Heat 5 tablespoons of the fat in a large, heavy-bottomed saucepan over medium-high heat. Add the flour, stirring constantly with a wire whisk, until a dark brown roux is achieved. Add the onions, celery, and bell pepper, and sauté until wilted. Add the lemon zest and pieces, garlic, thyme, bay leaves, Tabasco, Worcestershire, Seasoned Salt, and salt to the pan, reduce the heat, and simmer for at least 45 minutes.

2. Cut the okra into small pieces, combine with the remaining 2 tablespoons of fat, and cook slowly in a small pot until the okra is no longer stringy. Stir to prevent scorching or browning, add to the gumbo mixture, and cook for at least 20 minutes.

3. Add the shrimp tails and crabmeat, cook for 10 minutes, then add the oysters.

4. Add water to create a soupy consistency. Bring the mixture to a boil and cook for 20 minutes. Serve over rice with parsley and chopped green onions.

Courtesy of the Senator Allen J. Ellender Archives at Nicholls State University.

JOHN FOLSE'S DEATH BY GUMBO

Chef Folse is among Louisiana's most creative chefs and he knows his gumbo. I chose this recipe for its use of an unusual ingredient—quail—and for its homage to Chef's roots in the River Parishes where generations of homegrown gumbo cooks have incorporated all manner of game into their recipes.

Chef's note: This gumbo was created for Craig Claiborne of the New York Times. *When he asked me to come to his home on Long Island to create a special dinner depicting the evolution of Cajun and Creole cuisine, I knew this unusual dish would be the perfect choice.*

INGREDIENTS FOR QUAIL:

12 boneless Bobwhite quail

Salt and cracked black pepper to taste

Granulated garlic to taste

1½ cups cooked white rice

1 teaspoon filé powder

2 tablespoons chopped parsley

12 (⅛-inch) slices andouille

12 oysters poached in their own liquid

INGREDIENTS FOR GUMBO:

12 stuffed and seasoned Bobwhite quail

1 cup vegetable oil

1½ cups flour

2 cups diced onions

2 cups diced celery

1 cup diced bell peppers

¼ cup minced garlic

1 cup sliced mushrooms

½ cup sliced tasso

3 quarts chicken stock

1 teaspoon thyme
Salt and cracked black pepper to taste
Granulated garlic to taste
1 cup sliced green onions
1 cup chopped parsley

In a 2-gallon stockpot, heat oil over medium-high heat. Whisk in flour, stirring constantly until a golden-brown roux is achieved. Add onions, celery, bell peppers, and minced garlic. Sauté 3–5 minutes or until vegetables are wilted. Stir in mushrooms and tasso. Cook an additional 3 minutes then add chicken stock, one ladle at a time, stirring constantly. Stir in thyme, bring to a rolling boil, reduce to simmer and cook 30 minutes. Season to taste using salt, pepper, and granulated garlic. Place stuffed quail into gumbo and allow to simmer 30 minutes. When quail are tender and legs separate from body easily, remove birds to a platter and keep warm. Strain all seasonings from gumbo through a fine sieve and reserve gumbo liquid. Return stock to pot, add quail, green onions, and parsley then bring to a low boil. To serve, place 1 quail in center of each soup bowl and cover with gumbo.

> **METHOD FOR QUAIL:** Although it is best to use boneless quail for this recipe, you may also use bone-in birds if boneless is not available. Season birds inside and out using salt, cracked black pepper, and granulated garlic. Season cooked white rice to taste with salt, pepper, granulated garlic, filé powder, and chopped parsley. Stuff cavity of each quail with 1 tablespoon rice mixture, 1 slice andouille, 1 oyster, and a second tablespoon of rice mixture. Continue this process until all birds have been stuffed. Cover with plastic wrap and set aside.

Courtesy of Chef John Folse.

PEG AND BEV FREEMAN'S
POULE D'EAU AND OYSTER GUMBO

Most readers outside the Gumbo Belt are unlikely to have access to fresh coots (poules d'eau) for their gumbos (or an inclination to cook such a gumbo even if they did). But I felt it was important to document this recipe as a matter of historical and cultural significance as the number of Cajun and Creole cooks who continue to cook it are dwindling.

SERVES 6 TO 8

1 cup vegetable oil
1 cup flour
3 large onions, diced
8 poules d'eau dressed, plus gizzards
Salt
Black pepper
Tony Chachere's Original Creole Seasoning
4 garlic cloves, minced
8 green onion tops, chopped
1 quart fresh oysters, shucked
3 sprigs fresh parsley, chopped
Hot white rice for serving

1. In an 8-quart saucepan, make a dark brown roux with the oil and flour. Add the onion and stir until caramelized. Remove the saucepan from the heat and set aside.

2. Put a little oil in a skillet and brown the poules d'eau and gizzards. Transfer to an 8-quart saucepan, add 4 quarts water, salt, pepper, and Tony Chachere's Original Creole Seasoning to taste. Simmer, stirring occasionally, for at least two hours, until the birds are ten-

der and the mixture has cooked down to a dark, almost chocolate brown.

3. Reheat the roux over medium heat and pour it directly into the poule d'eau pot, stirring to combine. Bring the pot to a low boil and reduce the heat to medium. After about 15 minutes, stir in the garlic. Cook for 15 minutes, stir in the green onion, and bring to a low boil again. Reduce the heat to medium and cook for 15 minutes. Add the oysters and parsley and simmer for 45 minutes. Serve over white rice.

Courtesy of Carla Jane Freeman, the Freemans' daughter.

GOMBO AUX CRABES (ROUXLESS CRAB GUMBO)

When the Picayune—*now the New Orleans* Times-Picayune—*published this exhaustive compendium of Creole cooking in 1901, it noted that the recipes were those collected from both the white owners of households and the black Creole cooks that often served in the kitchens. Some of these recipes could date back "nearly two hundred years" to the very founding of the Louisiana colony. Of the nine gumbo recipes it includes, only two—shrimp gumbo and oyster gumbo—were made with a roux. That's an indication that early Creole/New Orleans gumbos were mostly rouxless and took their cue from the rouxless African okra stews, recipes that were brought orally by West Africans, who were the majority of the slaves in the Louisiana colony.*

SERVES 4 TO 6

1 dozen hard-shell or soft-shell crabs
Salt
Black pepper
1 tablespoon lard or 2 level tablespoons butter
6 large tomatoes, skinned and juice reserved
1 onion, chopped
1 sprig fresh thyme or parsley
2 pints okra (about 50), sliced thin
1 bay leaf, chopped finely
½ hot red pepper, without the seeds
Cayenne pepper to taste
Hot white rice for serving

According to the introduction to this recipe, "This is a great fast-day or *maigre* dish with the Creoles. Hard- or soft-shell crabs may be used, though more frequently the former, as they are always procurable and far cheaper than the latter article, which is considered a luxury. Crabs are always sold alive."

1. Scald the hard-shell crabs and clean, "taking off the dead man's fingers" and the spongy substances and being careful to remove the sandbags on the underpart. Cut off the claws, crack and cut the body of the crab in quarters, and season with salt and pepper.

2. Put the lard into the pot, heat over medium-high heat, and when hot, throw in the crab bodies and claws. Cover closely, cook for 5 to 10 minutes, and add the skinned tomatoes, chopped onion, and thyme or parsley, stirring occasionally to prevent scorching. Cook for 5 minutes and add the okra. When the okra is well browned, without the semblance of scorching, add the bay leaf, and the juice from the tomatoes. Pour over about 2½ quarts boiling water, add the hot pepper, reduce the heat to low, and let it simmer well for about 1 hour. When nearly ready to serve, season according to taste with cayenne and salt; pour into a tureen and serve with boiled rice.

From *The Picayune Creole Cook Book* (1901).
Courtesy of the American Antiquarian Society.

LI'L DIZZY'S CAFE'S CREOLE GUMBO

This "everything-but-the-kitchen sink" Creole gumbo breaks all of my mother's rules about not mixing meat and seafood in gumbo, and the taste is mind-bogglingly good. Wayne Baquet Sr., founder and owner of Li'l Dizzy's in New Orleans' historic Treme District, says he's refined the recipe from one passed down to him by his father, Eddie Baquet, who himself presided for years over one of the city's great neighborhood Creole eateries.

SERVES 10 TO 12

1¼ pounds seasoning ham

1¼ pounds smoked sausage

½ pound hot sausage

⅔ cup vegetable oil

2 cups chopped onion

1½ pounds chicken pieces

1½ pounds peeled shrimp

¼ cup chopped garlic

3 green onions, chopped

½ green bell pepper, chopped

2 teaspoons dried thyme

5 bay leaves

4 to 5 tablespoons flour

10 cups water

Salt

Black pepper

6 to 8 gumbo crabs

1 dozen oysters

Filé powder to taste

Hot white rice for serving

1. Cube the ham and slice the smoked and hot sausages. Heat the oil in an 8- to 10-quart pot. Add the ham to brown.

2. Add the onion and cook until tender. Add the chicken and all the sausage, and brown. Add the shrimp and the garlic, green onions, bell pepper, thyme, and bay leaves, and cook for 5 minutes.

3. Sprinkle the flour into the pot and stir well to combine.

4. Add the water and bring to a simmer. Add salt and pepper to taste.

5. Add the gumbo crabs and cook over low to medium fire for about 45 minutes. Add the oysters and cook for 5 minutes. Turn off the heat.

6. Add filé powder to taste and stir it into the gumbo. Serve over hot rice.

Courtesy of Wayne Baquet Sr.

MAINE LOBSTER AND ANDOUILLE ROUXLESS GUMBO

When my brother, Pershing Wells, and his wife, April White Wells, visited us in Maine in September 2017, the weather had turned fall–like, perfect for gumbo. We wanted to cook an experimental gumbo based on April's rouxless gumbo method and, being in Maine, of course we decided it had to be lobster! Having never cooked a lobster gumbo, we did a lot of improvising. But our four lobsters produced less meat than we anticipated and, with company coming, we needed to add andouille. It was the right move; the smoky sausage flavor completely complemented the sweetish taste of the lobster, giving the gumbo great balance and a signature taste of its own.

SERVES 8 TO 10

4 large steamed lobsters

Salt and pepper to taste

4 tablespoons vegetable oil

Two 8-ounce cans Rotel tomatoes (or equivalent)

8 large onions, chopped

4 large bell peppers, chopped

½ celery stalk, chopped

About 2 tablespoons of garlic salt

About 2 tablespoons of Tony Chachere's Original Creole Seasoning

2 pounds cut okra (frozen can be substituted for fresh)

Two 12-ounce packages Aidells Organic Cajun Style Andouille Smoked
Chicken Sausage (or equivalent), cut into ½-inch pieces

Hot white rice for serving

1. To make the seafood stock, pick the lobsters, setting aside all the meat. Preserve the head and shells, and place them in an 8-quart stockpot. Fill it two-thirds with water, season with salt and pepper, bring to a boil, and lower the heat to a simmer.

2. In another 8-quart stockpot heat the oil over medium heat. Add 1 can of the tomatoes and the onion, bell pepper, and celery so that they fill up three-quarters of the pot. Season lightly with garlic salt and Creole Seasoning. Cook over medium heat, stirring constantly, until the veggies reach a deep chocolate color and are reduced to a 1½-inch "paste" that covers the bottom of the pot. (This is a vital step of the recipe and can take 45 to 60 minutes.) Occasionally add a few tablespoons of water to prevent the mixture from sticking.

3. Put the okra in another pot together with the second can of tomatoes. Add them to the veggie paste. Continue to stir and cook for 5 to 10 minutes.

4. Add the lobster meat and the sausage, and cook for 10 minutes, stirring often. Bring to a boil, reduce the heat to a simmer, and cook for 30 minutes. Serve over white rice.

Courtesy of the author and April White Wells and Pershing Wells.

PAT MOULD'S SMOKED WILD DUCK-AND-ANDOUILLE GUMBO

Lafayette, Louisiana–native Pat Mould invented this recipe when he was cooking for that city's popular Southern- and Cajun-influenced restaurant, Charley G's, which specializes in wood-fire grilled beef and fresh Louisiana seafood. Mould, a duck hunter who spent considerable time at some of the hunting camps that dot the southwest Louisiana wetlands, told me he developed the dish in part to honor the long gumbo-cooking traditions that come out of those camps.

Here's the recipe as sent to me by Chef Mould: The creative twist on this recipe is to smoke the ducks prior to adding them to the gumbo. At the time I did this it hadn't been done before, unusual considering how much we smoke meat in Louisiana. If you don't have a hunter in the family, don't worry. I use a domesticated duck for this recipe.

Smoking meats is not as difficult as one might imagine. You can intensify the smoky flavor of any dish by making a stock out of the smoked meat bones, as I have done in this dish.

SERVES 8

One 5- to 7-pound duckling

3 tablespoons Pat's Cajun Seasoning (see recipe below)

¾ gallon Smoked Duck Stock (see recipe below)

1 cup dark roux

1 pound smoked andouille sausage, cut in ½ inch-cubes

1 cup chopped onion

½ cup chopped celery

½ cup chopped green bell pepper

1 tablespoon minced garlic

1 tablespoon Worcestershire sauce

2 teaspoons hot sauce

1 teaspoon salt

½ cup chopped green onion

¼ cup minced parsley

4 cups hot white rice for serving

1. Season the duckling with 1 tablespoon Pat's Cajun Seasoning and smoke in a conventional smoker. Allow the duck to cool, remove the bones, and reserve the meat, discarding any fat and reserving the bones for stock. Dice the meat and set aside.

2. Place the smoked duck stock in a large saucepot and bring to a boil. Add the dark roux, lower the heat, and simmer for 30 minutes.

3. Add the smoked andouille, onion, celery, bell pepper, garlic, the remaining 2 tablespoons of Pat's Cajun Seasoning, the Worcestershire sauce, hot sauce, and salt. Simmer for 30 minutes.

4. Add the diced duck meat and simmer for 15 minutes.

5. Stir in the green onion and parsley.

6. Divide the rice among 8 large bowls and serve the gumbo over it.

PAT'S CAJUN SEASONING: Combine 3 cups salt, ½ cup cayenne pepper, ½ cup paprika, ½ cup granulated garlic, ½ cup granulated onion, and ¼ cup black pepper. Keep in an airtight container.

SMOKED DUCK STOCK: Cover the smoked duck bones with 1½ gallons water. Add the end pieces from the onion, celery, and bell pepper, and bring to a boil. Reduce the heat and simmer for 1½ hours. Strain out the solids and reserve the stock. This can be done the day before cooking the gumbo. After the stock is chilled, skim off the fat that rises to the surface.

Courtesy of Chef Pat Mould.

MR. B'S BISTRO GUMBO YA-YA

People constantly ask me if I had a favorite gumbo after spending two years researching this book and sampling about one hundred restaurant and home-cooked gumbos. I had at least ten gumbos that were over the moon, but this one has stuck with me. When I sampled it at the bar of Mr. B's in the New Orleans French Quarter, I sent this note to myself: "The most beautiful gumbo so far with an intense, almost mahogany dark roux with a medium thick consistency. Liberal amounts of andouille and chicken float in the succulent broth. The aroma is deliciously smoky with hints of pepper."

Mr. B's credits the gumbo to Jimmy Smith, a former chef who worked there and "who grew up eating it in Cajun country. Its name is said to come from women who would cook the gumbo all day long while talking, or "ya-ya-ing." In my research, I found two alternate explanations for the "ya-ya" appendage. Some gumbo people say it's a Creole designation for "your momma's gumbo." But some culinary historians say "ya-ya" is an African dialect term for rice, so Gumbo Ya-Ya is gumbo served over rice.

This recipe makes a lot of gumbo, so you'll have enough for a big party or you can freeze some for later.

MAKES 6 QUARTS

  1 pound (4 sticks) unsalted butter

  3 cups flour

  2 red bell peppers, diced

  2 green bell peppers, diced

  2 medium onions, diced

  2 celery stalks, diced

  1¼ gallons (20 cups) chicken stock

  1 pound andouille sausage, cut into ¼-inch slices

  2 tablespoons Mr. B's Creole Seasoning (see recipe below)

  2 tablespoons kosher salt plus more to taste

  1 teaspoon ground black pepper

1 teaspoon hot red pepper flakes

1 teaspoon chili powder

1 teaspoon dried thyme

1 tablespoon minced garlic

2 bay leaves

One 3½-pound chicken, roasted and boned

Hot sauce to taste

Hot white rice for serving

1. Melt the butter in a 12-quart stockpot over low heat. Gradually add 1 cup of the flour, stirring constantly with a wooden spoon, and cook for 30 seconds. Add another cup of the flour and stir constantly for 30 seconds. Add the remaining cup of flour and stir constantly for 30 seconds. Continue to cook the roux, stirring constantly, until it is the color of dark mahogany, 45 to 60 minutes.

2. Add the red and green bell pepper and stir constantly for 30 seconds. Add the onion and celery and stir constantly for 30 seconds. Gradually add the stock to the roux, stirring constantly with a wooden spoon to prevent lumps.

3. Add the andouille, Creole Seasoning, salt, black pepper, red pepper flakes, chili powder, thyme, garlic, and bay leaves, and bring to a boil. Simmer the gumbo, uncovered, for 45 minutes, skimming off any fat and stirring occasionally.

4. Add the chicken and simmer for 15 minutes. Adjust the seasoning with salt and hot sauce. Serve over rice.

MR. B'S CREOLE SEASONING: Combine 1½ cups paprika, ¾ cup ground black pepper, ½ cup kosher salt, ⅓ cup granulated garlic, ⅓ cup dried thyme, ⅓ cup dried oregano, ⅓ cup dried basil, ¼ cup granulated onion, ¼ cup cayenne. Keep in an airtight container.

Courtesy of Mr. B's Bistro's website.

ACKNOWLEDGMENTS

It took a gumbo of family and friends, editors, and advisors to make this book possible and I'm grateful to them all. Especially:

To my Louisiana family: Brother Bill for an interesting gumbo excursion in Geismar, Louisiana.; to the Houma branch, Brother Bob Wells and wife, Mandy, Brother Chris Wells and his significant other, Carla Jane Freeman, and Brother Persh and his wife, April. They variously provided me with lodging, cooked great meals (including gumbos), took me fishing, and introduced me to gumbo-cooking friends. And to Chris and Carla Jane, in particular, for setting up that wonderful session with Carla Jane's poule d'eau gumbo–cooking parents, Peg and Bev Freeman. Peg and Bev have both passed away since that interview and I'm honored to have recorded their gifts for posterity.

To my New Orleans friends, Virginia Miller and Bruce Wallis; Roy Blount Jr. and Joan Griswold; and John Pearce for their incalculable hospitality while in that fair and delicious city.

To my cousins, Thad and Ellie Toups; my old and dear friends, Chris Cheramie Knobloch and Jimmy Knobloch; and my mentor, Al

Delahaye, all in Thibodaux, who shared their gumbos and gumbo enthusiasm, and to Al for his journalistic feedback.

To my lifelong friends, Steve and Cherry Fisher May, in Lafayette (since removed to New Orleans), who put me up and put up with me as the houseguest who seemed to have moved in with no intention of leaving.

To Judy Williams in Shreveport and my former *Wall Street Journal* colleague Tom Herman in New York City for providential introductions.

To my brother from another mother, Mark Robichaux, for his help and feedback.

To Monique Verdin in St. Bernard Parish for inviting me to gumbo with Matine "Maw-Maw" Verdin to share their gumbos and stories. Matine, one hundred years old at the time of that interview, passed away at one hundred and one in April 2016—one of the most beautiful people I've ever met.

To Dr. Chris Cenac in Houma, gifted surgeon and author-historian, who introduced me to another wonderful cast of poule d'eau gumbo–cooking characters and inspired the chapter on "The Meaning of T-Man."

To the chefs, restaurateurs, raconteurs, and gumbo aficionados and historians who opened their doors to me, most notably Ti Martin, Lally Brennan and Tory McPhail at Commander's Palace; John Folse whose gumbo empire spans much of the Gumbo Belt; Wayne Baquet Sr. of Li'l Dizzy's; Paul Miller of K-Paul's Louisiana Kitchen; Marcelle Bienvenu and Randy Cheramie of the Chef John Folse Culinary Institute; Patrick Singley of Gautreau's; Chef Pat Mould whose smoked-duck-and-andouille gumbo provided inspiration; Acadian historian and folklorist, Barry Jean Ancelet, and the African-and-Creole food historian, Jessica Harris. I also owe a debt to McIlhenny Company historian Shane Bernard for his heads-up on the Gwendolyn Midlo Hall gumbo discovery and to Dr. Midlo Hall for sharing her discovery in rich detail.

To Hollis Heimboch, who originally gave me the idea that this could actually be a book; to Maria Guarnaschelli, who signed it up at Norton; and to Melanie Tortoroli, who so ably took over the editing duties there.

To my agent, Carrie Hannigan, who takes care of all the details.

And last, and certainly not least, to my wife, Lisa, and daughters, Sara and Becca—my inspirations for gumbo, literature, and life.

NOTES ON SOURCES

This book is heavily autobiographical and where I draw from memory, these memories are mine and mine alone. While I accept the imprecision of memory, I present these as my best and honest recollection of events without embellishment. Whatever else I was as a child, I was observant. I loved stories and listened carefully. My parents and grandparents were avid, even vivid, storytellers and nothing pleased me more than to sit and absorb my family's history through the stories they told.

Readers will note the granular detail of my father's Arkansas childhood, move to Louisiana, and experiences during World War II (and his early fascination with gumbo and the people who cooked it). This comes in part from listening carefully but also from a single-spaced, one-hundred-forty-page memoir my dad left behind. This book came about because in 1987, as a reporter in the San Francisco bureau of the *Wall Street Journal*, I was sent on assignment to Guam, where my father had landed in World War II with G Company of the 2nd Marine Division. Before I flew off, I called him to get details of exactly where he had come ashore so I could walk the very beach he had occupied.

When I saw it, I couldn't understand how anyone had survived. The Marines had waded ashore at low tide across a broad coral reef while the Japanese were ensconced on cliffs above with mortars and machine guns. Back in San Francisco, I called Dad and said, "You've got to write this down or it will be lost." Though never published, his memoir is titled, "The Right Place at the Right Time."

Much of *Gumbo Life* is based on original reporting. From my home base in Chicago, I made five lengthy trips to the Gumbo Belt over a roughly two-year period to conduct more than eighty interviews, rummage through archives and sample a lot of gumbo. I dined in sixty separate restaurants spread across fifteen South Louisiana cities as a way of capturing a representative cross-section of Gumbo Belt restaurant cooking. Lots of Gumbo Belt friends and relatives invited me to eat gumbo in their homes. All told, I probably consumed one hundred gumbos during the reporting of this book.

I cite a number of useful websites below, but one whose archives I spent much time browsing is the nonprofit Oxford, Mississippi–based Southern Foodways Alliance, whose interviews with important Louisiana chefs and restaurateurs proved hugely helpful.

In the notes on sources that follow, I have omitted chapters that reflect wholly original reporting.

Preface

C. C. Robin's observations come from his memoir, *Voyage to Louisiana 1803–1805*, starting on page 115.

One of the first mentions of Midlo Hall's discovery can be found here on the blog of McIlhenny Co. historian Shane Bernard: http://bayoutechedispatches.blogspot .com/2011/10/gumbo-in-1764.html.

2. Academic Gumbo

Further explication of Chef Folse's view of the theory of the seven nations can be found in the foreword of the thirteenth edition of his *Encyclopedia of Cajun and Creole Cuisine*, and here: http://revolutionnola blogspot.com/2010/12/seven-nations-defining-creole.html.

Lolis Eric Elie's essay, "The Origin Myth of New Orleans Cuisine," published in *Oxford American*, can be found here: https://www.oxfordamerican.org/magazine/ item/206-lolis-eric-elie-explores-the-origin-myth-of-new-orleans-cuisine.

The preface to *The Picayune Creole Cook Book* can be found on page 5 of the first edition.

I found useful data on the timeline of Louisiana slavery during a visit to Whitney Planation, an antebellum home in Wallace, Louisiana, which in 2014 opened its doors as the only Louisiana plantation museum focusing on the lives of the state's slaves. Much of its research can be found on its highly useful website: http://whitneyplantation.com/.

I also consulted the voluminous slavery archives of the Schomburg Center for the Research of Black Culture, which can be found here: https://www.nypl.org/ locations/schomburg.

Dr. Midlo Hall shared by email her six-thousand-word account of her findings concerning 1764 in a book-in-progress titled *Maroons: In Search of the Invisible Africans*.

The evidence for the African roots of gumbo and Mrs. Fisher's gumbo recipes can be found in the facsimile edition on pages 22 and 23 of her cookbook *What Mrs. Fisher Knows About Old Southern Cooking* or digitally here: https://archive.org/details /whatmrsfisherkno00fishrich.

An interesting account of Madame Langlois, who opened the first cooking school in colonial Louisiana in 1718—and the possibility that she might have been an archetype instead of a real person—can be found here in an essay on the website of the New Orleans Bar Association by Ned Hémard: http://www.neworleansbar.org/uploads /files/Madame%20Langlois,%20Fact%20or%20Fiction.pdf.

An informative discussion of the mirepoix and its relation to gumbo's Trinity can be found on the Serious Eats website here: https://www.seriouseats.com/2014/05/all -about-mirepoix.html.

Moss's essay on the arguments against a bouillabaisse-gumbo connection can be found here: https://www.seriouseats.com/2014/09/history-new-orleans-gumbo-okra -file-powder.html.

I consulted multiple sources for my exploration of fusion foods, including this discussion of vindaloo on National Public Radio's website: https://www .npr.org/2013/07/25/205464472/tasting-the-shared-spicy-history-of-asian-and -latin-food.

Laussat's observations during the period when Louisiana was transferred from France to the United States can be found on page 86 of in his book, *Memoirs of My Life to My Son During the Years 1803 and After*.

Moss's essay on the roux can be found in full here: https://www.seriouseats .com/2014/09/history-new-orleans-gumbo-roux.html.

See interesting observations on the roux here from Southern Foodways Alliance board member Stanley Dry: https://www.southernfoodways.org/interview/a-short -history-of-gumbo/.

Leah Chase had some gumbo advice for President Obama when he came to dine on her gumbo in 2017. You can see it here; http://wgno.com/2017/01/19/what-advice -does-world-famous-chef-leah-chase-have-for-president-obama/.

The recipe for boiled calf brains appears on page 88 of the *Housekeeper's Encyclopedia of Useful Information for the Housekeeper*. You can find it digitally here: https://archive .org/details/housekeepersency00hask.

Information on Spain's rule of the Louisiana colony comes from many sources, among them the archives of the Library of Congress at: https://www.loc.gov /collections/louisiana-european-explorations-and-the-louisiana-purchase/articles -and-essays/louisiana-as-a-spanish-colony/. A second useful website is Know Louisiana, the Digital Encyclopedia of Louisiana, at: http://www.knowlouisiana.org/entry /spanish-colonial-louisiana.

A helpful article on Spain's Louisiana influence titled "Luisiana: The Spanish," appeared in the fall 2000 edition of the *Historic New Orleans Collection Quarterly*. You can read it here: https://www.hnoc.org/sites/default/files/quarterly/HNOC_Q4_2k.pdf.

For Spanish food and cultural contributions to Louisiana cooking, I drew from multiple sources, among them Folse's *Encyclopedia of Cajun and Creole Cuisine,* Susan Tucker's *New Orleans Cuisine: Fourteen Signature Dishes and Their Histories,* and a number of helpful food blogs, including this one by Restaurant R'evolution NOLA, http://revolutionnola.blogspot.com/2011/01/seven-nations-spain.html.

The *American Heritage* magazine piece I cite about the use of Spanish peppers among early Cajuns can be found here. https://www.americanheritage.com/content/true-and-delectable-history-creole-cooking.

An account of the Great Fire of 1788 in New Orleans can be read here: http://www.nola.com/300/2017/01/great_new_orleans_fire_1788_0099861.html.

Brasseaux's essay about how the Spanish welcomed Acadian immigrants is archived on the website of AcadianMemorial.org: http://www.acadianmemorial.org/ensemble_encore2/immigration.htm.

I consulted numerous sources in framing John Law's pivotal role in bringing the Germans to Louisiana, and the life of the Germans once they settled in, including the J. Hanno Deiler and Ellen Merrill books cited in the bibliography.

There is also a good account in the Library of Congress digital archives: http://international.loc.gov/intldl/fiahtml/fiatheme2c2.html and this one on the website of the Mississippi Historical Society: http://www.mshistorynow.mdah.ms.gov/articles/70/john-law-and-the-mississippi-bubble-1718–1720.

A description of Law's recruitment pamphlets can be found on page 13 of Deiler's book.

On Native American contributions to the Louisiana pot and culture in general, I found the digital archives of the Louisiana Folklife Program, operated under the Louisiana Division of Arts, to be particularly helpful. Two essays are worth reading, both by Maida Owens: http://www.louisianafolklife.org/LT/CSE/creole_food_trad.html, and http://www.louisianafolklife.org/LT/Maidas_Essay/main_introduction_onepage.html.

Another authoritative source on the history and culture of Louisiana's French Indians, as they call themselves, can be found at: http://www.biloxi-chitimacha.com/history.htm.

3. Gumbo Gets Going

As a fan of Louisiana's Hackberry Ramblers, I first learned that Williams had based "Jambalaya" on a traditional Cajun song, "Grand Texas," when I was listening to the

Ramblers' 1992 album, *Cajun Boogie*. They introduce "Grand Texas" by specifically mentioning Hank's adaptation of it. You can see them perform Grand Texas in this YouTube video: https://www.youtube.com/watch?v=hz7OfVdIG48.

I don't normally rely on Wikipedia as a source, but this history of how Williams came to do the song seems quite well documented: https://en.wikipedia.org/wiki /Jambalaya_%28On_the_Bayou%29.

I first heard of Senator Ellender's Washington gumbo cookery in the late 1960s when I was a young reporter on the *Houma Courier*. Indeed, Ellender visited our offices during his 1972 re-election campaign, shortly before he died, and we talked gumbo for a while. It also gets a mention in his *New York Times* obituary: https://www.nytimes .com/1972/07/28/archives/allen-j-ellender-of-louisiana-dies-senate-president-pro-tem -held.html.

Eddie Baquet's son, Wayne Baquet Sr., recalled for me in an interview how the Cosby mention drove even larger crowds to Eddie's. It also is chronicled in this May, 2014 NOLA.com piece, "The Importance of Eddie's": http://www.nola.com/dining /index.ssf/2014/05/the_importance_of_eddies_the_1.html.

This history of Jazz Fest can be found here: http://www.nojazzfest.com/info /history/.

During the early 1980s, I frequently visited Louisiana and had the good fortune to go eating, drinking, and dancing at Mulate's a number of times during its early incarnation. Granular details on Boutté's route to opening and running the restaurant, and its cultural importance to the Cajun movement, were recorded by the Southern Foodways Alliance during a seventy-seven-minute interview with Boutté in July 2007. It can be found in full here: https://www.southernfoodways .org/interview/mulates/.

A good discussion of the roots of Cajun and Creole French and how they differ from standard French can be found on the Louisiana State University's College of Humanities and Social Sciences website at: http://www.lsu.edu/hss/french /undergraduate_program/cajun_french/what_is_cajun.php.

You can read about CODOFIL's French preservation efforts here: https://www.crt .state.la.us/cultural-development/codofil/index.

An interesting piece on how Cajun music is helping to revive Cajun French can be found here on the *France-Amérique* website: https://france-amerique.com/the-musical -revival-of-cajun-french/.

Paul Prudhomme died in October 2015, a few months before I began researching this book, so I never got to interview him. The accounts of the chef's role in gumbo and the revolution in Cajun/Creole cuisine that appear here and a later chapter come from interviews I did with Ti Martin and Lally Brennan at Commander's Palace and Chef Paul Miller at K-Paul's Louisiana Kitchen, the French Quarter restaurant that

Prudhomme founded. The New Orleans *Times-Picayune* also published a lengthy oral history of Prudhomme's role in a piece published in June 2005 and updated in September 2016. You can find it here: http://www.nola.com/dining/index.ssf/2005/06 /paul_prudhomme_an_oral_history.html.

I also relied upon a fifty-three-minute interview Prudhomme gave to the Southern Foodways Alliance in June, 2011. You can find it here: https://www.southernfoodways .org/interview/paul-prudhomme/.

Woody Falgoux's *Rise of the Cajun Mariners*, listed in the bibliography, is a must-read for those interested in how Cajuns led the world in inventing oil-field workboat technology.

I interviewed Chef Folse at length at his Donaldsonville gumbo factory in April 2016 and also consulted his biographies in his books and website.

A fun account of the Disney kale gumbo disaster can be found here on Nola.com: http://www.nola.com/dining/index.ssf/2016/09/disney_gumbo_kale_quinoa.html.

4. Gumbo Inc. and the Gumbo Identity Crisis

You can see Louisiana's tourism statistics here: https://www.crt.state.la.us/tourism /louisiana-research/index.

The supplemental report can be found here: https://www.crt.state.la.us/Assets /Tourism/research/documents/2017-2018/2017%20Louisiana%20Tourism%20 Economic%20Impact%20revised.pdf.

According to the McIlhenny book, the company's revenue estimates include sales from salt mines and oil and gas revenues, even though hot sauce and related food products are the big revenue drivers.

I shop almost exclusively at Rouses when I visit Houma and Thibodaux, and often peruse the gumbo aisles. Corporate information comes from the company's website: https://www.rouses.com/.

On Prudhomme's food empire and influence as a chef, I interviewed Prudhomme company officials Marty Cosgrove and Chef Paul Miller in April 2016 and also gleaned a great deal of supplemental information from the company's website: https://chefpaul .com/site1.php.

5. The Meaning of "T"-Man in the Land of a Zillion Chefs

Trillin's essay appears here: https://www.newyorker.com/magazine/2002/01/28 /missing-links.

10. Gumbo Hunting in Treme

Other than sources I cite in this chapter, much of the information on the Baquet family and its restaurants and cooking history come from my interview with Wayne Baquet Sr. in November 2017. I gleaned supplemental information from an in-depth interview Baquet gave to the Southern Foodways Alliance in June 2007. You can read it here: https://www.southernfoodways.org/interview/lil-dizzys-cafe/.

Every professional chef and gumbo historian I interviewed spoke with admiration of Leah Chase and her iconic place in the New Orleans Creole food scene and the evolution of gumbo. Though I was not granted an interview, her fame has generated a great deal of press and interest among food historians. One source I relied upon was an interview she gave to the Southern Foodways Alliance in June 2014. It appears here: https://www.southernfoodways.org/interview/leah-chase/.

In 2014, New Orleans' Loyola University also embarked on an oral history project to document the contributions of the Chase family and Dooky Chase's to the New Orleans food scene. It is also catalogued on the SFA website here: https://www .southernfoodways.org/a-haven-for-all-of-us-loyola-university-documents-dooky -chase-restaurant/.

Also, a great deal of the Chase family history and the history of how Dooky Chase's restaurant got started appears on the restaurant website: http://www .dookychaserestaurant.com/.

A description of her famous gumbo z'herbes, which appears in the recipe section of this book, can be found on the SFA website here: https://www.southernfoodways.org /leah-chases-gumbo-zherbes/.

12. The Glory of Gumbo's Pantry

Figures on the size and value of Louisiana's wetlands and the annual rate of wetland loss come from several digital sources:

The United States Geological Survey: https://www.usgs.gov/news/usgs-louisiana -s-rate-coastal-wetland-loss-continues-slow.

The LaCoast.Gov website: https://lacoast.gov/reports/rtc/1997/4.htm.

Efforts to stem coastal losses are catalogued on the website of Louisiana's Coastal Wetlands Planning, Protection and Restoration Act: https://www.lacoast.gov/new /Default.aspx.

A 2002 state report that detailed the extent of the problem and first mapped out plans to stem losses can be found here: https://www.lacoast.gov/cwppra/reports /saving_coastal_louisiana.pdf.

13. Gumbo as Destiny

A treatise on the official effort to eradicate French in Louisiana can be found here: https://digitalcommons.law.lsu.edu/cgi/viewcontent.cgi?referer=https://www.bing .com/&httpsredir=1&article=5694&context=lalrev.

15. Bayou Black Today

As a reporter for the *Wall Street Journal* and later Bloomberg News, I wrote extensively on Louisiana's coastal wetlands loss, a subject I also deal with in detail in my book, *The Good Pirates of the Forgotten Bayous*. While much of my reportage is now behind paywalls at those publications, one article that sums up the unfolding disaster can be found here: http://www.cleanwaterlandcoast.com/collapsing-marsh-dwarfs-bp-oil -blowout-ecological-disaster/.

The $161 billion estimate for Katrina's losses are from the National Oceanic and Atmospheric Administration's Office for Coastal Management. See here: https://coast .noaa.gov/states/fast-facts/hurricane-costs.html.

The Coastal Protection and Restoration Authority's database, including estimates and projects, can be found here: http://coastal.la.gov/.

A fairly up-to-date story on how restoration efforts are proceeding can be found here at NOLA.com: http://www.nola.com/environment/index.ssf/2017/06/2017 _coastal_master_plan_2018.html.

You can read the Harte Research Institute report on the Gulf's resiliency here: https://www.harteresearchinstitute.org/news/gulf-resilient-five-years-after-deepwater -horizon-oil-spill.

BIBLIOGRAPHY AND FURTHER READING

Chefs, Cookbooks, and Foodways

Bienvenu, Marcelle. *Who's Your Mama, Are You Catholic, and Can You Make A Roux? A Cajun/Creole Family Album Cookbook.* Lafayette, LA: Acadian House Publishing, 2006.

Bienvenu, Marcelle, Carl Brasseaux, and Ryan Brasseaux. *Stir the Pot: A History of Cajun Cuisine.* New York: Hippocrene Books, 2005.

Brennan, Ella, and Ti Martin. *Miss Ella of Commander's Palace.* Layton, UT: Gibbs Smith, 2016.

Carney, Judith. *In the Shadow of Slavery: Africa's Botanical Legacy in the Atlantic World.* Berkeley: University of California Press, 2011.

Chase, Leah. *The Dooky Chase Cookbook.* Gretna, LA: Pelican Publishing Company, 1990.

———. *Listen, I Say Like This.* Gretna, LA: Pelican Publishing Company, 2002.

Fisher, Abby. *What Mrs. Fisher Knows About Old Southern Cooking* [1881 facsimile]. Carlisle, MA: Applewood, 1995.

Folse, John. *The Encyclopedia of Cajun and Creole Cuisine.* Gonzales, LA: Chef John Folse Company Publishing, 2015.

———. *The Evolution of Cajun & Creole Cuisine.* Gonzales, LA: Chef John Folse Company Publishing, 1989.

Gutierrez, C. Paige. *Cajun Foodways* [1864 facsimile]. Jackson: University Press of Mississippi, 1992.

Harris, Jessica. *High on the Hog: A Culinary Journey from Africa to America*. New York: Bloomsbury USA, 2012.

———. *Iron Pots & Wooden Spoons: Africa's Gifts to New World Cooking*. New York: Simon & Schuster, 1999.

Haskell, E. F. The *Housekeeper's Encyclopedia of Useful Information for the Housekeeper* [1864 facsimile]. New York: D. Appleton, 1861.

Hearn, Lafcadio. *Lafacadio Hearn's Creole Cook Book* [1885 facsimile]. Gretna, LA: Pelican Publishing Company 1995.

Junior League of New Orleans. *Plantation Cookbook*. New Orleans: B.E. Trice Publishing, 1992.

Martin, Addie K., and Jeremy Martin. *Southeast Louisiana Food: A Seasoned Tradition*. Mt. Pleasant, SC: The History Press, 2014.

Midlo Hall, Gwendolyn. *Africans in Colonial Louisiana: The Development of Afro-Creole Culture in the Eighteenth Century*. Baton Rouge: Louisiana State University Press, 1995.

National Council of Negro Women. *The Black Family Reunion Cookbook*. New York: Touchstone, 1993.

The Picayune Creole Cook Book [1901 facsimile]. American Antiquarian Cookbook Collection. Kansas City, MO: Andrews McMeel Publishing, 2013.

Prudhomme, Paul. *Chef Paul Prudhomme's Louisiana Kitchen*. New York: William Morrow, 1993.

St. Pierre, Todd-Michael. *Taste of Tremé: Creole, Cajun, and Soul Food from New Orleans' Famous Neighborhood of Jazz*. Berkeley, CA: Ulysses Press, 2012.

Southern Foodways Alliance Community Cookbook, The. Edited by Sarah Roahen and John T. Edge. Atlanta: University of Georgia Press, 2015.

Toups, Isaac, and Jennifer Cole. *Chasing the Gator: Isaac Toups and the New Cajun Cooking*. New York: Little Brown & Co., 2018.

Tucker, Susan. *New Orleans Cuisine: Fourteen Signature Dishes and Their Histories*. Jackson: University Press of Mississippi, 2009.

Ursuline Alumnae Association. *Recipes and Reminiscences of New Orleans*. New Orleans: Academy Cooperative Club, 1971.

The Gumbo Belt, Cajun and Creole History, and New Orleans

Ancelet, Barry Jean. *Cajun and Creole Folktales: The French Oral Tradition of South Louisiana*. Jackson: University Press of Mississippi, 1994.

Bernard, Shane K. *The Cajuns: Americanization of a People*. Jackson: University Press of Mississippi, 2003.

Brasseaux, Carl, and Donald W. Davis. *Ain't There No More: Louisiana's Disappearing Coastal Plain*. Jackson: University Press of Mississippi, 2017.

Brinkley, Douglas. *The Great Deluge: Hurricane Katrina, New Orleans, and the Mississippi Gulf Coast*. New York: Harper Perennial, 2007.

Cenac, Christopher Everette, and Claire Domangue Joller. *Hard Scrabble to Hallelujah, Volume 1. Bayou Terrebonne: Legacies of Terrebonne Parish, Louisiana*. Jackson: University Press of Mississippi, 2017.

Crété, Lilian. *Daily Life in Louisiana, 1815–1830*. Translated by Patrick Gergory. Baton Rouge: Louisiana State University Press, 1981.

Daigle, Jules O. *A Dictionary of the Cajun Language*. Ville Platte: Swallow Publications, 1993.

Deiler, J. Hanno. *The Settlement of the German Coast of Louisiana and the Creoles of German Descent* [1909]. Baltimore: Clearfield Company, 2009.

De Laussat, Pierre Clément. *Memoirs of My Life to My Son During the Years 1803 and After, Which I Spent in Public Service in Louisiana as Commissioner of the French Government for the Retrocession to France of That Colony and for Its Transfer to the United States* [1831]. Translated by Sister Agnes-Josephine Pastwa. Baton Rouge: Louisiana State University Press, 1978.

———. *Memoirs of My Life: Beyond the Bayou* [1831?]. Translated by Sister Agnes-Josephine Pastwa. Baton Rouge: Louisiana State University Press, 2003.

Falgoux, Woody. *Rise of the Cajun Mariners: The Race for Big Oil*. Stockard James, 2007.

Faragher, John Mack. *A Great and Noble Scheme: The Tragic Story of the Expulsion of the French Acadians from Their American Homeland*. New York: W. W. Norton, 2006.

Groom, Winston. *Patriotic Fire: Andrew Jackson and Jean Lafitte at the Battle of New Orleans*. New York: Knopf, 2006.

Hallowell, Christopher. *Holding Back the Sea: The Struggle on the Gulf Coast to Save America*. New York: Harper Perennial, 2005.

James, Rosemary. *My New Orleans: Ballads to the Big Easy by the Sons, Daughters and Lovers*. New York: Harper Touchstone, 2006.

Jones, Terry L. *The Louisiana Journey*. Layton, UT: Gibbs Smith, 2007.

Merrill, Ellen. *Germans of Louisiana*. Gretna, LA: Pelican Publishing Company, 2004.

Piazza, Tom. *Why New Orleans Matters*. New York: Harper Perennial, 2015.

Reed, Julia. *The House on First Street: My New Orleans Story*. New York: Harper Perennial, 2009.

Robin, C. C. *Voyage to Louisiana 1803–1805*. Translated by Stuart O. Laudry Jr. Gretna, LA: Pelican Publishing Company, 1966.

Rothfeder, Jeffrey. *McIlhenny's Gold: How a Louisiana Family Built the Tabasco Empire*. New York: HarperCollins, 2007.

Rushton, William Faulkner. *Cajuns: From Acadia to Louisiana*. New York: Farrar, Straus & Giroux, 1980.

Seck, Ibrahima. *Bouki Fait Gombo: A History of the Slave Community of Habitation Haydel (Whitney Plantation), Louisiana, 1750–1860*. New Orleans: University of New Orleans Press, 2014.

Tidwell, Mike. *Bayou Farewell: The Rich Life and Tragic Death of Louisiana's Cajun Coast*. New York: Vintage, 2004.

Toups, Neil J. *The Toups Clan and How It All Began*. Lafayette, LA: Neilson Publishing Company, 1969.

INDEX

ABOUT THE AUTHOR

Ken Wells is a journalist and novelist who grew up in Cajun country on the banks of Bayou Black deep below New Orleans, hunting, fishing, wrangling snakes, and eating his momma's gumbo. Second of six sons, Wells began his writing career as a nineteen-year-old college dropout covering car wrecks and gator sightings for his semiweekly hometown paper, the *Houma Courier*. He would return to college and go on to an illustrious career in journalism: a Pulitzer Prize finalist for the *Miami Herald* and a twenty-four-year stint on the *Wall Street Journal* as both a feature writer and a page-one editor. Wells is also the author of five well-received novels of the Cajun bayous. *Gumbo Life* is his third book of narrative nonfiction. An avid hiker, fisherman, and photographer, Wells divides his time between Chicago and a summer cabin in the wilds of Maine. He also dabbles in blues and jazz guitar and songwriting, and cooks a mean Cajun gumbo.